Machine Interpretation of Patterns
Image Analysis and Data Mining

T0324964

Statistical Science and Interdisciplinary Research

Series Editor: Sankar K. Pal *(Indian Statistical Institute)*

Description:

In conjunction with the Platinum Jubilee celebrations of the Indian Statistical Institute, a series of books will be produced to cover various topics, such as Statistics and Mathematics, Computer Science, Machine Intelligence, Econometrics, other Physical Sciences, and Social and Natural Sciences. This series of edited volumes in the mentioned disciplines culminate mostly out of significant events — conferences, workshops and lectures — held at the ten branches and centers of ISI to commemorate the long history of the institute.

Vol. 3   Algorithms, Architectures and Information Systems Security
         edited by Bhargab B. Bhattacharya, Susmita Sur-Kolay,
         Subhas C. Nandy & Aditya Bagchi
         (Indian Statistical Institute, India)

Vol. 4   Advances in Multivariate Statistical Methods
         edited by A. SenGupta (Indian Statistical Institute, India)

Vol. 5   New and Enduring Themes in Development Economics
         edited by B. Dutta, T. Ray & E. Somanathan
         (Indian Statistical Institute, India)

Vol. 6   Modeling, Computation and Optimization
         edited by S. K. Neogy, A. K. Das and R. B. Bapat
         (Indian Statistical Institute, India)

Vol. 7   Perspectives in Mathematical Sciences I: Probability and Statistics
         edited by N. S. N. Sastry, T. S. S. R. K. Rao, M. Delampady and
         B. Rajeev (Indian Statistical Institute, India)

Vol. 8   Perspectives in Mathematical Sciences II: Pure Mathematics
         edited by N. S. N. Sastry, T. S. S. R. K. Rao, M. Delampady and
         B. Rajeev (Indian Statistical Institute, India)

Vol. 9   Recent Developments in Theoretical Physics
         edited by S. Ghosh and G. Kar (Indian Statistical Institute, India)

Vol. 11 Machine Interpretation of Patterns: Image Analysis and Data Mining
         edited by R. K. De, D. P. Mandal and A. Ghosh
         (Indian Statistical Institute, India)

Vol. 12 Recent Trends in Surface and Colloid Science
         edited by Bidyut K. Paul (Indian Statistical Institute, India)

Platinum Jubilee Series

Statistical Science and
Interdisciplinary Research — Vol. 11

Machine
Interpretation
of Patterns
Image Analysis and
Data Mining

Editors

Rajat K. De
Deba Prasad Mandal
Ashish Ghosh

Indian Statistical Institute, India

Series Editor: **Sankar K. Pal**

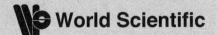

World Scientific

NEW JERSEY · LONDON · SINGAPORE · BEIJING · SHANGHAI · HONG KONG · TAIPEI · CHENNAI

Published by

World Scientific Publishing Co. Pte. Ltd.

5 Toh Tuck Link, Singapore 596224

USA office: 27 Warren Street, Suite 401-402, Hackensack, NJ 07601

UK office: 57 Shelton Street, Covent Garden, London WC2H 9HE

British Library Cataloguing-in-Publication Data
A catalogue record for this book is available from the British Library.

Statistical Science and Interdisciplinary Research — Vol. 11
MACHINE INTERPRETATION OF PATTERNS
Image Analysis and Data Mining

ISBN-13 978-981-4299-18-3
ISBN-10 981-4299-18-9

Printed in Singapore.

Foreword

The Indian Statistical Institute (ISI) was established on 17th December, 1931, by a great visionary Prof. Prasanta Chandra Mahalanobis to promote research in the theory and applications of statistics as a new scientific discipline in India. In 1959, Pandit Jawaharlal Nehru, the then Prime Minister of India introduced the ISI Act in the parliament and designated it as an Institution of National Importance because of its remarkable achievements in statistical work as well as its contribution to economic planning.

Today, the Indian Statistical Institute occupies a prestigious position in the academic firmament. It has been a haven for bright and talented academics working in a number of disciplines. Its research faculty has done India proud in the arenas of Statistics, Mathematics, Economics, Computer Science, among others. Over seventy five years, it has grown into a massive banyan tree, like the institute emblem. The Institute now serves the nation as a unified and monolithic organization from different places, namely Kolkata, the Headquarters, Delhi, Bangalore and Chennai, three centers, a network of five SQC-OR Units located at Mumbai, Pune, Baroda, Hyderabad and Coimbatore, and a branch (field station) at Giridih.

The platinum jubilee celebrations of ISI have been launched by Honorable Dr. Manmohan Singh on December 24, 2006, and the Government of India has declared 29th June as the "Statistics Day" to commemorate the birthday of Prof. Mahalanobis nationally.

Prof. Mahalanobis, was a great believer in interdisciplinary research because he thought that this will promote the development of not only Statistics, but also the other natural and social sciences. To promote interdisciplinary research, major strides were made in the areas of computer science, statistical quality control, economics, biological and social sciences, physical and earth sciences.

The Institute's motto of "unity in diversity" has been the guiding principle of all its activities since its inception. It highlights the unifying role of statistics in relation to various scientific activities.

In tune with this hallowed tradition, a comprehensive academic programme, involving Nobel Laureates, Fellows of the Royal Society, Abel prize winner and other dignitaries, has been implemented throughout the Platinum Jubilee year, highlighting the emerging areas of ongoing frontline research in its various scientific divisions, centers, and outlying units. It includes international and national-level seminars, symposia, conferences and workshops, as well as series of special lectures. As an outcome of these events, the Institute is bringing out a series of comprehensive volumes in different subjects under the title Statistical Science and Interdisciplinary Research, published by the World Scientific Press, Singapore.

The present volume titled "Machine Interpretation of Patterns — Image Analysis and Data Mining" is the eleventh one in the series. The volume consists of fifteen chapters, written by eminent scientists from different parts of the world. These chapters provide a current perspective of different areas of research and development, both from theoretical and application points of view, emphasizing the major challenging issues primarily in pattern recognition, computer vision, machine learning and data mining. Interesting application areas covered include mapping earthquake damage in urban areas, personalization and context modeling in web mining, human fall detection from videos of multiple persons in computer vision, and prediction of soluble proteins in bioinformatics. Tools used are both classical and modern including case based reasoning, granular support vector machine, decision tree, parallel genetic algorithms and bipolar fuzzy sets. I believe the state-of-the art studies presented in this book will be very useful to students, researchers as well as practitioners.

Thanks to the contributors for their excellent research contributions and to the volume editors Dr. Rajat K. De, Dr. D. P. Mandal and Prof. Ashish Ghosh for their sincere effort in bringing out the volume nicely. Initial design of the cover by Mr. Indranil Dutta is acknowledged. Sincere efforts by Prof. Dilip Saha and Dr. Barun Mukhopadhyay for editorial assistance are appreciated. Thanks are also due to World Scientific for their initiative in publishing the series and being a part of the Platinum Jubilee endeavor of the Institute.

January 2010   Sankar K. Pal
Kolkata   Series Editor and Director

Preface

This book provides some recent developments and state of the art review in various areas of pattern recognition, image processing, machine learning, data mining and web intelligence, both from theoretical and application points of view. It is a peer-reviewed research monograph under the ISI Platinum Jubilee Series on Statistical Science and Interdisciplinary Research. The book may be considered as an integrated volume to the researchers interested in doing interdisciplinary research where computer science is a component. Since a wide variety of current topics are covered in the book, the readers are expected to have some basic idea of pattern recognition, machine learning, image processing, data mining and web intelligence; but will be able to follow each of the chapters independent of the others. The book contains a total of 15 chapters. The first 5 chapters deal with development of a few methodologies for various tasks of pattern recognition and image processing, along with some theoretical aspects. Chapters 6, 7 and 8 consider text processing and other related tasks. The next four chapters (Chapters 9–12) consider various issues of computer vision from application points of view. The last 3 chapters (Chapters 13–15) describe the classification task of pattern recognition, involving signal processing, case-based reasoning and support vector machines. These chapters are on applications of pattern recognition to speech processing, broker system designing and protein classification.

Chapter 1 deals with the design of a probabilistic multi-class multi-kernel machine based on a kernel combination methodology. The classifier is able to combine diverse sources of information and multiple feature spaces. The methodology follows a well-founded hierarchical Bayesian paradigm that models uncertainty in the parameters via a hierarchy of prior and hyper-prior distributions. Chapter 2 presents an image quality metric which integrates the notions of structural similarity measure mimicking the overall functionality of the human visual system and perceptually important regions based on the characteristics of intermediate and higher level visual processes. In Chapter 3, a new approach for image entropy reduction is described, which is based on two-dimensional fractional differentiation. Chapter 4 deals with the development of two novel methods for object-background classification using the notion of parallel genetic algorithms. Chapter 5 addresses the issue of bipolarity in spatial domains. It introduces mathematical morphological operations on bipolar fuzzy sets.

Chapter 6 describes the present day scenario of the area of information retrieval. The main focus is on the problem of personalization and context modelling, and on the definition of new paradigms for content representation. An online archiving and retrieving system is developed in Chapter 7. This is followed by the development of a two stage recognition scheme, in Chapter 8, for recognition of handwritten Devanagari words.

Chapter 9 is concerned with a problem of computer vision. It deals with the development of a model based approach for human fall detection from videos in the presence of multiple persons. Chapter 10 shows how multi-temporal SAR data allows mapping earthquake damage in urban areas with an acceptable accuracy, provided the ancillary information defining urban blocks are available. Chapters 11 and 12 describe the designs of safety related systems based on the theories of machine learning.

In Chapter 13, a methodology is developed for signal reconstruction using the notion of non-linear quantization based on logarithmic and Incomplete Beta Function (IBF) which dynamically assign the number of quantization levels exploiting the auditory motivation. Chapter 14 addresses some discovery tasks as correlated with supervised learning. Textual case-based and decision tree induction approaches are considered to these tasks, and the use of multiple representations is explored. The performance evaluation is made on a broker system that discovers and mediates requests, and responses for meteorological and oceanographic data. Finally in Chapter 15, an important bioinformatics problem is considered where a Granular Support Vector Machine (GSVM) is used for prediction of soluble proteins based on over expression in *Escherichia coli*.

Rajat K. De
Deba Prasad Mandal
Ashish Ghosh
Editors

Contents

Foreword   v

Preface   vii

1. Combining Information with a Bayesian Multi-class   1
    Multi-kernel Pattern Recognition Machine
    T. Damoulas and M. A. Girolami

2. Image Quality Assessment Based on Weighted Perceptual   29
    Features
    D. V. Rao and L. P. Reddy

3. Quasi-reversible Two-dimension Fractional Differentiation   57
    for Image Entropy Reduction
    A. Nakib, A. Nait-Ali, H. Oulhadj and P. Siarry

4. Parallel Genetic Algorithm Based Clustering for Object and   69
    Background Classification
    P. Kanungo, P. K. Nanda and A. Ghosh

5. Bipolar Fuzzy Spatial Information: First Operations in the   91
    Mathematical Morphology Setting
    I. Bloch

6. Approaches to Intelligent Information Retrieval   113
    G. Pasi

7. Retrieval of On-line Signatures   131
    H. N. Prakash and D. S. Guru

8. A Two Stage Recognition Scheme for Offline Handwritten   145
    Devanagari Words
    B. Shaw and S. K. Parui

9. Fall Detection from a Video in the Presence of Multiple   167
    Persons
    V. Vishwakarma, S. Sural and C. Mandal

10. Fusion of GIS and SAR Statistical Features for Earthquake   195
    Damage Mapping at the Block Scale
    G. Trianni, G. Lisini, P. Gamba and F. Dell'Acqua

11. Intelligent Surveillance and Pose-invariant 2D Face   207
    Classification
    B. C. Lovell, C. Sanderson and T. Shan

12. Simple Machine Learning Approaches to Safety-related   231
    Systems
    C. Moewes, C. Otte and R. Kruse

13. Nonuniform Multi Level Crossings for Signal Reconstruction   251
    N. Poojary, H. Kumar and A. Rao

14. Adaptive Web Services Brokering   269
    K. M. Gupta and D. W. Aha

15. Granular Support Vector Machine Based Method for   289
    Prediction of Solubility of Proteins on Over Expression in
    Escherichia Coli and Breast Cancer Classification
    P. Kumar, B. D. Kulkarni and V. K. Jayaraman

Chapter 1

Combining Information with a Bayesian Multi-class Multi-kernel Pattern Recognition Machine

Theodoros Damoulas and Mark A. Girolami

Inference Group,
Department of Computing Science, FIMS, University of Glasgow,
18 Lilybank Gardens, SWA Building, G12 8QQ, Glasgow, Scotland, UK,
{theo, girolami}@dcs.gla.ac.uk

In this contribution we offer a multi-class multi-kernel machine based on the multinomial probit likelihood which is able to informatively combine diverse sources of information and multiple feature spaces. The proposed methodology follows a well-founded hierarchical Bayesian paradigm that models uncertainty in the parameters via a hierarchy of prior and hyper-prior distributions that are well described and justified. We offer the full Markov chain Monte Carlo (MCMC) solution via a Metropolis-Hastings (MH) within Gibbs sampling approach and a Variational Bayes (VB) approximation to the solution which enables efficient CPU times and reduced computational complexity. We also provide and examine different combination strategies that can be employed with the model, including a weighted summation, a binary switch and a weighted product rule. The proposed approach provides the current *state-of-the-art* in a variety of domains such as protein fold prediction, remote homology detection and handwritten numerals classification, and matches or outperforms previous ensemble learning methods that are based on the popular support vector machines (SVM) methodology. Finally, we examine the efficiency of the VB approximation against the full MCMC solution and the insight our method offers on these problems by inferring the significance of various sources of information and string kernels.

Contents

1.1 Introduction 2
1.2 Intuition and Motivation 5
1.3 Multinomial Probit Kernel Combination 5
    1.3.1 Markov chain Monte Carlo solution 9

      1.3.2   Variational Bayes approximation   11

1.4   Experiments and Results   14

      1.4.1   Proof of concept on an artificial data-set   15

      1.4.2   UCI and handwritten numerals data-sets   18

      1.4.3   Protein fold recognition and remote homology detection   21

1.5   Discussion and Future Directions   24

References   26

1.1. Introduction

Problem area

In a large number of pattern recognition and machine learning problems we encounter the situation where different sources of information and different representations are available for the specific object that we are trying to classify. For example consider different representations of an image (i.e. pixel grey-scale values, gabor coefficients, fourier coefficients), different attributes of a signal or even more heterogeneous sources such as an image of a physical object, its response to specific radiation and the concentration of iron in its constitution. In these cases the underlying problem is how to combine all the available sources, in an informative way, in order to achieve a superior classification performance for the task in hand while at the same time dealing with the "curse of dimensionality"[5,7,30] inherited in the domain.

When multiple feature spaces/sources S are available for a multinomial classification task there are broadly three distinct approaches available:

a) Concatenate all the features together into a large dimensional space and employ a multinomial classifier[a]. *b)* Employ a multinomial classifier[a] on each feature space and then combine. *c)* Combine first the feature spaces and then employ a multinomial classifier[a].

First of all it is easy to understand the computational drawbacks if we employ binary classifiers instead of multinomials in all cases. Next, although concatenating might work fine in certain problems, the possible excessive dimensionality of the final augmented space will be forbidding for most problems and classifiers. At the same time, scaling issues and inability to control the contribution of each individual space is another problem, especially when suspect or degraded features might be included.

---

[a]Or combine binary classifiers

Past methods

The typical preferred approach so far has been to combine multinomial or even binary classifiers, namely *ensemble learning* methods.[13] The idea behind that approach is to train one classifier in every feature space and then combine their class predictive distributions. Different ways of combining the output of the classifiers have been studied[21,22,41] and also meta-learning an overall classifier on these distributions[43] has been proposed.

The *drawbacks* of that approach lies on the theoretical justification, on the processing loads incurred as multiple training has to be performed and on the fact that the individual classifiers operate independently on the data. Their performance has been shown to significantly improve over the best individual classifier in many cases but the extra load of training multiple classifiers may possibly restrain their application when resources are limited. The typical combination rules for classifiers are *ad hoc* methods[6] that are based on the notions of the *linear* or *independent* opinion pools.

Recently, *kernel combination* methodologies that follow the third approach, are being proposed that seem suitable for such problems. Previous work on kernel combination includes[23] where semidefinite programming is used to learn the composite kernel matrix,[34] where a hyper-kernel space is defined on the space of kernels in order to learn the composite kernel within a specific parametric family,[25] where Gaussian kernels under a Support Vector Machine (SVM) framework are combined into an expanded composite kernel,[35] in which the composite kernel is a summation of base kernels, without however learning the combinatorial weights or the kernel parameters and work by[15] where hierarchic Bayesian models are employed to infer the combinatorial weights and perform kernel learning. Furthermore, in recent work by[27] a nonstationary kernel combination approach was presented which allows for variation on the relative weights of the base kernels among the input examples. In this case the kernel combination weights are a function of the input.

The *drawbacks* of the above methods are their foundation on binary classifiers by nature (mostly SVMs) that leads to bad scaling for multi-class problems (We need for example 4,350 classifiers for a 10-fold cross validation on a 30 class problem employing an all-versus-all method). Also, the majority of them are based on SVMs that are non-probabilistic classifiers and these two restrictions together with associated scaling problems create the need for an efficient multi-kernel multi-class probabilistic classifier.

To that end, another related approach within the non-parametric Gaussian process (GP) methodology[33,36] has been proposed by,[17] where instead of kernel combination the integration of information is achieved via combination of the GP covariance functions. However, a first order approximation for inverting the composite kernel is needed to obtain estimates of the values for the kernel weights and the method is restricted to kernel-type covariance functions.

Proposed method

Having identified the problem area we offer a principled solution via a multi-class multi-kernel pattern recognition machine that is able to combine feature sets and kernel spaces in an informative manner while at the same time inferring their significance and predictive contribution. The proposed methodology is general and can also be employed outside the "kernel-domain", i.e without the need to embed the features into Hilbert spaces, by allowing for combination of basis function expansions. That is useful in the case of multi-scale problems and wavelets.[3] The combination of kernels or dictionaries of basis functions as an alternative to classifier combination offers the advantages of reduced computational requirements, the ability to learn the significance of the individual sources and an improved solution based on the inferred significance.

Our work further develops the work of,[15] which we generalize to the multi-class case by employing a multinomial probit likelihood and introducing latent variables that give rise to efficient Metropolis-Hastings within Gibbs sampling from the parameter posterior distribution through the introduction of auxiliary variables as demonstrated in the seminal paper by[1] and further extended by.[20] This enables us to retain the efficient hierarchical Bayesian structure of our model and provides us with an elegant solution for the multiclass setting.

Furthermore, we bound the marginal likelihood or model evidence[31] and derive the Variational Bayes (VB) approximation for the proposed model, providing a fast and efficient solution to accompany the standard MCMC aforementioned approach. We are able to combine kernels in a general way via linear, product or binary rules and learn the associated weights to infer the significance of the sources.

In a summary our contribution[b] offers:

---

[b]Parts of this work have been submitted for publication, see[8–10]

- A hierarchical Bayesian model with probabilistic output predictions.
- An explicit multi-class multi-kernel classifier.
- The ability to infer knowledge on three levels (regressors, importance of information channels, parameters of kernels), within the training of the classifier.
- A general framework for combining different sources of information, not dependent on the use of kernels and on a specific kernel type.
- A multitude of combination rules from linear and binary to product ones.

1.2. Intuition and Motivation

The intuition behind kernel combination methods is to create the same type of information in all feature spaces and then to combine them instructively via an appropriate rule. The proposed approach, as can be seen from Fig. 1.1 for the protein fold prediction problem, is based on the ability to embed each object description via the kernel trick[38,39] into a kernel space (Hilbert space). This produces a similarity measure between objects in every feature space and then, having a common measure, we can combine informatively these similarities onto a composite kernel space.

Hence now, a single multiclass kernel machine can operate on that composite space effectively "disregarding" the number of feature spaces used. Inference by Bayes theorem on our hierarchical multiclass model enables us to learn the significance of each source and their predictive power by the corresponding kernel weights β, to learn the regressors and the kernel parameters without resorting to *ad-hoc* ensemble learning, combination of binary classifiers or parameter tuning. It is also worth noting that the type of kernel employed does not need to be same across feature spaces nor of a specific form as long as it is a valid kernel function ensuring a positive semi-definite symmetric matrix.

1.3. Multinomial Probit Kernel Combination

Consider S sources of information; From each one we have input variables $\mathbf{x}_n^s$ as D^s- dimensional vectors[c] for $s = 1, \ldots, S$ and corresponding

---

[c]The superscripts denote "function of" unless otherwise specified. Matrices are denoted by $\mathbf{M}$, vectors by $\mathbf{m}$ and scalars by m.

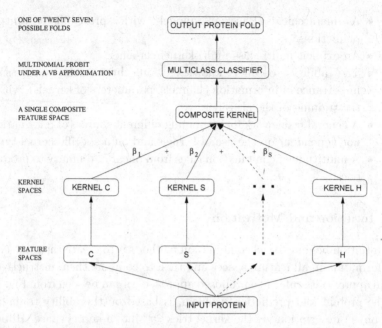

Figure 1.1. Diagrammatic representation of the linear kernel combination methodology for the specific problem of protein fold prediction. The original feature spaces are first embedded into kernels (Hilbert spaces) and then combined into a composite kernel where the multiclass kernel machine operates on.

real-valued target variables $t_n \in \{1, \ldots, C\}$ for $n = 1, \ldots, N$ where N is the number of observations and C the number of classes. By applying the *kernel trick* on the individual feature spaces created by the S sources we can define the $N \times N$ composite kernel as

$$\mathbf{K}^{\beta\Theta} = \sum_{s=1}^{S} \beta_s \mathbf{K}^{s\theta_s}$$

with each element analysed as

$$K^{\beta\Theta}\left(\mathbf{x}_i, \mathbf{x}_j\right) = \sum_{s=1}^{S} \beta_s K^{s\theta_s}\left(\mathbf{x}_i^s, \mathbf{x}_j^s\right)$$

where β is an $S \times 1$ column vector and Θ is an $S \times D^s$ matrix, describing the D^s−dimensional kernel parameters θ_s of all the base kernels $\mathbf{K}^s$. Now as we can see the composite kernel is a weighted summation[d] of the base

---

[d]We present the more general linear kernel combination method first as our baseline approach.

kernels with β_s as the corresponding weight for each one. In the case where instead of kernels we employ the original feature spaces or expansions of them[e], we would still define the composite feature space as a weighted summation of the individual ones and proceed in a similar manner as below, with the appropriate dimensions for the corresponding sub-sets of regressors.

Following the standard approach for the multinomial probit by[1] we introduce auxiliary variables $\mathbf{Y} \in \mathcal{R}^{C \times N}$ and define the relationship between the auxiliary variable y_{cn} and the target variable t_n as

$$t_n = i \text{ if } y_{in} > y_{jn} \; \forall \; j \neq i \tag{1.1}$$

Now, the model response regressing on the variable y_{cn} with model parameters $\mathbf{W} \in \mathcal{R}^{C \times N}$ and employing a standardized normal noise model as in[1,16] is given by

$$y_{cn} | \mathbf{w}_c, \mathbf{k}_n^{\beta\Theta} \sim \mathcal{N}_{y_{cn}} \left(\mathbf{w}_c \mathbf{k}_n^{\beta\Theta}, 1 \right) \tag{1.2}$$

where $\mathcal{N}_x (m, v)$ denotes the normal distribution of x with mean m and variance v, $\mathbf{W}$ and $\mathbf{Y}$ are $C \times N$ matrices, $\mathbf{w}_c$ is a $1 \times N$ row vector and $\mathbf{k}_n^{\beta\Theta}$ is an $N \times 1$ column vector from the nth column of the composite kernel $\mathbf{K}^{\beta\Theta}$. Hence now, the multinomial likelihood, can be expressed as the following by simply marginalizing over the auxiliary variable $\mathbf{y}_n$ and making use of relations 1.1 and 1.2:

$$P \left(t_n = i | \mathbf{W}, \mathbf{k}_n^{\beta\Theta} \right) = \int P \left(t_n = i | \mathbf{y}_n \right) P \left(\mathbf{y}_n | \mathbf{W}, \mathbf{k}_n^{\beta\Theta} \right) d\mathbf{y}_n$$

$$= \int \delta \left(y_{in} > y_{jn} \; \forall \; j \neq i \right) \prod_{c=1}^{C} \mathcal{N}_{y_{cn}} \left(\mathbf{w}_c \mathbf{k}_n^{\beta\Theta}, 1 \right) d\mathbf{y}_n$$

$$= \mathcal{E}_{p(u)} \left\{ \prod_{j \neq i} \Phi \left(u + (\mathbf{w}_i - \mathbf{w}_j) \mathbf{k}_n^{\beta\Theta} \right) \right\} \tag{1.3}$$

where the expectation $\mathcal{E}$ is taken with respect to the standardised normal distribution $p(u) = \mathcal{N}(0, 1)$. Hence, we can easily calculate the likelihood

---

[e]Consider for example polynomial expansions.

by averaging the quantity inside the expectation for a certain number of random samples[f] of u.

In the graphical model in Fig. 1.2, the conditional relation of the model parameters and associated hyper and hyper-hyper-parameters can be seen for the case of the *mean composite* kernel with the accompanied variations in Fig. 1.3 for the *binary* and *product composite* kernel. We place a product of zero mean Gaussian distributions on the regressors $\mathbf{W} \sim \prod_{c=1}^{C} \prod_{n=1}^{N} \mathcal{N}_{w_{cn}}(0, \zeta_{cn})$ with variance ζ_{cn} (described by the variable $\mathbf{Z}$ in the graph) and a gamma distribution on the inverse of each scale with hyper-hyper-parameters τ, υ, reflecting our lack of prior knowledge and taking advantage of the conjugacy of these distributions.

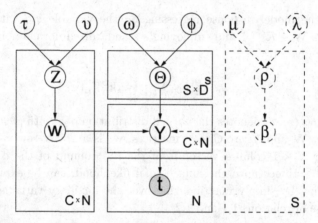

Figure 1.2.   Plates diagram of the model for *linear composite* kernel.

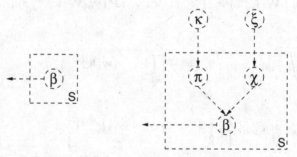

Figure 1.3.   Modification for *binary composite* (left) and *product composite* kernel (right).

---

[f]Typically 1000 samples have been employed which has been sufficient to approximate the expectation to a high degree of accuracy.

Furthermore, we place a gamma distribution on each kernel parameter since $\theta_{sd} \in \Re_+$. In the case of the *mean composite* kernel, a Dirichlet distribution with parameters ρ is placed on the combinatorial weights in order to satisfy the constraints imposed on the possible values which are defined on a simplex. A further gamma distribution is placed on each ρ_s with associated hyper-hyper-parameters μ, λ. The hyper-hyper-parameters $\Xi = \{\tau, \upsilon, \omega, \phi, \mu, \lambda, \kappa, \xi\}$ can be set by type-II maximum likelihood or set to uninformative values and the hyper and first level parameters $\Psi = \{Y, W, \beta, \rho, \Theta, Z\}$ are sampled accordingly.

In the *product composite* kernel case we employ the right dashed plate in Fig. 1.3 which places a gamma distribution on the combinatorial weights β, that do not need to be defined on a simplex anymore, with an exponential hyper-prior distribution on each of the parameters π_s, χ_s.

Finally, in the *binary composite* kernel case we employ the left dashed plate in Fig. 1.3 which places a binomial distribution on each β_s with equal probability of being 1 or zero (unless prior knowledge says otherwise). The small size of the possible 2^S states of the β vector allows for their explicit consideration in the inference procedure and hence there is no need to place any hyper-prior distributions.

1.3.1. *Markov chain Monte Carlo solution*

Inference on the model parameters is performed via Bayes rule in order to obtain the posterior distributions. In that way we update the probabilities of parameter values based on the data as our prior distributions (prior beliefs) are multiplied by the likelihood (evidence from data). We present here the resulting posterior distributions which are adoptions, for our problem, of standard results in the statistics literature, for a full treatment see.[12,18] The conditional posterior distribution for the regression parameters $p\left(W|Y, K^{\beta\Theta}, \zeta\right) \propto p\left(Y|W, K^{\beta\Theta}\right) p\left(W|\zeta\right)$ is a product of Gaussian distributions $\prod_{c=1}^{C} \mathcal{N}_{w_c}\left(m_c, V_c\right)$ where

$$m_c = V_c \left(K^{\beta\Theta} y_c^T\right) \text{ and } V_c = \left(K^{\beta\Theta} K^{\beta\Theta} + Z_c^{-1}\right)^{-1}$$

Z_c is a diagonal matrix with ζ_c in the main diagonal and y_c is an $1 \times N$ vector of the auxiliary variables for a specific class c. The posterior $p\left(Y|W, K^{\beta\Theta}, t\right) \propto p\left(t|Y\right) p\left(Y|W, K^{\beta\Theta}\right)$ over the auxiliary variables is a product of N $C-$dimensional conically truncated Gaussians given by

$$\prod_{n=1}^{N} \delta\left(y_{in} > y_{jn} \ \forall \ j \neq i\right) \delta\left(t_n = i\right) \mathcal{N}_{y_n}\left(Wk_n^{\beta\Theta}, I\right)$$

Furthermore, the posterior distribution $p(\zeta|\mathbf{W}, \tau, \upsilon)$ $\propto$ $p(\mathbf{W}|\zeta) p(\zeta|\tau, \upsilon)$ over the variances ζ is of the same form as the prior with updated parameters $\tau^* = \tau + \frac{1}{2}$ and $\upsilon^* = \upsilon + \frac{1}{2}w_{cn}^2$ and finally the combinatorial weights $\boldsymbol{\beta}$, the associated hyper-parameter $\boldsymbol{\rho}$ and the base kernel parameters $\boldsymbol{\Theta}$ are inferred via three Metropolis-Hastings,[19] MH hereafter, subsamplers with appropriate acceptance ratios,.[9]

$$\text{where} \quad \Phi(\boldsymbol{\rho}) = \frac{\Gamma\left(\sum_{s=1}^{S} \rho_s\right)}{\prod_{s=1}^{S} \Gamma(\rho_s)}$$

with the proposed move symbolised by $*$ and the current state with i.

In the case of the *binary* combination method, $\boldsymbol{\beta}$ becomes a binary vector switching base kernels on or off. The approach has been motivated by the work of[20] on covariate set uncertainty where they employed a MH subsampler to learn a binary covariate indicator vector switching features on or off. We modify the approach, as a *kernel set uncertainty* by infering the binary vector with an extra Gibbs step that depends on the conditional distribution of the auxiliary variable $\mathbf{Y}$ given $\boldsymbol{\beta}$ and marginalised over the model parameters $\mathbf{W}$.

The prior distribution over $\boldsymbol{\beta}$ is now a binomial distribution $\boldsymbol{\beta} \sim \prod_{s=1}^{S} \text{Bi}(\sigma_s)$ with $\sigma_s = 0.5$ reflecting our lack of prior knowledge. The conditional distribution which is the extra Gibbs step introduced, here for switching off kernels, $p\left(\beta_i = 0|\boldsymbol{\beta}_{-i}, \mathbf{Y}, \mathbf{K}^{s\boldsymbol{\theta}_s} \, \forall s \in \{1, \ldots, S\}\right)$ is given by

$$\frac{p\left(\mathbf{Y}|\beta_i = 0, \boldsymbol{\beta}_{-i}, \mathbf{K}^{s\boldsymbol{\theta}_s} \, \forall s \in \{1, \ldots, S\},\right) p\left(\beta_i = 0|\boldsymbol{\beta}_{-i}\right)}{\sum_{j=0}^{1} p\left(\mathbf{Y}|\beta_i = j, \boldsymbol{\beta}_{-i}, \mathbf{K}^{s\boldsymbol{\theta}_s} \, \forall s \in \{1, \ldots, S\},\right) p\left(\beta_i = j|\boldsymbol{\beta}_{-i}\right)}$$

where $\mathbf{K}^{s\boldsymbol{\theta}_s} \, \forall s \in \{1, \ldots, S\}$ are all the base kernels. The case for switching on kernels follows logically from the above.

Finally, the marginal likelihood term $p\left(\mathbf{Y}|\boldsymbol{\beta}, \mathbf{K}^{s\boldsymbol{\theta}_s} \, \forall s \in \{1, \ldots, S\}\right)$, that the Gibbs step depends on, is derived based on standard procedures from the literature,[12] as

$$\prod_{c=1}^{C} (2\pi)^{-\frac{N}{2}} |\boldsymbol{\Omega}_c|^{-\frac{1}{2}} \exp\left\{-\frac{1}{2}\mathbf{y}_c\boldsymbol{\Omega}_c\mathbf{y}_c^T\right\}$$

where $\boldsymbol{\Omega}_c = \mathbf{I} + \mathbf{K}^{\boldsymbol{\beta\Theta}}\mathbf{Z}_c^{-1}\mathbf{K}^{\boldsymbol{\beta\Theta}}$

The *product composite* kernel employs two MH subsamplers to sample β, from a gamma distribution this time, and the hyper-parameters π, χ from exponential distributions. The kernel parameters Θ are inferred in all cases via an extra MH subsampler, see[9] for details).

The MH subsamplers only need to sample once every step as the main Gibbs sampler, which always accepts the proposed move, will lead them towards convergence. The overall method in pseudo-algorithmic format can be seen in algorithm 1.1

Algorithm 1.1 Gibbs sampler

1:   Initialize Hyper-hyper-parameters $\tau, \upsilon, \omega, \phi, \mu, \lambda$
2:   Sample hyper-parameters ζ, ρ
3:   Sample parameters $\mathbf{W}, \Theta, \beta, \mathbf{Y}$
4:   Create train kernels
5:   **for** Gibbs iterations **do**
6:      Update posterior distributions (Bayes rule)
7:      Sample hyper-parameters and parameters
8:      Update kernels (if needed)
9:   **end for**
10: Discard Burn-in period samples
11: Create test kernels $\mathbf{K}^*$ given β, Θ posteriors
12: Monte Carlo estimation of Eq. 1.3 with $\mathbf{K}^*$ given $\mathbf{W}$ posterior

---

1.3.2. *Variational Bayes approximation*

An approximation to the exact solution for the multinomial probit composite kernel model can be offered, in similar manner to previous work by,[16] via the variational methodology[4] which offers a lower bound on the model evidence by using an ensemble of factored posteriors to approximate the joint parameter posterior distribution. The joint likelihood of the model[g] is defined as $p\left(\mathbf{t}, \boldsymbol{\Psi}|\mathbf{X}, \boldsymbol{\Xi}\right) = p\left(\mathbf{t}|\mathbf{Y}\right)p\left(\mathbf{Y}|\mathbf{W}, \boldsymbol{\beta}, \boldsymbol{\Theta}\right)p\left(\mathbf{W}|\mathbf{Z}\right)p\left(\mathbf{Z}|\tau, \upsilon\right)p\left(\boldsymbol{\beta}|\boldsymbol{\rho}\right)p\left(\boldsymbol{\Theta}|\omega, \phi\right)p\left(\boldsymbol{\rho}|\mu, \lambda\right)$
and the factorable ensemble approximation of the required posterior is $p\left(\boldsymbol{\Psi}|\boldsymbol{\Xi}, \mathbf{X}, \mathbf{t}\right) \approx Q\left(\boldsymbol{\Psi}\right) = Q\left(\mathbf{Y}\right)Q\left(\mathbf{W}\right)Q\left(\boldsymbol{\beta}\right)Q\left(\boldsymbol{\Theta}\right)Q\left(\mathbf{Z}\right)Q\left(\boldsymbol{\rho}\right)$. We can bound the model evidence using Jensen's inequality

$$\log p\left(\mathbf{t}\right) \geq \mathcal{E}_{Q(\boldsymbol{\Psi})}\{\log p\left(\mathbf{t}, \boldsymbol{\Psi}|\boldsymbol{\Xi}\right)\} - \mathcal{E}_{Q(\boldsymbol{\Psi})}\{\log Q\left(\boldsymbol{\Psi}\right)\} \qquad (1.4)$$

and minimise it (the lower bound is given in[9]) with distributions of the form $Q\left(\boldsymbol{\Psi}_i\right) \propto \exp\left(\mathcal{E}_{Q(\boldsymbol{\Psi}_{-i})}\{\log p\left(\mathbf{t}, \boldsymbol{\Psi}|\boldsymbol{\Xi}\right)\}\right)$ where $Q\left(\boldsymbol{\Psi}_{-i}\right)$ is the factorable ensemble with the ith component removed.

---

[g]The *linear composite* kernel is considered as an example. Modifications for the *binary* and *product composite* kernel are straightforward.

The resulting posterior distributions for the approximation are given below with full details of the derivations in.[9] First, the approximate posterior over the auxiliary variables is given by

$$Q\left(\mathbf{Y}\right) \propto \prod_{n=1}^{N} \delta\left(y_{i,n} > y_{k,n} \forall k \neq i\right) \delta\left(t_n = i\right) \mathcal{N}_{\mathbf{y}_n}\left(\widetilde{\mathbf{W}}\mathbf{k}_n^{\widetilde{\beta}\widetilde{\Theta}}, \mathbf{I}\right) \qquad (1.5)$$

which is a product of N C−dimensional conically truncated Gaussians. The shorthand tilde notation denotes posterior expectations in the usual manner, i.e. $\widetilde{f(\beta)} = \mathcal{E}_{Q(\beta)}\{f(\beta)\}$, and the posterior expectations for the auxiliary variable follow as

$$\widetilde{y}_{cn} = \widetilde{\mathbf{w}}_c \mathbf{k}_n^{\widetilde{\beta}\widetilde{\Theta}} - \frac{\mathcal{E}_{p(u)}\{\mathcal{N}_u\left(\widetilde{\mathbf{w}}_c \mathbf{k}_n^{\widetilde{\beta}\widetilde{\Theta}} - \widetilde{\mathbf{w}}_i \mathbf{k}_n^{\widetilde{\beta}\widetilde{\Theta}}, 1\right) \Phi_u^{n,i,c}\}}{\mathcal{E}_{p(u)}\{\Phi\left(u + \widetilde{\mathbf{w}}_i \mathbf{k}_n^{\widetilde{\beta}\widetilde{\Theta}} - \widetilde{\mathbf{w}}_c \mathbf{k}_n^{\widetilde{\beta}\widetilde{\Theta}}\right) \Phi_u^{n,i,c}\}} \qquad (1.6)$$

$$\widetilde{y}_{in} = \widetilde{\mathbf{w}}_i \mathbf{k}_n^{\widetilde{\beta}\widetilde{\Theta}} - \left(\sum_{c \neq i} \widetilde{y}_{cn} - \widetilde{\mathbf{w}}_c \mathbf{k}_n^{\widetilde{\beta}\widetilde{\Theta}}\right) \qquad (1.7)$$

where Φ is the standardized cumulative distribution function (CDF) and $\Phi_u^{n,i,c} = \prod_{j \neq i,c} \Phi\left(u + \widetilde{\mathbf{w}}_i \mathbf{k}_n^{\widetilde{\beta}\widetilde{\Theta}} - \widetilde{\mathbf{w}}_j \mathbf{k}_n^{\widetilde{\beta}\widetilde{\Theta}}\right)$. Next, the approximate posterior for the regressors can be expressed as

$$Q\left(\mathbf{W}\right) \propto \prod_{c=1}^{C} \mathcal{N}_{\mathbf{w}_c}\left(\widetilde{\mathbf{y}_c}\mathbf{K}^{\widetilde{\beta}\widetilde{\Theta}}\mathbf{V}_c, \mathbf{V}_c\right) \qquad (1.8)$$

where the covariance is defined as

$$\mathbf{V}_c = \left(\sum_{i=1}^{S}\sum_{j=1}^{S} \widetilde{\beta_i \beta_j} \mathbf{K}^{i\widetilde{\theta}_i} \mathbf{K}^{j\widetilde{\theta}_j} + \left(\widetilde{\mathbf{Z}}_c\right)^{-1}\right)^{-1} \qquad (1.9)$$

and $\widetilde{\mathbf{Z}}_c$ is a diagonal matrix of the expected variances $\widetilde{\zeta}_i \ldots \widetilde{\zeta}_N$ for each class. The associated posterior mean for the regressors is therefore $\widetilde{\mathbf{w}}_c = \widetilde{\mathbf{y}_c}\mathbf{K}^{\widetilde{\beta}\widetilde{\Theta}}\mathbf{V}_c$ and we can see the coupling between the auxiliary variable and regressor posterior expectation.

The approximate posterior for the variances $\mathbf{Z}$ is an updated product of inverse-gamma distributions and the posterior mean is given by $2\tau + 1/2\upsilon + \widetilde{w_{cn}^2}$, for details see.[12] Finally, the approximate posteriors for the kernel parameters $Q\left(\Theta\right)$, the combinatorial weights $Q\left(\beta\right)$ and the associated hyper-prior parameters $Q\left(\rho\right)$, or $Q\left(\pi\right), Q\left(\chi\right)$ in the product composite kernel case, can be obtained by importance sampling[2] in a similar manner to[16] since no tractable analytical solution can be offered.

Having described the approximate posterior distributions of the parameters and hence obtained the posterior expectations we turn back to our original task of making class predictions $\mathbf{t}^*$ for N_{test} new objects $\mathbf{X}^*$ that are represented by S different information sources $\mathbf{X}^{s*}$ embedded into Hilbert spaces as base kernels $\mathbf{K}^{*s\theta_s,\beta_s}$ and combined into a composite *test* kernel $\mathbf{K}^{*\Theta,\beta}$. The predictive distribution for a single new object $\mathbf{x}^*$ is given by $p\left(t^* = c|\mathbf{x}^*, \mathbf{X}, \mathbf{t}\right) = \int p\left(t^* = c|\mathbf{y}^*\right) p\left(\mathbf{y}^*|\mathbf{x}^*, \mathbf{X}, \mathbf{t}\right) dy^* = \int \delta_c^* p\left(\mathbf{y}^*|\mathbf{x}^*, \mathbf{X}, \mathbf{t}\right) dy^*$ which ends up as

$$p\left(t^* = c|\mathbf{x}^*, \mathbf{X}, \mathbf{t}\right) = E_{p(u)} \left\{ \prod_{j \neq c} \Phi \left[\frac{1}{\widetilde{\nu_j^*}} \left(u\widetilde{\nu_c^*} + \widetilde{m_c^*} - \widetilde{m_j^*} \right) \right] \right\} \qquad (1.10)$$

where,
for the general case of N_{test} objects, $\widetilde{m_c^*} = \widetilde{\mathbf{y}}_c \mathbf{K} \left(\mathbf{K}^* \mathbf{K}^{*T} + \mathbf{V}_c^{-1} \right)^{-1} \mathbf{K}^* \widetilde{\mathbf{\mathcal{V}}_c^*}$ and $\widetilde{\mathbf{\mathcal{V}}_c^*} = \left(\mathbf{I} + \mathbf{K}^{*T} \mathbf{V}_c \mathbf{K}^* \right)$ while we have dropped the notation for the dependance of the train $\mathbf{K}\,(N \times N)$ and test $\mathbf{K}^*\,(N \times N_{test})$ kernels on Θ, β for clarity. In algorithm 1.2 we summarize the VB approximation in a pseudo-algorithmic fashion.

Inference and intuition

Finally, the intuition behind the main model parameters is:

W The regressors indicate the weight with which data point n "votes" for class c. With appropriate sparsity-enducing priors on the distribution of their variance, a relevance vector machine[42] version of our model can be implemented. Furthermore, in the case of imbalanced problems separate prior distributions on the variance of the regressors can be enforced to induce sparsity on the over-represented class and improve predictive performance.

β The combinatorial weights indicate the significance of individual sources and their predictive ability based on the model likelihood.

Θ The kernel parameters control the applied smoothing on each feature set and through them we can infer the significance of the original dimensions **D**.

Algorithm 1.2 Variational Bayes approximation

1: Initialize $\boldsymbol{\Xi}$, sample $\boldsymbol{\Psi}$, create $\mathbf{K}_s|\beta_s, \theta_s$ and hence $\mathbf{K}|\boldsymbol{\beta}, \boldsymbol{\Theta}$
2: **while** Lower Bound changing **do**
3:     $\widetilde{\mathbf{w}}_c \leftarrow \widetilde{\mathbf{y}_c} \mathbf{K} \mathbf{V}_c$
4:     $\widetilde{y}_{cn} \leftarrow \widetilde{\mathbf{w}}_c \mathbf{k}_n^{\widetilde{\beta}\widetilde{\Theta}} - \dfrac{\mathcal{E}_{p(u)}\{\mathcal{N}_u\left(\widetilde{\mathbf{w}}_c \mathbf{k}_n^{\widetilde{\beta}\widetilde{\Theta}} - \widetilde{\mathbf{w}}_i \mathbf{k}_n^{\widetilde{\beta}\widetilde{\Theta}}, 1\right)\Phi_u^{n,i,c}\}}{\mathcal{E}_{p(u)}\{\Phi\left(u + \widetilde{\mathbf{w}}_i \mathbf{k}_n^{\widetilde{\beta}\widetilde{\Theta}} - \widetilde{\mathbf{w}}_c \mathbf{k}_n^{\widetilde{\beta}\widetilde{\Theta}}\right)\Phi_u^{n,i,c}\}}$
5:     $\widetilde{y}_{in} \leftarrow \widetilde{\mathbf{w}}_i \mathbf{k}_n^{\widetilde{\beta}\widetilde{\Theta}} - \left(\sum_{j\neq i}\widetilde{y}_{jn} - \widetilde{\mathbf{w}}_j \mathbf{k}_n^{\widetilde{\beta}\widetilde{\Theta}}\right)$
6:     $\widetilde{\zeta}_{cn} \leftarrow \dfrac{\tau + \frac{1}{2}}{v + \frac{1}{2}w_{cn}^2}$
7:     $\widetilde{\rho}, \widetilde{\beta}, \widetilde{\Theta} \leftarrow \widetilde{\rho}, \widetilde{\beta}, \widetilde{\Theta}|\widetilde{\mathbf{w}}_c, \widetilde{\mathbf{y}}_n$ by importance sampling
8:     Update $\mathbf{K}|\widetilde{\beta}, \widetilde{\Theta}$ and $\mathbf{V}_c$
9: **end while**
10: Create composite test kernel $\mathbf{K}^*|\widetilde{\beta}, \widetilde{\Theta}$
11: $\widetilde{\mathcal{V}_c^*} \leftarrow \left(\mathbf{I} + \mathbf{K}^{*T}\mathbf{V}_c\mathbf{K}^*\right)$
12: $\widetilde{\mathbf{m}_c^*} \leftarrow \widetilde{\mathbf{y}}_c \mathbf{K}\left(\mathbf{K}^*\mathbf{K}^{*T} + \mathbf{V}_c^{-1}\right)^{-1}\mathbf{K}^*\widetilde{\mathcal{V}_c^*}$
13: **for** $n = 1$ to N_{test} **do**
14:     **for** $c = 1$ to C **do**
15:         **for** $i = 1$ to K Samples **do**
16:             $u_i \leftarrow \mathcal{N}(0,1), \quad p_{cn}^i \leftarrow \prod_{j\neq c}\Phi\left[\frac{1}{\nu_j^*}\left(u_i\widetilde{\nu_c^*} + \widetilde{m_c^*} - \widetilde{m_j^*}\right)\right]$
17:         **end for**
18:     **end for**
19:     $P\left(t_n^* = c|\mathbf{x}_n^*, \mathbf{X}, \mathbf{t}\right) = \frac{1}{K}\sum_{i=1}^K p_{cn}^i$
20: **end for**

1.4. Experiments and Results

In this section we present experimental results from both the MCMC and the VB methods, a direct comparison between them and an examination of their differences with respect to the resulting posterior distributions of the parameters. We monitor convergence of the VB approximation via the progression of the lower bound and assume convergence when there is less than 0.1% increase on the bound or a maximum number of 100 iterations has been reached. All results are repeated over a number of random initializations in order to report statistical measures. Finally, throughout the different data sets employed, we use the kernel function that was found to perform better after an initial examination and in the case of radial basis function kernels we fix the kernel parameters to $1/D$ where D the dimensionality of the corresponding features.

We first compare the MCMC solution and the approximation on two synthetic data sets, then we consider some publicly available UCI data sets and then we report results from the VB approximation on two important problems arising in the bioinformatics research area. The reported CPU times are for a 1.6 GHz Intel based PC with 2Gb RAM running Matlab codes.

1.4.1. *Proof of concept on an artificial data-set*

In order to illustrate the performance of the VB approximation against the full Gibbs sampling solution, we employ two low dimensional datasets which enable us to visualise the decision boundaries and posterior distributions produced by either method. First we consider a linearly seperable case in which we construct the dataset by fixing our regressors $\mathbf{W} \in \Re^{C \times D}$, with $C = 3$ and $D = 3$, to known values and sample two dimensional covariates $\mathbf{X}$ plus a constant term. In that way, by knowing the true values of our regressors, we can examine the accuracy of both the Gibbs posterior distribution and the approximate posterior estimate of the VB. In Fig. 1.4.1 the dataset together with the optimal decision boundaries constructed by the known regressor values can be seen.

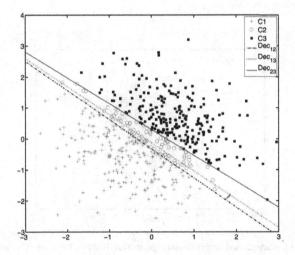

Figure 1.4.   Linearly seperable dataset with known regressors defining the decision boundaries. Cn denotes the members of class n and Dec_{ij} is the decision boundary between classes i and j.

In Figs. 1.5 and 1.6 we present the posterior distributions of one decision bounary's (Dec_{12}) slope and intercept based on both our obtained Gibbs samples and the approximate posterior of the regressors $\mathbf{W}$. As we can see, the variational approximation is in agreement with the mass of the Gibbs posterior and it successfuly captures the pre-determined regressors values.

However, as it can be observed in Eq. 1.11 the approximation is over-confident in the prediction and produces a smaller covariance

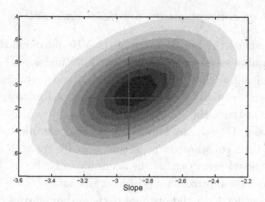

Figure 1.5.   Gibbs posterior distribution of a decision boundary's (Dec_{12}) slope and intercept for a chain of 100,000 samples. The cross shows the original decision boundary employed to sample the dataset.

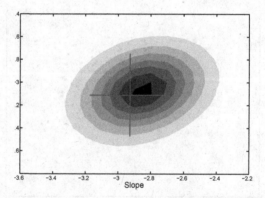

Figure 1.6.   The variational approximate posterior distribution for the same case as above. Employing 100,000 samples from the approximate posterior of the regressors **W** in order to estimate the approximate posterior of the slope and intercept.

for the posterior distribution as expected Furthermore, the probability mass is concentrated in a very small area due to the very nature of VB approximation and similar mean field methods that make extreme "judgments" as they do not explore the posterior space by Markov chains.

$$C_{\text{Gibbs}} = \begin{bmatrix} 0.16 & 0.18 \\ 0.18 & 0.22 \end{bmatrix} \quad C_{\text{VB}} = \begin{bmatrix} 0.015 & 0.015 \\ 0.015 & 0.018 \end{bmatrix} \tag{1.11}$$

The second synthetic dataset we employ is a 4-dimensional 3-class dataset $\{\mathbf{X}, \mathbf{t}\}$ with $N = 400$, first described by,[33] which defines the first class as points in an ellipse $\alpha > x_1^2 + x_2^2 > \beta$, the second class as points below a line $\alpha x_1 + \beta x_2 < \gamma$ and the third class as points surrounding these areas, see Fig. 1.7.

We approach the problem by: 1) introducing a second order polynomial expansion on the original dataset $F(\mathbf{x}_n) = [1 \ x_{n1} \ x_{n2} \ x_{n1}^2 \ x_{n1}x_{n2} \ x_{n2}^2]$ while disregarding the uninformative dimensions x_3, x_4, 2) modifying the dimensionality of our regressors $\mathbf{W}$ to $C \times D$ and analogously the corresponding covariance and 3) substituting $F(\mathbf{X})$ for $\mathbf{K}$ in our derived methodology. Due to our expansion we now have a $2-D$ decision plane that we can plot and a $6-$dimensional regressor $\mathbf{w}$ per class. In Fig. 1.7 we plot the decision boundaries produced from the full Gibbs solution by averaging over the posterior parameters after 100,000 samples and in Fig. 1.8 the corresponding decision boundaries from the VB approximation after 100 iterations.

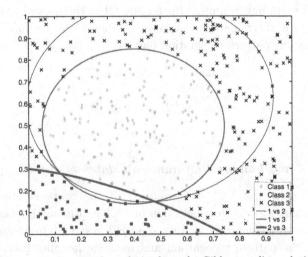

Figure 1.7.   Decision boundaries from the Gibbs sampling solution.

As it can be seen, both the VB approximation and the MCMC solution produce similar decision boundaries leading to good classification performances - 2% error for both Gibbs and VB for the above decision boundaries and training size. However, the Gibbs sampler produces tighter boundaries due to the Markov Chain exploring the parameter posterior space more efficiently than the VB approximation.

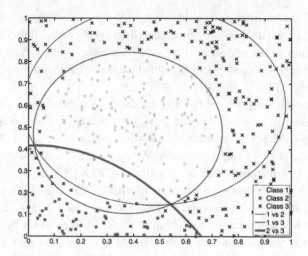

Figure 1.8.   Decision boundaries from the VB approximation.

The corresponding training plus testing CPU times (sec) are given in Table 1.1 and it is straightforward to see the benefit of the approximation as an employable pattern recognition method.

Table 1.1.   CPU times.

Gibbs	VB
41,720 (s)	120.3 (s)

1.4.2. UCI and handwritten numerals data-sets

To further assess the VB approximation of the proposed multinomial probit classifier, we explore a selection of UCI multinomial datasets. The performances are compared against reported results[32] from well-known methods in the pattern recognition and machine learning literature. We employ an RBF (VB RBF), a 2nd order polynomial (VB P) and a linear kernel (VB L) with the VB approximation and report 10-fold cross-validated (CV) error percentages, in Table 1.2, and CPU times, in Table 1.3, for a maximum of 50 VB iterations unless convergence has already occured. The comparison with the K-nn and PK-nn is for standard implementations of these methods, see[32] for details.

As we can see the VB approximation to the multinomial probit outperforms in most cases both the K-nn and PK-nn although not always

Table 1.2.   10-fold CV error % (mean±std) on standard UCI multinomial datasets.

Dataset	VB RBF	VB L	VB P	K-nn	PK-nn
Balance	8.8 ± 3.6	12.2 ± 4.2	$\mathbf{7.0 \pm 3.3}$	11.5 ± 3.0	10.2 ± 3.0
Crabs	23.5 ± 11.3	$\mathbf{13.5 \pm 8.2}$	21.5 ± 9.1	15.0 ± 8.8	19.5 ± 6.9
Glass	27.9 ± 10.1	35.8 ± 11.8	28.4 ± 8.9	29.9 ± 9.2	$\mathbf{26.7 \pm 8.8}$
Iris	$\mathbf{2.7 \pm 5.6}$	11.3 ± 9.9	4.7 ± 6.3	5.3 ± 5.3	4.0 ± 5.6
Soybean	6.5 ± 10.6	6 ± 9.7	$\mathbf{4 \pm 8.4}$	14.50 ± 16.7	4.5 ± 9.6
Vehicle	$\mathbf{25.6 \pm 4}$	29.7 ± 3.3	26 ± 6.1	36.3 ± 5.2	37.2 ± 4.5
Wine	4.5 ± 5.1	2.8 ± 4.7	$\mathbf{1.1 \pm 2.3}$	3.9 ± 3.8	3.4 ± 2.89

Table 1.3.   VB running times (seconds) for computing 10-fold cross-validation results.

Dataset	Balance	Crabs	Glass	Iris	Soybean	Vehicle	Wine
CPU time (s)	2,285	270	380	89	19	3,420	105

offering statistical significant improvements as the variance of the 10-fold CV errors is quite large in most cases.

In the following paragraphs we report results demonstrating the efficiency of our kernel combination approach when multiple sources of information are available. Comparisons are made against combination of classifiers and also between different ways to combine the kernels as we have described previously. In order to assess the above, we make use of a data-set that has multiple feature spaces describing the objects to be classified. It is a large $N = 2000$, multinomial $C = 10$ and "multi-featured" $S = 4$ UCI data-set, named "Multiple Features". The objects are handwritten numerals, from 0 to 9, and the available features are the Fourier descriptors (FR), the Karhunen-Loéve features (KL), the pixel averages (PX) and the Zernike moments (ZM).[41] have previously reported results on this problem by combining classifiers but have employed a different test set which is not publicly available. Furthermore, we allow the rotation invariance property of the ZM features to cause problems in the distinction between digits 6 and 9. The hope is that the remaining feature spaces can compensate on the discrimination.

In Tables 1.4, 1.5 and 1.6, we report experimental results over 50 repeated trials where we have randomly selected 20 training and 20 testing objects from each class. For each trial we employ 1) A single classifier on each feature space, 2) the proposed classifier on the composite feature

Table 1.4. Classification percentage error (mean±std) of individual classifiers trained on each feature space.

Full MCMC Gibbs sampling - *Single F.S*			
FR	KL	PX	ZM
27.3 ± 3.3	11.0 ± 2.3	7.3 ± 2	25.2 ± 3

Table 1.5. Combinations of the individual classifiers based on four widely used rules: Product (Prod), Mean (Sum), Majority voting (Maj) and Maximum (Max).

Full MCMC Gibbs sampling - *Comb. Classifiers*			
Prod	Sum	Max	Maj
5.1 ± 1.7	5.3 ± 2	8.4 ± 2.3	8.45 ± 2.2

Table 1.6. Combination of feature spaces. VB approximation.

VB approx. - *Comb. Kernels*				
Bin	FixSum	WSum	FixProd	WProd
5.53 ± 1.7	4.85 ± 1.5	6.1 ± 1.6	5.35 ± 1.4	6.43 ± 1.8

space. This allows us to examine the performance of combinations of classifiers versus combination of feature spaces. We report results from the VB approximation and in all cases we employ the multinomial probit kernel machine using a Gaussian kernel with fixed parameters.

As we can see from Table 1.4 and 1.5 the two best performing ensemble learning methods outperform all of the individual classifiers trained on seperate feature spaces. With a p-value of $1.5e^{-07}$ between the Pixel classifier and the Product rule, it is a statistical significant difference. At the same time, all the kernel combination methods in Table 1.6 match the best performing classifier combination approaches, with a p-value of approximately 0.9 between the Product classifier combination rule and the linear (sum) kernel combination method.

Furthermore, the variants of our method that employ combinatorial weights offer the advantage of infering the significance of the contributing sources of information. In Fig. 1.9, we can see that the pixel (PX) and zernike moments (ZM) feature spaces receive large weights and hence contribute significantly in the composite feature space. This is in accordance with our expectations, as the pixel feature space seems to be the best perfoming individual classifier and complementary predictive power mainly from the ZM channel is improving on that.

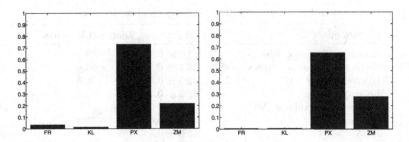

Figure 1.9. Typical combinatorial weights from Mean (left) and Product (right) composite kernel.

The results indicate that there is no benefit in the zero-one loss when weighted combinations of feature spaces are employed. This is in agreement with past work by[27] and.[17] The clear benefit however remains the ability to infer the relative significance of the sources and hence gain a better understanding of the problem.

1.4.3. *Protein fold recognition and remote homology detection*

Fold recognition

The original dataset from[14] (based on SCOP PDB-40D) consists of 313 proteins for training and 385 proteins for testing with less than 35% sequence identity between any two proteins in the train and the test set. Furthermore, the extensions proposed by[40] exclude 4 proteins from the original dataset, namely proteins 2SCMC and 2GPS from the training set plus 2YHX_1 and 2YHX_2 from the test set, due to lack of sequence records.

Reported results are averaged over 20 (fold recognition) and 10 (RHD) randomly initialized trials in order to obtain statistical measures of accuracy and precision. Throughout this problem we have employed second order polynomial kernels for the global characteristics and inner product kernels for the local characteristics (SW) as they were found to provide a better embeding of the feature spaces.

First we examine the performance from individual feature spaces to gain an overall understanding of their predictive abilities. This however does not draw the complete picture as complementary information may be shared across sources achieving low performances. In Table 1.7 we present the mean percentage accuracy with standard deviations from our method (VBKC) together with the *best* ones reported by[14] on the original dataset.

Table 1.7.   Average individual F.S percentage accuracy.

Feature Space	VBKC	Ding and Dubchak
Amino Acid Composition (C)	51.2 ± 0.5	44.9
Predicted Secondary Structure (S)	38.1 ± 0.3	35.6
Hydrophobicity (H)	32.5 ± 0.4	36.5
Polarity (P)	32.2 ± 0.3	32.9
van der Waals volume (V)	32.8 ± 0.3	35
Polarizability (Z)	33.2 ± 0.4	32.9
PseAA $\lambda = 1$ (λ_1)	41.5 ± 0.5	—
PseAA $\lambda = 4$ (λ_4)	41.5 ± 0.4	—
PseAA $\lambda = 14$ (λ_{14})	38 ± 0.2	—
PseAA $\lambda = 30$ (λ_{30})	32 ± 0.2	—
SW with BLOSUM62 (SW_1)	59.8 ± 1.9	—
SW with PAM50 (SW_2)	49 ± 0.7	—

— Not employed in the Ding and Dubchak data-set.

Regarding the original features employed by[14] we are in agreement with their observations as the best performing feature space, seems to be the amino acid composition (C). The $\lambda = 1$ and $\lambda = 4$ PseAA achieve the second best *global* individual performance and as the "step" λ increases further, the individual performances decrease. Although according to[40] the PseAA composition "has the same form as the conventional amino acid composition, but contains much more information" it seems at this stage that none of the PseAA is as predictive as the conventional amino acid composition. Furthermore, the local characteristics (SW) surprisingly outperform every global one and SW_1 achieves a higher accuracy than the best SVM-combinations proposed by.[14] This is because although most of the proteins have less than 35% sequence similarity, this still seems to be an adequate similarity level to achieve a good accuracy.

In Table 1.8 we report the effect of sequentially adding the feature spaces in the order of,[14] extending that to the addition of the PseAA compositions and finally adding the sequence similarity based features. We compare against the best performing SVM combination methodology as reported in[14] and the ensemble method of.[40] As we can see in all the steps the proposed method outperforms the best reported accuracies and offers the current *state-of-the-art* in this data-set.

The best performances can be seen in Table 1.9 in comparison with the best ones reported in the cited past work. We achieve an improvement over both past methods while we employ a single multiclass kernel machine without resorting to ensemble learning techniques or combining multiple binary classifiers.

Table 1.8.   Effect of F.S combination. % Accuracy reported.

Feature Spaces	VBKC	Ding & Dubchak (AvA)
C	51.2 ± 0.5	44.9
CS	55.7 ± 0.5	52.1
CSH	57.7 ± 0.6	56.0
CSHP	57.9 ± 0.9	56.5
CSHPV	58.1 ± 0.8	55.5
CSHPVZ	58.6 ± 1.1	53.9
CSHPVZλ_1	60 ± 0.8	—
CSHPVZ$\lambda_1\lambda_4$	60.8 ± 1.1	—
CSHPVZ$\lambda_1\lambda_4\lambda_{14}$	61.5 ± 1.2	—
CSHPVZ$\lambda^1\lambda^4\lambda^{14}\lambda^{30}$	62.2 ± 1.3	—
CSHPVZ$\lambda^1\lambda^4\lambda^{14}\lambda^{30}SW_1$	66.4 ± 0.8	—
CSHPVZ$\lambda^1\lambda^4\lambda^{14}\lambda^{30}SW_1SW_2$	68.1 ± 1.2	—
		Shen & Chou
SHPVZ$\lambda_1\lambda_4\lambda_{14}\lambda_{30}$	61.0 ± 1.4	62.1

— Not employed in the Ding and Dubchak dataset.

Table 1.9.   Best single run performances (% Accuracy).

Feature Spaces	Ding & Dubchak	Shen & Chou	VBKC
CSHPVZ	56	—	60.5
SHPVZ$\lambda_1\lambda_4\lambda_{14}\lambda_{30}$	—	62.1	63.5
CSHPVZ$\lambda_1\lambda_4\lambda_{14}\lambda_{30}$	—	—	63.9
CSHPVZ$\lambda^1\lambda^4\lambda^{14}\lambda^{30}SW_1SW_2$	—	—	**70**
No. of Classifiers	2,106	9	1

In Fig. 1.10 we plot a summary of the weights over 20 runs depicting the lower quartile, median, and upper quartile values.

As we can observe, the amino acid composition and the secondary structure are judged as more important, followed by the PseAA $\lambda = 1$. However, it is worth noting that by taking out the amino acid composition we have only a small loss in performance as we have seen in Table 1.8. These two observations suggest that the original amino acid (C) and the pseudo-ones (λ_i) carry redundant information. Furthermore, despite the individual accuracies of the SW features, they are not heavily weighted. This is because they depend solely on the sequence similarity between proteins and their quality of discriminative information is strongly related to which end of the 0-35% sequence similarity the two proteins will belong. In reality, for the real "twilight-zone" of low-homology proteins (much less than 35% similarity) such features have little effect by definition.

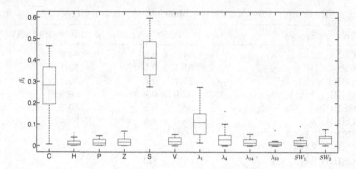

Figure 1.10.   Combinatorial weights when all the feature spaces are employed.

Remote homology detection (RHD)

The SCOP 1.53 benchmark data-set[h] as described in[28] is employed to simulate the RHD problem. It consists of 4,352 proteins belonging to one of 54 families and the positive training is performed on low-homologs while the positive testing on members of the same family. We consider four state-of-the-art string kernels, namely a *local alignment* (LA) kernel,[37] a *mismatch* (MM) kernel,[26] an *oligomer* kernel (Mono)[29] and a *pairwise* (PW) kernel,[28] taking the best performing case from each string kernel category as a separate informational source. We follow the above past works within the kernel machine paradigm by adding a class-dependent regularization parameter to the diagonal of the kernels to improve performance on this highly imbalanced problem.

The results from the combination of the string kernels are depicted in Table 1.10 together with the best previously reported results within the SVM methodology. We achieve a state-of-the-art performance via the combination of the kernels and match the overall best performing SVM method outperforming other string kernels. In Fig. 1.11 the number of families that achieve certain ROC scores is depicted in comparison with some of the best performing methods reported in the literature.

1.5. Discussion and Future Directions

In this contribution we offer a probabilistic multi-class multi-kernel machine that is able to operate simultaneously in multiple feature sets via a kernel

---

[h]Available from http://www.ccls.columbia.edu/compbio/svm-pairwise

Table 1.10. ROC, ROC50 and median RFP averaged over 54 families.

Method	Mean ROC	Mean ROC50	Mean mRFP
VBKC	**0.924**	**0.567**	**0.0661**
SVM (SW)	0.896	0.464	0.0837
SVM (LA)	**0.925**	**0.649**	**0.0541**
SVM (MM)	0.872	0.400	0.0837
SVM (Mono)	**0.919**	**0.508**	**0.0664**

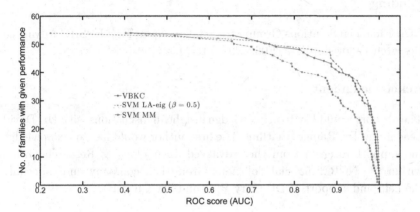

Figure 1.11. ROC score (AUC) distributions for the proposed string combination method and two state-of-the-art string kernels with SVMs.

combination methodology. Furthermore, we illustrate the capabilities of our method on two artificial data-sets, several benchmark UCI data-sets and finally on the challenging problems of protein fold and remote homology detection.

We provide the current state-of-the-art in the protein fold prediction problem and also achieve state-of-the-art performances in the majority of the considered data-sets, demonstrating the benefit of an explicit multi-class kernel machine for multi-featured problems. Furthermore, our methodology offers a significant reduction in computational resources, via the VB approximation, as it is based on a single classifier operating over a composite space which retains the dimensionality $(N \times N)$ of any of the individual contributing feature spaces $(N \times N)$. This, in contrast with the past work of employing thousands of binary classifiers or ensembles of individually trained classifiers is a significant improvement.

The computational complexity of the MCMC solution is $\sim \mathcal{O}\left(SN^3\right)$ per sample, with the VB approximation alleviating the sample size dependance. We are planning to offer the MAP solution to our model as a further approximate solution and to extend the method to an explicit multi-class multi-kernel RVM algorithm and also an informative vector machine (IVM)[24] adaptation which would offer further insight on the advantages and drawbacks of these frameworks.

Funding

NCR Financial Solutions Group Ltd. Scholarship to T.D; EPSRC Advanced Research Fellowship (EP/E052029/1) to M.A.G

Acknowledgment

The authors would like to acknowledge insightful discussions with Dr. David Leader and Dr. Rainer Breitling. The first author would like to acknowledge the support received from the Advanced Technology & Research Group within the NCR Financial Solutions Group Ltd company and especially the help and support of Dr. Gary Ross and Dr. Chao He.

References

1. Albert, J. and Chib, S. (1993). Bayesian analysis of binary and polychotomous response data, *Journal of the American Statistical Association* **88**, pp. 669–679.
2. Andrieu, C. (2003). An introduction to MCMC for machine learning, *Machine Learning* **50**, pp. 5–43.
3. Bai, L. and Shen, L. (2003). Combining wavelets with hmm for face recognition, in *Proceedings of the 23rd Artificial Intelligence Conference*.
4. Beal, M. J. (2003). *Variational Algorithms for approximate Bayesian Inference*, Ph.D. thesis, The Gatsby Computational Neuroscience Unit, University College London.
5. Bellman, R. (1961). *Adaptive Control Processes: A Guided Tour* (Princeton University Press).
6. Berger, J. O. (1985). *Statistical Decision Theory and Bayesian Analysis* (Springer Series in Statistics, Springer).
7. Bishop, C. M. (2006). *Pattern Recognition and Machine Learning* (Springer, New York, USA).
8. Damoulas, T. and Girolami, M. A. (2008a). A bayesian multi-class multi-kernel pattern recognition machine, *Pattern Recognition Letters* Under Review.

9. Damoulas, T. and Girolami, M. A. (2008b). Combining feature spaces for multinomial classification with bayesian inference, *Pattern Recognition* Under Review.

10. Damoulas, T. and Girolami, M. A. (2008c). Probabilistic multi-class multi-kernel learning: On protein fold recognition and remote homology detection, *Bioinformatics* Under Review.

11. de Freitas, N., Højen-Sørensen, P., Jordan, M. and Russell, S. (2001). Variational MCMC, in *Proceedings of the 17th conference in Uncertainty in Artificial Intelligence*.

12. Denison, D. G. T., Holmes, C. C., Mallick, B. K. and Smith, A. F. M. (2002). *Bayesian Methods for Nonlinear Classification and Regression* (Wiley Series in Probability and Statistics, West Sussex, UK).

13. Dietterich, T. G. (2000). Ensemble methods in machine learning, in *Proceedings of the 1st International Workshop on Multiple Classifier Systems*, pp. 1–15.

14. Ding, C. and Dubchak, I. (2001). Multi-class protein fold recognition using support vector machines and neural networks, *Bioinformatics* **17**, 4, pp. 349–358.

15. Girolami, M. and Rogers, S. (2005). Hierarchic Bayesian models for kernel learning, in *Proceedings of the 22nd International Conference on Machine Learning*, pp. 241–248.

16. Girolami, M. and Rogers, S. (2006). Variational Bayesian multinomial probit regression with Gaussian process priors, *Neural Computation* **18**, 8, pp. 1790–1817.

17. Girolami, M. and Zhong, M. (2007). Data integration for classification problems employing Gaussian process priors, in *Twentieth Annual Conference on Neural Information Processing Systems*.

18. Hastie, T., Tibshirani, R. and Friedman, J. (2001). *The Elements of Statistical Learning* (Springer Series in Statistics, Springer), ISBN 0-387-95284-5.

19. Hastings, W. K. (1970). Monte Carlo sampling methods using Markov chains and their applications, *Biometrika* **57**, pp. 97–109.

20. Holmes, C. C. and Held, L. (2006). Bayesian auxiliary variable models for binary and multinomial regression, *Bayesian Analysis* **1**, pp. 145–168.

21. Kittler, J., Hatef, M., Duin, R. P. W. and Matas, J. (1998). On combining classifiers, *IEEE Transactions on Pattern Analysis and Machine Intelligence* **20**, 3, pp. 226–239.

22. Kuncheva, L. I. (2004). *Combining Pattern Classifiers. Methods and Algorithms* (Wiley).

23. Lanckriet, G. R. G. (2004). Learning the kernel matrix with semidefinite programming, *Journal of Machine Learning Research* **5**, pp. 27–72.

24. Lawrence, N., Seeger, M. and Herbrich, R. (2003). Fast sparse gaussian process methods: The informative vector machine, in *Advances in Neural Information Processing Systems 15*, pp. 625–632.

25. Lee, W.-J., Verzakov, S. and Duin, R. P. (2007). Kernel combination versus classifier combination, in *7th International Workshop on Multiple Classifier Systems*.
26. Leslie, C. S., Eskin, E., Cohen, A., Weston, J. and Noble, W. S. (2004). Mismatch string kernels for discriminative protein classification, *Bioinformatics* **20**, 4, pp. 467–476.
27. Lewis, D. P., Jebara, T. and Noble, W. S. (2006). Nonstationary kernel combination, in *23rd International Conference on Machine Learning*.
28. Liao, L. and Noble, W. S. (2003). Combining pairwise sequnce similarity and support vector machines for detecting remote protein evolutionary and structural relationships, *Journal of Computational Biology* **6**, 6, pp. 857–868.
29. Lingner, T. and Meinicke, P. (2004). Remote homology detection based on oligomer distances, *Bioinformatics* **22**, 18, pp. 2224–2231.
30. MacKay, D. (2003). *Information Theory, Inference and Learning Algorithms* (Cambridge University Press).
31. MacKay, D. J. C. (1992). The evidence framework applied to classification networks, *Neural Computation* **4**, 5, pp. 698–714.
32. Manocha, S. and Girolami, M. A. (2007). An empirical analysis of the probabilistic k-nearest neighbour classifier, *Pattern Recognition Letters*.
33. Neal, R. M. (1998). Regression and Classification using Gaussian process priors, *Bayesian Statistics* **6**, pp. 475–501.
34. Ong, C. S., Smola, A. J. and Williamson, R. C. (2005). Learning the kernel with hyperkernels, *Journal of Machine Learning Research* **6**, pp. 1043–1071.
35. Pavlidis, P., Weston, J., Cai, J. and Grundy, N. W. (2001). Gene functional classification from heterogenous data, in *5th Annual International Conference on Computational Molecular Biology*, pp. 242–248.
36. Rasmussen, C. E. and Williams, C. K. I. (2006). *Gaussian Processes for Machine Learning* (MIT Press, Cambridge, Massachusetts, USA), ISBN 0-262-18253-X.
37. Saigo, H., Vert, J.-P., Ueda, N. and Akutsu, T. (2004). Protein homology detection using string alignment kernels, *Bioinformatics* **20**, 11, pp. 1682–1689.
38. Schölkopf, B. and Smola, A. (2002). *Learning with Kernels* (The MIT Press).
39. Shawe-Taylor, J. and Cristianini, N. (2004). *Kernel Methods for Pattern Analysis* (Cambridge University Press).
40. Shen, H.-B. and Chou, K.-C. (2006). Ensemble classifier for protein fold pattern recognition, *Bioinformatics* **22**, 14, pp. 1717–1722.
41. Tax, D. M. J., van Breukelen, M., Duin, R. P. W. and Kittler, J. (2000). Combining multiple classifiers by averaging or by multiplying? *Pattern Recognition* **33**, pp. 1475–1485.
42. Tipping, M. E. (2001). Sparse Bayesian learning and the relevance vector machine, *Journal of Machine Learning Research* **1**, pp. 211–244.
43. Wolpert, D. H. (1992). Stacked generalization, *Neural Networks* **5**, 2, pp. 241–259.

Chapter 2

Image Quality Assessment Based on Weighted Perceptual Features

D. Venkata Rao[1] and L. Pratap Reddy[2]

[1] *Vignan's Engineering College, Guntur*
E-mail: dv2002@yahoo.co.in

[2] *JNTU College of Engineering, Hyderabad*
E-mail: prataplr@rediffmanil.com

A novel method of image quality assessment is proposed in this work integrating the intermediate and higher visual processes of human visual perception with structural distortion measurement. The intermediate and higher visual processes are known to select a subset of available sensory information reducing the complexity of scene analysis and facilitate cognition. This subset of sensory information forms perceptual important regions. In this work the perceptually important regions are modeled based on three image parameters viz., edge strength, texture content and local contrast. A new image quality assessment metric is formulated by weighing the structural distortions in local regions in proportional to the perceptual importance of the region, evaluated based on edge strength in the respective region. Perceptual weights of the local regions are also calculated individually based on texture content and local contrast of the respective regions. These perceptual weights are used to weigh the structural distortions in the local regions and to arrive at the respective perceptual quality metrics. A perceptual importance map is obtained by combining the perceptual weights of the local regions based on edge strength, texture content and local contrast. An enhanced image quality assessment metric, Perceptual Structural SIMilarity 'PSSIM' is proposed by weighing the structural distortion map with the perceptual importance map. The performance of the proposed method is compared with the state of the art image quality metrics namely Peak Signal to Noise Ratio (PSNR), Universal image Quality Index (UQI) and Structural SIMilarity index (SSIM).

Contents

2.1 Introduction 30
   2.1.1 Statistical metrics 31
   2.1.2 Error sensitivity metrics 32
   2.1.3 Coder specific metrics 33
   2.1.4 Transform based metrics 34
   2.1.5 Structural approaches 34
2.2 A Model for Weighted Perceptual Features on SSIM 37
   2.2.1 Image distortion model 38
2.3 Perceptual Structural Similarity Model 41
   2.3.1 Weighing function based on edge strength 42
   2.3.2 Perceptual structural similarity based on edge strength 43
   2.3.3 Weighing function based on texture 43
   2.3.4 Perceptual structural similarity based on texture 44
   2.3.5 Weighing function based on contrast 44
   2.3.6 Perceptual structural similarity based on local contrast 45
   2.3.7 Weighing function of perceptual features 45
   2.3.8 Perceptual Structural Similarity index 47
2.4 Performance Evaluation of PSSIM 47
2.5 Conclusions and Future Scope 51
References 52

2.1. Introduction

The role of images in present day communication has been steadily increasing. In this context the quality of an image plays a vital role. Different stages and multiples design choices at each stage exist in any image processing system. They have direct bearing on the quality of the resulting image. Unless we have a quantitative measure for the quality of an image, it becomes difficult to design an ideal image processing system. Measurement of image quality plays an important role in every stage of image processing systems. An image acquisition system can use the quality metric to adjust itself automatically for obtaining improved quality images. It can be used to compare and evaluate image processing systems and algorithms. A quality metric can as well be embedded into an image-processing algorithm to optimize its performance.

The image quality assessment methods can be classified as subjective and objective methods. For several years, the image quality assessment (QA) has been performed subjectively using human observers based on their satisfaction. It depends on the type, size, range of images, observer's background and motivation and experimental conditions like lighting, display quality etc. The human visual system (HVS) is enormously complex with optical, synaptic, photochemical and electrical phenomena. The International Telecommunication Union (ITU) has recommended a 5-point scale using the adjectives bad, poor, fair, good and excellent. A numerical category scaling also can be used as an alternative, which is linear and hence more convenient to use. Subjective quality measurement techniques provide numerical values that quantify viewer's satisfaction, however are time-consuming and observer responses may vary. They provide no constructive methods for performance improvement and are difficult to use as a part of design process.

The objective image quality measurement seeks to measure the quality of images algorithmically. Objective image quality metrics can be classified as Full-reference in which the algorithm has access to the perfect (considered to be distortion free) image, No-reference in which the algorithm has access only to the distorted image and Reduced-reference in which the algorithm has partial information regarding the perfect image.

2.1.1. *Statistical metrics*

In,[1] a number of simple statistical metrics on numerical errors are compared for gray scale image compression. These metrics include average difference, maximum difference, absolute error, MSE, peak MSE, Laplcian MSE, histogram, Hosaka plot (a graphical quality measure, the area and shape of the plot gives information about the type and amount of degradation) etc. It is observed that although some numerical measures correlate well with the observers response for a specific compression technique, they are not found to be reliable for evaluation across various methods of compression. The most widely adopted statistical feature is the Mean Squared Error (MSE). However, MSE and its variants may not correlate well with subjective quality measures because human perception of image distortions and artifacts is unaccounted for. MSE is treated as ineffective measure because; the residual image is not uncorrelated additive noise. It contains components of the original image. A detailed discussion on MSE is presented by Girod.[2] These facts led to the development of quality metrics based on error sensitivity, which aims at quantifying the strength of the errors between the reference and the distorted signals in an image plane.

2.1.2. *Error sensitivity metrics*

These methods are proposed with multiple stages among Pre-processing, Contrast Sensitivity Function (CSF) filtering, Channel decomposition, Error normalization, Masking and Error pooling.

A well-known method for image quality under this paradigm that incorporates majority of these stages is, Visible Differences Predictor (VDP)[3,4] proposed by Dally. VDP by Dally aims at computation of a probability-of-detection map between the reference and the distorted signal. The value at each point in the map is modeled as the probability that a human observer will perceive a difference between the reference and the distorted images (expressed in luminance values instead of pixels) are passed through a series of processes: point non-linearity, CSF filtering, channel decomposition, contrast calculation, masking effect modeling, and probability-of-detection calculation. A modified cortex transform[5] is used for channel decomposition, which transforms the image signal into five spatial levels followed by six orientation levels, leading to a total of 31 independent channels (including the baseband). For each channel, a threshold elevation map is computed from the contrast in that channel. A psychometric function is used to convert error strengths (weighted by the threshold elevations) into a probability-of-detection map for each channel. Pooling is carried out across channels to obtain the overall detection map. It is basically developed for high quality imaging systems.

Lubins visual discrimination model[6] also estimates the detection probability of the error in terms of differences between the original and the distorted versions. A laplacian pyramid[7] is used to decompose the image into seven resolutions (each resolution is one-half of the immediately higher one), followed by band-limited contrast calculations.[8] A set of orientation filters implemented through steerable filters of Freeman and Adelson[9] is then applied for orientation selectivity in four different orientations. The CSF is modeled by normalizing the output of each frequency-selective channel by the base-sensitivity for that channel. Masking is implemented through a sigmoid non-linearity, after which the errors are convolved with disk-shaped kernels at each level before being pooled into a distortion map using Minkowski pooling across frequency.

Teo and Heeger's perceptual distortion metric[10] is similar in character to Lubin's model. This model uses pyramid transform[11] which decomposes the image into several spatial frequency and orientation bands. However, unlike the previous two models, it does not attempt to separate the base sensitivity and the other masking effects. Instead, this model proposes a normalization model that explains baseline contrast sensitivity, contrast masking, as well as masking that occurs when the orientations of the target and masker are different.

2.1.3. *Coder specific metrics*

Some measures have been developed specifically for image compression applications. These models adopt the frequency decomposition of a given coder, which is chosen to provide high compression efficiency. These are considerably simpler than the general models discussed above, as they only have to consider the properties of HVS that are relevant for this application. Watson's DCT metric[12] is based on an 8x8 DCT transform commonly used in image and video compression. Unlike the models above, this method partitions the spectrum into 64 uniform subbands (8 in each Cartesian dimension). After the block-based DCT and the associated sub band contrasts are computed, a visibility threshold is calculated for each subband coefficient within each block using the base-sensitivity for that subband. The base sensitivities are derived empirically. The thresholds are corrected for luminance and texture masking. The error in each subband is weighted by the corresponding visibility threshold and pooled using Minkowski pooling spatially. Pooling across subbands is then performed using the Minkowski formulation with a different exponent. This metric has been shown to be effective in predicting the performance of block-based coders. However, it is not as effective in predicting performance across different coders.

Safranek-Johnston's perceptual image coder[13] incorporates a quality metric using a similar strategy as in Watson's DCT metric. The channel decomposition uses a generalized quadrature mirror filter (GQMF)[14] for analysis and synthesis. This transform splits the spectrum into 16 uniform sub bands (four in each Cartesian dimension). Masking and pooling methods are similar to those in Watson's DCT metric. This metric is specifically developed for perceptual image coder (PIC). It uses an empirically derived perceptual masking model that is obtained for a given cathode ray tube (CRT) display and viewing conditions (six times image height). However, the real challenging task is to predict the performance of coders with different structures.

2.1.4. *Transform based metrics*

Fast Fourier Transform: a no-reference scalar measure[15] that estimates horizontal and vertical blocking artifacts in images. The overall blockiness of the distorted image is given by the arithmetic mean of the two estimates. JPEG compressed gray-scale images are used to test the measure. Because of the computational requirements of the FFT, a pixel domain approach was also proposed.[16]

Discrete Cosine Transform: a no-reference scalar measure[17] that defines a new block across any two adjacent blocks in horizontal and vertical directions. Computations on these overlap blocks result in a map of artifact visibility for the whole image. The set of values in the map can be combined to have a numerical value predicting the overall image quality. The proposed measure is applied to JPEG compressed gray-scale images.

Discrete Wavelet Transformation: a full-reference measure[18] based on integer wavelet transformation presents a graphical representation of image distortion using relative wavelet subband energy. The proposed measure can also be represented as a single numerical value by computing a weighted sum of the subband values. The distortion types for gray-scale images are blur, noise, and lossy compression (JPEG, wavelet, and vector quantization). A more recent wavelet-based full-reference distortion measure[19] utilizes linear-phase wavelets (namely, biorthogonal Daubechies 9/7 and cubic spline wavelets). The measure is tested with three types of degradation – Gaussian noise, JPEG compression, and a grid pattern.

2.1.5. *Structural approaches*

One distinct feature that makes natural image signals different from a "typical" image randomly picked from the image space is that they are highly structured - the signal samples exhibit strong dependencies amongst themselves. These dependencies carry important information about the structures of objects in the visual scene. An image-quality metric that ignores such dependencies may fail to provide effective predictions of image quality.

Structural similarity based methods[20,21] of image quality assessment claim to account for such dependencies in assessing the image quality. Structural similarity based methods replace the Minkowski error metric with different measurements that are adapted to the structures of the reference image signal, instead of attempting to develop an ideal transform that can fully decouple signal dependencies.

Zhou Wang et al. proposed a new universal objective image quality index UQI,[20] which is easy to calculate and applicable to various image processing applications. Though no human visual system model is employed explicitly in designing the metric, it is mathematically defined based on the philosophy that the main function of the human eyes is to extract structural information from the viewing field and the human visual system is highly adapted for this purpose. The index is designed by modeling any image distortion as a combination of three factors: loss of correlation, luminance distortion, and contrast distortion. The metric when applied on various image distortion types proves to be significantly better than the widely used MSE.

In[21] a more generalized and stable version of the universal quality index was proposed named as Structural SIMilarity quality measure (SSIM). Figure 1 demonstrates the model for the calculation of structural similarity measure. The luminance of the surface of an object being observed is the product of illumination and reflectance, but the structures of the object in the scene are independent of the illumination. The structural information in an image was expressed independent of the average luminance and contrast. The mathematical definition of SSIM measure is similar to that of universal quality index but for the fact that the former introduces specific constants for better stability of the measure.

In[22] a multi scale structural similarity for image quality assessment has been proposed which provides more flexibility than the single scale methods in incorporating the variations of viewing conditions. Taking the reference and distorted signals as the input the system iteratively applies a low pass filter and down samples the filtered image by a factor of 2. Each iteration results in a scale. The contrast measure and the structure measure are made after every iteration. The luminance comparison is computed only after the final scale. The multi scale SSIM index of scale M is obtained by combining the measurements at M different scales.

The structural methods of quality assessment quantify image quality based on the assumption that HVS is highly adapted extract structural information from the viewing field. These methods consider the overall functionality of the HVS in assessing image quality. They ignore the specific characteristics of intermediate and higher visual processes which play an important role in scene analysis. SSIM treats the distortions in the image uniformly, though HVS behaves quite contrary to this.

Vision models,[23–26] which treat visible distortions equally, regardless of their location in the image, may not be powerful enough to accurately

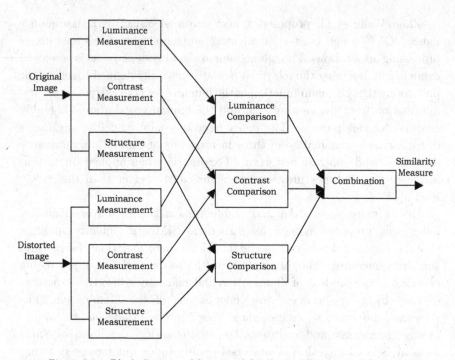

Figure 2.1.   Block diagram of Structural Similarity Measurement System.

predict picture quality in such cases. This is because we are known to be more sensitive to distortions in areas of the image to which we are paying attention than to errors in peripheral areas.

In this chapter we present an image quality metric which integrates the notions of structural similarity measure mimicking the overall functionality of HVS and perceptually important regions based on the characteristics of intermediate and higher visual processes. We observed that the proposed index correlates effectively with subjective scores and found to posses superior performance when compared with other metrics discussed in this paper.

This chapter is organized as follows. Section 2.2 explains model for weighted perceptual features on SSIM, Section 2.2 and 2.3 explains the performance of the Perceptual Structural Similarity Index (PSSIM). Finally, in Section 2.4, the conclusions and future scope are presented.

2.2. A Model for Weighted Perceptual Features on SSIM

Full-reference HVS based image quality assessment methods are mainly focused upon error quantification between the reference and distorted signals to achieve correlation with human perception. The signal samples of natural images are highly structured and exhibit strong dependencies[27] among themselves. This fact is un-attempted in various HVS based full reference image quality assessment methods and several other problems associated with these approaches are reported[27] in literature.

Structural similarity based image quality assessment methods[27] emphasize quantification of the distortion caused due to signal dependencies between the original and distorted images. However these methods ignore the fact that intermediate and higher visual processes select a subset of the available sensory information before further processing.[28-32] Recently SSIM index is improved[33] upon by incorporating bottom up HVS mechanism into it. The top down SSIM method is extended to a region based algorithm. The concept of bottom up visual importance is associated with structural similarities obtained from the region-based algorithm.   It is observed that the SSIM lacks behind measuring the quality of highly blurred images. An improved quality assessment called edge-based structural similarity (ESSIM) is proposed in[34] considering the edge information as another important image structure.

A novel method of image quality assessment is proposed in the present work combining the key perceptual features of HVS in the local regions of interest with that of structural similarity measurement. The structural similarity index proposed by Wang et al. decomposes the image structure into three parts viz. luminance, contrast and structure. These three characteristics of the original image are computed by evaluating the mean of all the regions defined in the image. This representation provides a measure of index with respect to the distorted image, where these features are obtained in a similar fashion. In this process, the regions of interest reflecting the perceptual importance are ignored.

In this work, a novel algorithm is proposed emphasizing the regions of interest (perceptual importance) in the form of weights. Contrast information in the regions of interest is obtained with the help of Michaelson contrast reflecting contrast variation. The structure information is further divided into edge strength and texture. Similar approach is adopted for obtaining the weights of the features associated with the regions of interest. Combination of these weights is formulated in the form of perceptual weights. Structural similarity is re-adjusted adopting a weighing function leading to the proposed Perceptual Structural Similarity index.

2.2.1. *Image distortion model*

Based on the assumption that the HVS is highly adapted to extract structural information from the viewing field, the philosophy of SSIM for image quality measurement is proposed by Wang et al.[21] Let the reference image be represented as a vector in the image space. Image distortion is interpreted as a distortion vector to the reference image vector. In particular, the distortion vectors with same length define an equal mean squared error hyper sphere in the image space. However, images that reside on the same hyper sphere may possess dramatically different visual quality. This implies that length of a distortion vector does not suffice as useful image quality where as the directions of these vectors defines perceptual meaning.

From the perception of image formation, luminance of the surface of an object being observed is the product of illumination and reflectance. Structures of these objects are independent of illumination. The impact of illumination change in the image is defined as variation of average luminance, and contrast.

Luminance and contrast changes and their separation from structural distortion in the image space are illustrated in Figure 2.3. Luminance changes can be characterized by moving along the direction defined by $x_1 = x_2 = \dots\dots = x_N$, which is perpendicular to the hyper plane of $\sum_{i=1}^{N} x_i = 0$. Contrast changes are identified in the direction $X - \bar{x}$. In the image space, the two vectors that determine luminance and contrast changes span a 2D subspace (a plane), which is adapted to the reference image vector X.

Let x and y be two discrete non-negative signals where $x = \{x_i \,|\, i = 1, 2, ..., N\}$ and $y = \{y_i \,|\, i = 1, 2, ..., N\}$ are aligned with each other (e.g., two image patches extracted from the same spatial location of original image and distorted image being compared, respectively).

First, the luminance of each signal is estimated as mean intensity using equation 2.1.

$$\mu_x = \bar{x} = \frac{1}{N} \sum_{i=1}^{N} x_i \qquad (2.1)$$

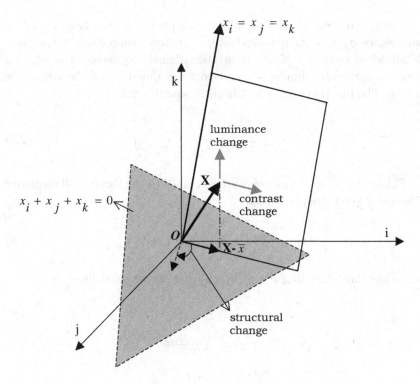

Figure 2.2.   Separation of luminance, contrast and structural changes from a reference image **x** in the image space.

The luminance comparison function $l(x, y)$ is expressed as a function of μ_x and μ_y using equation 2.2.

$$l(x, y) = l(\mu_x, \mu_y) \tag{2.2}$$

Second, the standard deviation is used as an estimate of signal contrast. An unbiased estimate in discrete form is expressed in equation 2.3.

$$\sigma_x = \left(\frac{1}{N-1} \sum_{i=1}^{N} (x_i - \bar{x}) \right)^{1/2} \tag{2.3}$$

The contrast comparison function $c(x, y)$ is obtained by comparing σ_x and σ_y, defined in equation 2.4.

$$c(x, y) = c(\sigma_x, \sigma_y) \tag{2.4}$$

Third, the signal is normalized (divided) by its own deviation parameters σ_x and σ_y independently. Structure comparison $s(x,y)$ is a deviation of distorted signal from the original expressed of a relation between normalized luminance and contrast functions of the respective signals. The function $s(x,y)$ is defined in equation 2.5.

$$s(x,y) = s\left(\frac{x - \mu_x}{\sigma_x}, \frac{y - \mu_y}{\sigma_y}\right) \qquad (2.5)$$

Finally, the three components are combined to yield an overall similarity measure defined in equation 2.6.

$$(x,y) = f(\, l(x,y),\ c(x,y),\ s(x,y)\,) \qquad (2.6)$$

where the three functions $l(x,y)$, $c(x,y)$ and $s(x,y)$ are defined as

$$l(x,y) = \frac{2\mu_x\mu_y + C_1}{\mu_x^2 + \mu_y^2 + C_1}$$

$$c(x,y) = \frac{2\sigma_x\sigma_y + C_2}{\sigma_x^2 + \sigma_y^2 + C_2}$$

$$s(x,y) = \frac{2\sigma_{xy} + C_3}{\sigma_x\sigma_y + C_3}$$

The emphasis on these three components can be treated as signal dependency functions. The overall Structural Similarity measure is defined considering these signal dependencies using equation 2.7.

$$SSIM(x,y) = [l(x,y)]^\alpha \cdot [c(x,y)]^\beta \cdot [s(x,y)]^\gamma \qquad (2.7)$$

Where α, β and γ are parameters to define the relative importance of the three components. The simplest case $\alpha = \beta = \gamma = 1$ is considered assuming that the three components posses equal importance, and the resulting SSIM index is given in the equation 2.8.

$$SSIM(x,y) = \frac{(2\mu_x\mu_y + C_1)(2\sigma_{xy} + C_2)}{(\mu_x^2 + \mu_y^2 + C_1)(\sigma_x^2 + \sigma_y^2 + C_2)} \qquad (2.8)$$

Evaluation of SSIM is carried out on moving pixel window by Wang et al. Local regions of interest and their associated weight metric demands for block based approach, where a window size of N x N will be the point of interest. In the proposed work the original and distorted images are divided into N x N non-overlapping blocks.

First SSIM for each block is computed using equation 2.8. All the computed indices of the image are collected in the form of a matrix S (equation 2.9), where each element s_{ij} represents the distortion measure between the respective blocks of the original and distorted images with the coordinates $(i,j), 1 \leq i \leq m = \lfloor H/N \rfloor, 1 \leq j \leq m = \lfloor W/N \rfloor$, where H and W represent the height and width of the image respectively.

$$
S = \begin{pmatrix}
s_{11} & s_{12} & \cdots & s_{1n} \\
s_{21} & s_{22} & \cdots & s_{2n} \\
\cdot & \cdot & \cdots & \cdot \\
\cdot & \cdot & \cdots & \cdot \\
s_{m1} & s_{m2} & \cdots & s_{mn}
\end{pmatrix}
\tag{2.9}
$$

2.3. Perceptual Structural Similarity Model

Eye movements are essential part of human vision because they carry the fovea and, consequently, the visual attention to each part of an image to be fixated upon and processed with high resolution. An average of three eye fixations per second generally occurs during active perception where these eye fixations are intercalated by rapid eye jumps (saccades), during which vision is suppressed. Only a small set of eye fixations (human detected Regions-of-Interest), are usually required by the brain to recognize a complex visual input.

Visual attention and eye movements have shown that humans generally attend to few areas[35-37] in the image. Even though unlimited viewing time is provided, subjects will continue to focus on few areas rather than scanning the whole image. These areas are often highly correlated amongst different subjects, when viewed in the same context. In order to determine the parts of an image that a human is likely to attend to, it is necessary to adapt a model that correlate the operation of human visual attention and eye movements.

Perceptual regions of interest can be modeled based on various features of the natural image. Different criteria can be adopted to divide the image into local regions and local maxima. A normalized set of the quantified data is considered as an indicative of the degree of interest for each region of the image, which results in perceptual importance map of the image.

2.3.1. *Weighing function based on edge strength*

The studies of neural and perceptual responses[38] on visual spatiotemporal edges, It is well known that in a lateral inhibitory network such as the retina, the lateral geniculate nucleus of the thalamus (LGN), or the primary visual cortex (area V-1), the spatial edges of stimuli excite neurons strongly, whereas the interiors of stimuli evoke relatively little response.

The early vision physical responses of the HVS are used as a basis for knowledge of the visual scene which is combined in the later vision mental processes to yield scene understanding. The work carried out in[39,40] indicate the fact that humans use the same principles when exploring an outline picture by touch or by sight, leading to the conclusion that any system that represents boundaries of surfaces is useful. Way[41] showed that by applying boundary detection (by means of Edge Detection or Segmentation) in the generation of tactile pictures, ones ability to discriminate, identify, and comprehend them improved greatly. The boundaries of objects within an image are often manifested by sharp color transitions commonly referred to as edges. By extracting the edges, the boundaries are obtained.

Considering number of edge pixels in a local block as a measure of edge strength information in that block, the degree of its perceptual importance is determined. The edge map of the original image is obtained by using the Canny extension of the sobel operator.[42] The edge map is divided into N x N blocks. The number of edge pixels 'e' in each block is determined. The edge strengths obtained for all the N x N blocks of the original image are normalized to obtain values ranging from 0 to 1. These normalized edge strengths are collected as a matrix 'E' where each element e_{ij} represents the edge strength for the block with coordinates (i, j), $1 \leq i \leq m = \lfloor H/ N \rfloor$, $1 \leq j \leq m = \lfloor W/ N \rfloor$, where H and W represent the height and width of the image respectively. The perceptual importance map 'E' obtained based on edge strength for the original image is defined in equation 2.10.

$$
E = \begin{pmatrix}
e_{11} & e_{12} & \cdots & e_{1n} \\
e_{21} & e_{22} & \cdots & e_{2n} \\
\cdot & \cdot & \cdots & \cdot \\
\cdot & \cdot & \cdots & \cdot \\
e_{m1} & e_{m2} & \cdots & e_{mn}
\end{pmatrix}
\tag{2.10}
$$

2.3.2. *Perceptual structural similarity based on edge strength*

Perceptual Structural Similarity index '$PSSIM^e$' is defined as the weighted average of the structural similarity indices s_{ij} in each local block with coordinates (i, j), where each s_{ij} is weighted with the respective perceptual weights e_{ij}. The expression for $PSSIM^e$ is defined in equation 2.11.

$$PSSIM^e = \frac{\sum_{i=1}^{m} \sum_{j=1}^{n} S(i,j) \, E(i,j)}{\sum_{i=1}^{m} \sum_{j=1}^{n} E(i,j)} \tag{2.11}$$

2.3.3. *Weighing function based on texture*

The information content of a generic image can be abstracted by different image parameters that are related to texture content in a local region signifying the human attention it calls for. The texture content in a local region is quantified by computing the entropy. Although no formal definition of texture exists; intuitively this descriptor provides measures of properties such as smoothness, coarseness, and regularity. Texture measure based on histogram,[43] of the image, which provides average entropy, is defined using equation 2.12.

$$\eta = -\sum_{i=0}^{L-1} p(z_i) \, \log_2 p(z_i) \tag{2.12}$$

where z_i is a random variable indicating intensity, $p(z_i)$ is the histogram of the intensity levels in a region, L is the number of possible intensity levels. L varies from 0 to 255 for gray scale images. Entropy is a measure of variability (randomness) and is zero for a constant image.

Perceptual weights based on texture[44,45] are obtained by computing the entropy 'n' in each N x N block of the original image, which emphasizes the texture content in the respective block. The entropies calculated for all the N x N blocks of the original image are normalized to obtain values ranging from 0 to 1. These normalized entropies are collected in matrix 'N' defined in equation 2.13, where each element n_{ij} represents the entropy value for the block with coordinates (i, j), $1 \le i \le m = \lfloor H/N \rfloor$, $1 \le j \le m = \lfloor W/N \rfloor$, where H and W represent the height and width of the image respectively.

$$N = \begin{pmatrix} n_{11} & n_{12} & \cdot\cdot & n_{1n} \\ n_{21} & n_{22} & \cdot\cdot & n_{2n} \\ \cdot & \cdot & \cdot\cdot & \cdot \\ \cdot & & \cdot\cdot\cdot & \\ n_{m1} & n_{m2} & \cdot\cdot & n_{mn} \end{pmatrix} \qquad (2.13)$$

2.3.4. *Perceptual structural similarity based on texture*

The Perceptual Structural similarity based on texture content, '$PSSIM^n$' is proposed in [107]. The weighted average of the quality indices s_{ij} in each local block with coordinates (i, j), where each s_{ij} is weighted with the respective degree of interest in that region n_{ij}, is expressed in equation 2.14, in the form of $PSSIM^n$.

$$PSSIM^n = \frac{\sum_{i=1}^{m} \sum_{j=1}^{n} N(i,j)S(i,j)}{\sum_{i=1}^{m} \sum_{j=1}^{n} N(i,j)} \qquad (2.14)$$

2.3.5. *Weighing function based on contrast*

Contrast is arguably the most fundamental local image property encoded[46] by the retina and transmitted to the brain. Visual perception is an adaptive process that alters sensitivity to the selected patterns and its ambient stimulus. Contrast adaptation plays a fundamental role in visual perception for the natural images. Because HVS responds to ratios of luminance (i.e., contrast) rather than to absolute luminance. It is natural to use contrast information to assess image quality, for example, using CSF (contrast threshold) to adjust[47] weighting values in multi-channel assessment system.

The HVS converts luminance into contrast at an early stage of processing. Region-wise contrast information is therefore a strong low level visual attractor. Regions which have a high contrast with their surrounds attract human attention[36,37] and are likely to be of greater visual importance.

Michaelson contrast 'c', is one of the most useful parameter in identifying high contrast regions, generally considered to be an important choice for human vision.[48] Michaelson contrast is calculated using equation 2.15.

$$c = \|(\ l_m - L_M)/(l_m + L_M \ )\| \qquad (2.15)$$

where l_m, the mean luminance is within an N x N block and L_M is the overall mean luminance of the image. 'c' is scaled to the range in between 0-1, a value of 1 indicating highest contrast block and 0 indicating lowest contrast block. Perceptual weights based on local contrast are obtained by computing the local contrast 'c' in each N x N block of the original image, which emphasizes the contrast information of the respective block. These normalized contrast values are collected as a matrix 'C' (equation 2.16), where each element c_{ij} represents the contrast value of the block with coordinates (i, j), $1 \leq i \leq m = \lfloor H/N \rfloor$, $1 \leq j \leq m = \lfloor W/N \rfloor$, where H and W represent the height and width of the image respectively.

$$C = \begin{pmatrix} c_{11} & c_{12} & \cdots & c_{1n} \\ c_{21} & c_{22} & \cdots & c_{2n} \\ \cdot & \cdot & \cdots & \cdot \\ \cdot & \cdot & \cdots & \cdot \\ c_{m1} & c_{m2} & \cdots & c_{mn} \end{pmatrix} \tag{2.16}$$

2.3.6. *Perceptual structural similarity based on local contrast*

Perceptual Structural Similarity index $PSSIM^c$ is defined as the weighted average of the structural similarity indices s_{ij} in each local block with coordinates (i, j), where each s_{ij} is weighted with the corresponding perceptual weights c_{ij}. $PSSIM^c$ is defined in equation 2.17.

$$PSSIM^c = \frac{\sum_{i=1}^{m} \sum_{j=1}^{n} C(i, j) \, S(i, j)}{\sum_{i=1}^{m} \sum_{j=1}^{n} C(i, j)} \tag{2.17}$$

2.3.7. *Weighing function of perceptual features*

Perceptual weights are obtained independently considering edge strength, texture content and local contrast of an N x N block of the original image. The resulting map in each case is viewed as perceptual importance map of that feature. Each of them in turn is used to evaluate the image quality by weighing the structural similarity.

In reality human perception is attentive for multiple features simultaneously. Human brain collects information in the form of independent variables from the visionary system evolving into a holistic nature. Multiple viewing angles infer multiple concepts, which is a specific phenomenon applicable to human beings. In the case of machine based algorithms a model towards this approach is in progress. In this context the present work perceived the model as holistic under the influence of local features. Keeping in view of this, the perceptual importance map is modeled[49] as a combination of the above three features within the local region of the respective block. This model provides a uniform approach for all the regions in the image as presented in Figure 2.3.

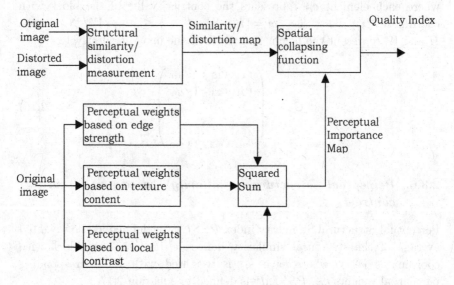

Figure 2.3.   Model for PSSIM (proposed model).

In this section, the perceptual importance of each block is formulated by combining the perceptual weights[49] determined with respect to each of 3 factors, viz., edge strength, texture content and local contrast.

In the present case a simple average of weights may not signify the overall weight factor of that region. To emphasize the perceptual weight, squared sum of all the weights is chosen for the current work. The perceptual weight 'p' of each local region is expressed using equation 2.18.

$$p = e^2 + n^2 + c^2 \tag{2.18}$$

where 'e', 'n', and 'c' are the perceptual weights evaluated independently based on edge strength, texture content and local contrast respectively. The perceptual weight 'p' calculated for all the N x N blocks of the original image are normalized to obtain values ranging from 0 to 1.

These normalized perceptual weights are collected as a matrix 'P', where each element p_{ij} represents the perceptual importance value for the block with coordinates (i, j), $1 \leq i \leq m = \lfloor H / N \rfloor$, $1 \leq j \leq m = \lfloor W / N \rfloor$, where H and W represent the height and width of the image respectively. The perceptual importance map 'P' obtained based on perceptual importance for the original image is expressed in equation 2.19. 'p_{ij}' represents perceptual importance of each block with coordinates (i, j) as defined earlier.

$$P = \begin{pmatrix} p_{11} & p_{12} & \cdots & p_{1n} \\ p_{21} & p_{22} & \cdots & p_{2n} \\ \cdot & \cdot & \cdots & \cdot \\ \cdot & \cdot & \cdots & \cdot \\ p_{m1} & p_{m2} & \cdots & p_{mn} \end{pmatrix} \tag{2.19}$$

2.3.8. *Perceptual Structural Similarity index*

Perceptual Structural Similarity index $PSSIM$ is defined as the weighted average of the structural similarity indices s_{ij} in each local block with coordinates (i, j), where each s_{ij} is weighted with the corresponding perceptual importance p_{ij}. $PSSIM$ is expressed in equation 2.20.

$$PSSIM = \frac{\sum_{i=1}^{m} \sum_{j=1}^{n} P(i,j) S(i,j)}{\sum_{i=1}^{m} \sum_{j=1}^{n} P(i,j)} \tag{2.20}$$

2.4. Performance Evaluation of PSSIM

The proposed model is evaluated on LIVE image database.[50] The database consists of twenty-nine high resolution 24-bits/pixel RGB color images (typically 768 x 512), distorted using five distortion types: JPEG2000, JPEG, White noise in the RGB components, Gaussian blur in the RGB components, and bit errors in JPEG2000 bit stream using a fast-fading Rayleigh channel model. Each image is distorted with each type, and for each type the perceptual quality covered the entire quality range. Observers are asked to provide their perception of quality on a continuous linear scale that was divided into five equal regions marked with adjectives "Bad", "Poor", "Fair", "Good", and "Excellent". About 20-29 human observers rated each image. The raw scores for each subject are converted to difference scores (between test and reference) and then converted to Z-scores, scaled back to 1-100 range, and finally a Difference Mean Opinion Score (DMOS) value for each distorted image is computed.

In order to provide quantitative measures on the performance of the objective quality assessment models, different evaluation metrics are adopted in the Video Quality Experts Group (VQEG) report on testing validation.[51] Non-linear mapping is performed between the objective and subjective scores, using 4-parameter logistic function of the form shown in equation 2.21.

$$y = a/(1.0 + e^{-(x-b)/c}) + d \qquad (2.21)$$

After the non-linear mapping, the Correlation Coefficient (CC), the Mean Absolute Error (MAE), and the Root Mean Squared Error (RMSE) between the subjective and objective scores are evaluated as measures of prediction accuracy. The prediction consistency is quantified using the Outlier Ratio (OR), which is defined as the percentage of the number of predictions outside the range of ± 2times the standard deviation. Finally, the prediction monotonicity is measured using the Spearman Rank-Order-Correlation Coefficient (ROCC).

Prediction accuracy infers us about the ability to predict the subjective quality ratings with low error. Prediction monotonicity indicates the degree to which the predictions agree with the relative magnitudes of subjective quality ratings and prediction consistency indicates the degree to which the model maintains prediction accuracy. The proposed model is compared with other quality assessment metrics PSNR, MSSIM using statistical performance indices viz., prediction accuracy, prediction monotonicity and prediction consistency as set by Video Quality Experts Group (VQEG). Comparison is also made with other perceptual metrics $PSSIM^e$, $PSSIM^n$, and $PSSIM^c$ in Table 2.1. Figure 2.4 shows the scatter plots of DMOS versus $PSSIM$ for different kinds of distortions. The performance is superior when the perceptual weight for a local block is calculated as a combination of edge strength, texture content and local contrast.

Table 2.1. Performance comparison of image quality assessment models on LIVE image database [50]. CC: non-linear regression correlation coefficient; ROCC: Spearman rank-order correlation coefficient; MAE: mean absolute error; RMS: root mean square error; OR: outlier ratio. (a) JPEG2000 (b) JPEG (c) White noise (d) Gaussian blur (e) Fast fading.

Model	CC	ROCC	MAE	RMS	OR%
PSNR	0.859	0.851	6.454	8.269	5.917
MSSIM	0.899	0.894	5.687	7.077	2.366
$PSSIM^e$	0.931	0.925	4.773	5.929	4.142
$PSSIM^n$	0.91	0.899	5.424	6.827	4.142
$PSSIM^c$	0.911	0.903	5.424	6.827	4.142
$PSSIM$	0.922	0.914	5.085	6.259	2.958
(a)					
Model	CC	ROCC	MAE	RMS	OR%
PSNR	0.842	0.828	6.636	8.622	6.285
MSSIM	0.891	0.863	5.386	7.236	5.714
$PSSIM^e$	0.917	0.882	4.563	6.377	6.857
$PSSIM^n$	0.905	0.875	5.077	6.783	5.714
$PSSIM^c$	0.904	0.871	5.416	6.663	5.325
$PSSIM$	0.916	0.882	4.839	6.402	6.285
(b)					
Model	CC	ROCC	MAE	RMS	OR%
PSNR	0.922	0.938	4.524	6.165	5.555
MSSIM	0.940	0.914	4.475	5.459	2.777
$PSSIM^e$	0.962	0.954	3.526	4.367	4.166
$PSSIM^n$	0.958	0.940	3.771	4.555	4.861
$PSSIM^c$	0.943	0.925	5.168	6.429	1.388
$PSSIM$	0.961	0.944	3.623	4.382	3.472
(c)					
Model	CC	ROCC	MAE	RMS	OR%
PSNR	0.744	0.725	8.395	10.50	3.448
MSSIM	0.947	0.940	3.992	5.027	3.448
$PSSIM^e$	0.9688	0.9636	3.168	3.894	4.137
$PSSIM^n$	0.961	0.9564	3.5278	4.3456	3.448
$PSSIM^c$	0.9569	0.9503	3.6646	4.5667	4.82
$PSSIM$	0.965	0.960	3.363	4.105	2.758
(d)					
Model	CC	ROCC	MAE	RMS	OR%
PSNR	0.857	0.859	6.383	8.476	6.896
MSSIM	0.956	0.945	3.806	4.799	5.517
$PSSIM^e$	0.962	0.960	3.656	4.467	2.758
$PSSIM^n$	0.962	0.952	3.473	4.456	4.137
$PSSIM^c$	0.961	0.951	3.479	4.521	4.827
$PSSIM$	0.967	0.957	3.274	4.173	4.137
(e)					

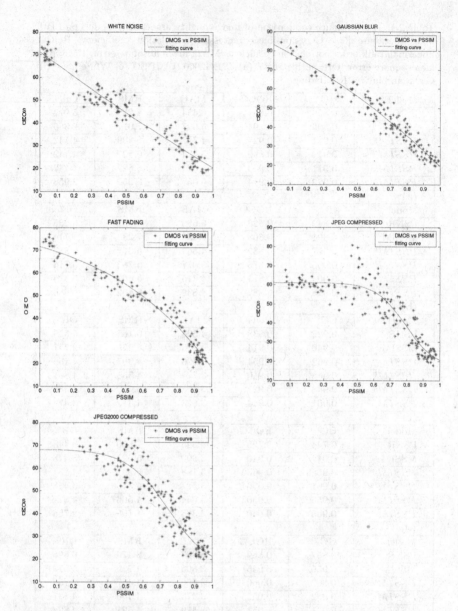

Figure 2.4.   Scatter plots for DMOS versus model prediction for (a) JPEG2000 (b) JPEG (c) white noise (d) Gaussian blur (e) fast fading distorted images.

2.5. Conclusions and Future Scope

The assessment of image quality demands for a consistent evaluation, correlating with human visual perception characteristics. In the present work a novel image quality assessment metric is proposed adopting perceptual weights on structural similarity model. One distinct feature that makes natural image signals different from "typical" image (randomly picked from image space) is that they are highly structured. Structural similarity metric is quantified as a distortion (deviation), viewed as loss of correlation, luminance distortion, and contrast distortion.

Visual processes select a subset of the available sensory information termed as perceptual regions of interest for further reduction in the complexity of scene analysis. Such regions are attentive than other parts of the image. This phenomenon of HVS is an important model for adoption of perceptual weights. Image quality is quantified using this model, where the computed structural distortions and the perceptual weights in all regions are combined together.

Human eye is sensitive to the edge and contour information and the human attention will be more in regions containing edges. Texture is another important characteristic that represents information about structural arrangement of surfaces. Human attention is more sensitive to the regions with high contrast compared to their surroundings in any image.

Perceptual importance map of original image is modeled as a combination of above three features, resulting into a form of perceptual importance map evaluated for local regions. By using these perceptual importance values to weigh the structural distortion in the respective region, the proposed image quality metric, Perceptual Structural SIMilarity index ($PSSIM$) is quantified.

The proposed metrics are evaluated on LIVE image quality assessment database. This database consists of 29 reference images and 779 distorted images classified into five categories viz., white noise corrupted, Gaussian blurred, distorted by fast fading, JPEG compressed, JPEG2000 compressed. The proposed model is compared with state of the art quality assessment metrics, PSNR, and MSSIM using statistical performance indices viz., prediction accuracy, prediction monotonicity and prediction consistency as set by Video Quality Experts Group (VQEG).

The human visual attention model is proposed in this work exploring a set of features namely texture content, edge strength and local contrast. Though these features are regarded as prominent perceptual features, the other image features resulting from convolution with different kinds of masks, local symmetry, and centre surround orientation differences are to be explored further as a future task for possible enhancement of the model. Image features in frequency domain are another parameter for consideration as candidate for perceptual importance model of the image. The present work is modeled on gray scale images. Inclusion of color as an important component of visual stimulus and an extension work is to be taken up as a future task.

References

1. A. M. Eskicioglu and P. S. Fisher, Image quality measures and their performance, *IEEE Transactions on Communications*, vol. 43, no. 12, pp. 2959-2965, Dec. 1995.
2. B. Girod, What's wrong with Mean-Squared Error, *Digital Images and Human Vision*, A. B. Watson Ed., Chapter 15, pp. 207-220, the MIT press, 1993.
3. S. Daly, The visible differences predictor: an algorithm for the assessment of image fidelity, *Digital Images and Human Vision, A. B. Watson Ed., Chapter 14*, pp. 179-206, the MIT press, 1993.
4. S. Daly, The visible difference predictor, An algorithm for the assessment of image fidelity, *in Proc. SPIE*, vol. 1616, pp. 2-15, 1992.
5. A. B. Watson, "The cortex transform: rapid computation of simulated neural images," *Computer Vision, Graphics, and Image Processing*, vol. 39, pp. 311-327, 1987.
6. J. Lubin, "The use of psychophysical data and models in the analysis of display system performance," in *Digital Images and Human Vision* (A. B. Watson, ed.), pp. 163-178, Cambridge, Massachusetts: The MIT Press, 1993.
7. P. J. Burt and E. H. Adelson, "The Laplacian pyramid as a compact image code," *IEEE Trans. Communications*, vol. 31, pp. 532-540, Apr. 1983.
8. E. Peli, "Contrast in complex images," *Journal of Optical Society of America*, vol. 7, pp. 2032-2040, Oct. 1990.
9. W. T. Freeman and E. H. Adelson, "The design and use of steerable filters," *IEEE Trans. Pattern Analysis and Machine Intelligence*, vol. 13, pp. 891-906. 1991.
10. P. C. Teo and D. J. Heeger, "Perceptual image distortion," in *Proc. SPIE*, vol. 2179, pp. 127-141, 1994.
11. E. P. Simoncelli, W. T. Freeman, E. H. Adelson, and D. J. Heeger, "Shiftable multi-scale transforms," *IEEE Trans. Information Theory*, vol. 38, pp. 587-607, 1992.
12. A. B. Watson, "DCTune: A technique for visual optimization of DCT quantization matrices for individual images," in *Society for Information Display Digest of Technical Papers*, vol. XXIV, pp. 946-949, 1993.

13. R.J. Safranek and J. D. Johnston, A perceptually tuned subband image coder with image dependent quantization and post-quantization data compression, *IEEE International Conference on Acoustics, Speech and Signal Processing,* vol. 3, pp. 1945-1948, May 1989.

14. R. J. Safranek and J. D. Johnston, "A perceptually tuned sub-band image coder with image dependent quantization and post-quantization data compression," in *Proc. IEEE Int. Conf. Acoust. Speech, and Signal Processing,* pp. 1945-1948, May 1989.

15. Z. Wang, A. C. Bovik and B. L. Evans, Blind measurement of blocking artifacts in images, *Proceedings of IEEE 2000 International Conferencing on Image Processing,* Vancouver, BC, Canada, September 10-13, 2000.

16. Z. Wang, H. R. Sheikh and A. C. Bovik, No-reference perceptual quality assessment of JPEG compressed images,*Proceedings of IEEE2002 International Conferencing on Image Processing,* Rochester, NY,September 22-25, 2002.

17. A. C. Bovik and S. Liu, DCT-domain blind measurement of blocking artifacts in DCT-coded images, *Proceedings of International Conference on Acoustics, Speech, and Signal Processing,* Salt Lake City, UT, May 7-11, 2001.

18. K. J. Hermiston and D. M. Booth, Image quality measurement using integer wavelet transformations,*Proceedings of 1999 International Conference on Image Processing,* Kobe, Japan, pp. 293-297, October 24-28, 1999.

19. A. Beghdadi and B. Pesquet-Popescu, A new image distortion measure based on wavelet decomposition, *7th International Symposium and Its Applications (ISSPA 2003),* Paris, France, July 1-4, 2003.

20. Z. Wang and A. C. Bovik, A universal image quality index, *IEEE Signal Processing Letters,* 2002.

21. Z. Wang, A. C. Bovik, H. R. Sheikh, and E. P. Simocelli, Image quality assessment: From error measurement to structural similarity, *IEEE Trans. Image Processing,* vol. 13, no.4, pp.600-612, Apr .2004.

22. Z. Wang, E.P. Simoncelli and A.C. Bovik, "Multi-scale structural similarity for image quality assessment", *Proc. 37th IEEE Asilomar conference on Signals, Systems and Computers,* vol. 2, Pacific Grove, California, Nov. 2002.

23. G. A. Geri and Y. Y. Zeevi. Visual assessment of variable-resolution imagery. *Journal of the OpticalSociety of America,* vol. 12, no. 10, pp. 2367-2375, October 1995.

24. P. Kortum and W. Geisler. Implementation of a foveated image coding system for image bandwidth reduction. In SPIE - Human Vision and ElectronicImaging, volume 2657, pages 350-360, February 1996.

25. L. B. Stelmach, W. J. Tam, and P. J. Hearty. Static and dynamic spatial resolution in image coding: An investigation of eye movements. In Proceedings of the SPIE, volume 1453, pages 147-152, San Jose, 1991.

26. A. L. Yarbus. Eye Movements and Vision.Press, New York, 1967.

27. Z.Wang, Alan C.Bovik and E.P.Simoncelli, Structural approaches to image quality assessment, in *Handbook of Image and video processing, 2nd Edition, (Al Bovik, ed.,),* Academic press, 2005.

28. D. Noton and L.W. Stark, Scanpaths in Eye Movements During Pattern Perception, *Science*, vol. 17, no. 1, pp. 308-311, 1971.

29. P.J. Locher and C.F. Nodine, Symmetry Catches the Eye, *Eye Movements: From Physiology to Cognition*, pp. 353-361, 1987.

30. S.K. Mannan, K.H. Ruddock, and D.S. Wooding, The Relationship between the Locations of Spatial Features and Those of Fixations Made during Visual Examination of Briefly Presented Images, *Spatial Vision*, vol. 10, no. 3, pp. 165-188, 1996.

31. E. Niebur and C. Koch, Control of Selective Visual Attention: Modeling the 'Where' Pathway, *Advances in Neural Information Processing Systems*, D.S. Touretzky, M.C. Mozer,and M.E. Hasselmo, eds., vol. 8, pp. 802-808, MIT Press, 1996.

32. L. Itti, C. Koch, and E. Niebur, A Model of Saliency-Based Visual Attention for Rapid Scene Analysis, *IEEE Trans. Pattern Analysis and Machine Intelligence*, vol. 20, no. 11, pp. 1,254-1,259, Nov. 1998.

33. Zhai, G. Zhang, W. Yang, X. Xu, Y., Image quality metric with an integrated bottom-up and top-down HVS approach, *IEE Proceedings-Vision, Image, and Signal Processing*, volume 153, Issue 4, pp.456-460, August 2006.

34. G. H. Chen, C. L. Yang, L. M. Po and S. L. Xie, "Edge-based Structural Similarity for Image Quality Assessment, *Proceeding of IEEE International Conference on Acoustics, Speech, and Signal Processing*, vol. 2, pp. 933-936, May 2006.

35. C. J. van den Branden Lambrecht, D. M. Costantini, G. L. Sicuranza, and M. Kunt, "Quality assessment of motion rendition in video coding," *IEEE Trans. Circuits and Systems for Video Tech.*, vol. 9, pp. 766-782. Aug. 1999.

36. J.Findlay, The visual stimulus for saccadic eye movement in human observers, *Perception*, vol. 9, pp. 7-21, Sept. 1980.

37. J. Senders. Distribution of attention in static and dynamic scenes, *Proceedings SPIE*, 3016, pages 186-194, San Jose, Feb 1997.

38. Hubel, D. H. & Wiesel, T. N. (1970) *J. Physiol (London)* 206, 419, 436.

39. M. Heller, Ed., "Touch, Representation, and Blindness," *Oxford University Press*, 2000.

40. W. Richards and L. Kaufman, Centre-of-Gravity Tendencies for Fixations and Flow Patterns, *Perception and Psychology*, vol. 5, pp. 81-84, 1969.

41. T. Way and K. Barner, "Automatic visual to tactile translation - part two," *IEEE Transactions on Rehabilitation Engineering*, 1997.

42. J. Canny, A Computational Approach to Edge Detection, *IEEE Trans. Pattern Analysis and Machine Intelligence*, vol. 8, no. 6, pp. 679-698, 1986.

43. Gonzalez and Woods, Digital Image Processing, *Prentice Hall*, 2002.

44. D.Venkata Rao, V.R.Rayalu, N.Sudhakar, L.Pratap Reddy, A visual region of interest weighted image quality index, *Proc. of IET international conference on visual information engineering(VIE'06)*, pp 594-599, Bangalore, September 2006.

45. D.Venkata Rao, N.Sudhakar, I.R.Babu, L.Pratap Reddy., Image quality assessment complemented with visual regions of interest, *Proc. Of ICCTA'07, IEEE Computer Society press.* pp 681-687, ISI Kolkata, March 2007.

46. E. C. Carterette and M. P. Friedman, Eds., *Handbook of Perception*, vol. 5, New York: Academic, 1975.
47. Stefan Winkler, Issues in vision modeling for perceptual video quality assessment, *Signal Processing*, Vol. 78, pp.231-252, 1999.
48. S.K. Mannan, K.H. Ruddock, and D.S. Wooding, The Relationship between the Locations of Spatial Features and Those of Fixations Made during Visual Examination of Briefly Presented Images, *Spatial Vision*, vol. 10, no. 3, pp. 165-188, 1996.
49. D.Venkata Rao, L.Pratap Reddy, Image quality assessment based on perceptual structural similarity, LNCS 4815, pp 87-94, *PReMI'07*, ISI, Kolkata, India, December 2007.
50. H. R. Sheikh, A. C. Bovik, L. Cormack, and Z. Wang, LIVE Image Quality Assessment Database, 2004. http://live.ece.utexas.edu/research/quality
51. VQEG, Final report from the video quality experts group on the validation of objective models of video quality assessment, http://www.vqeg.org/ http://www.vqeg.org/, Mar. 2000.

Chapter 3

Quasi-reversible Two-dimension Fractional Differentiation for Image Entropy Reduction

A. Nakib, A. Nait-Ali, H. Oulhadj and P. Siarry

Université de Paris XII, Laboratoire Images, Signaux et Systèmes Intelligents (LISSI, E. A. 3956), 61 avenue du Général De Gaulle 94010 Créteil, FRANCE

nakib@univ-paris12.fr

In order to reduce the entropy of a given image, we present a new approach based on a two-dimension fractional differentiation (2D-DFD). The entropy reduction is particularly interesting for increasing the performances of entropy coding algorithms. As it will be demonstrated, this transformation is theoretically reversible and quasi-reversible in practice, due to rounding errors. The proposed method can be used as a pre-processing technique for compression purpose.

Contents

3.1 Introduction 57
3.2 Fractional Differentiation 58
3.3 Extension of the Fractional Differentiation to the 2D Case and its Application in Entropy Reduction 60
3.4 Statistical Properties of the Differentiated Image 61
    3.4.1 Average value of the differentiated image 62
    3.4.2 Entropy 62
3.5 Choice of the Optimal Order 64
3.6 Conclusion 65
References 67

3.1. Introduction

Image compression is an important aspect of digital image processing.[1] It is used for instance, for image transmission, like television, and image storage, like biomedical images. Nowadays, research in this field is particularly active.

The theory of non-integer (fractional) order derivatives dates back to correspondence between Leibniz and L'Hospital in 1695 (see[2,3]). The basis for defining fractional derivatives is the relationship between the integer n and the nth order derivatives. A remarkable merit of fractional differentiation operators is that they may still be applied to functions which are not differentiable in the classical sense. Unlike the integer order derivative, the fractional order derivative at point x is not determined by an arbitrary small neighbourhood of x. In other words, the fractional derivative is not a local property of the function. The theory of fractional derivatives was primarily developed as a theoretical field of mathematics. More recently, fractional differentiation has found applications in various areas: in control theory it is used to determinate a robust command control;[4] it is also used to solve the inverse heat conduction problem;[5] other applications are reported for instance in neuronal modelling,[6] in image processing for edge detection,[7] in biomedical signal processing.[8]

This chapter highlights how the two-dimension fractional differentiation reduces the entropy of any given image. A detailed interpretation and a statistical analysis of the two-dimension fractional differentiation are proposed in terms of entropy and amplitude range variations. The application of the proposed method to real world images is presented through an application to brain Magnetic Resonance Images (MRI).

The rest of the paper is organized as follows. In section 3.2, the formalism of fractional differentiation calculus is given. In section 3.3, we present the properties of the fractional differentiated image histogram as well as some analysis results applied on "Lena" image. The choice of the optimal order of the 2D-DFD is discussed in section 3.4. Finally, we conclude this chapter in the last section.

3.2. Fractional Differentiation

For a fractional integral operator, output $y(t)$ is the integral of input $e(t)$:

$$y(t) = D^\alpha(t) \qquad (3.1)$$

where D is the differentiation operator, α is the fractional integration order. It can be any complex or real number.

When the real part of the fractional order (α) is negative, a fractional integral operator is in fact also defined by Eq. (3.1). We denote the αth integral operator by J.

The Riemann-Liouville operator D^α for fractional differentiation is defined by the formula:

$$D^\alpha f(x) = \frac{1}{\Gamma(\alpha)} \int_x^c (x-\xi)^{\alpha-1} f(\xi) d\xi \qquad (3.2)$$

where $f(x)$ is a real causal function, $Re(\alpha) > 0$, the integral reference and Γ the gamma function.

whereas the inverse fractional integral operator (fractional derivative operator) D is given by:

$$J^\alpha D^\alpha = f, m-1 \le \alpha \le m, m \in N \qquad (3.3)$$

The discrete form of fractional differentiation of order α presented by Grünwald is given by:

$$g(x) = D^\alpha f(x) = \frac{1}{h^\alpha} \sum_{k=0}^{M} \omega_k^{(\alpha)} f(x-k) \qquad (3.4)$$

where h is the sampling step, M is the number of samples and $\omega_k^{(\alpha)}$ are the binomial coefficients:

$$\omega_0^\alpha = 1, \omega_{k+1}^{(\alpha)} = \frac{k-\alpha}{k+1} \omega_k^{(\alpha)}, k = 0, 1, \ldots, M \qquad (3.5)$$

A positive real part for fractional differentiation order is chosen for Eq. (3.5), so the fractional integral Eq. (3.2) can be computed. Definition Eq. (3.4) shows that the fractional integral of a function takes into account the past of the function f. More details about the definition of the fractional differentiation are given in.[2,3]

The calculus of the αth derivatives at all points of the interval $[a, b]$ produces $N+1$ formulas, that can be written in the matrix form:

$$
\begin{bmatrix}
D^\alpha f(x_0) \\
D^\alpha f(x_1) \\
\vdots \\
D^\alpha f(x_{N-1}) \\
D^\alpha f(x_N)
\end{bmatrix}
= \frac{1}{h^\alpha}
\begin{bmatrix}
w_0^{(\alpha)} & 0 & 0 & \cdots & 0 \\
w_1^{(\alpha)} & w_0^{(\alpha)} & 0 & \cdots & 0 \\
\vdots & \ddots & \ddots & \cdots & \vdots \\
w_{N-1}^{(\alpha)} & \ddots & w_1^{(\alpha)} & w_0^{(\alpha)} & 0 \\
w_N^{(\alpha)} & w_{N-1}^{(\alpha)} & \ddots & w_1^{(\alpha)} & w_0^{(\alpha)}
\end{bmatrix}
\begin{bmatrix}
f(0) \\
f(1) \\
\vdots \\
f(N-1) \\
f(N)
\end{bmatrix}
\qquad (3.6)
$$

3.3. Extension of the Fractional Differentiation to the 2D Case and its Application in Entropy Reduction

The proposed method is based on the extension of the one-dimension fractional differentiation to the two-dimension case.

As an image can be considered as a two-dimension real bounded function $f(x, y)$, we propose to extend the one-dimension DFD to the two-dimension case, called 2D-DFD. Then, the approximation of the fractional differentiated function of an image is given by:

$$D^\alpha f(x, y) = (\frac{\partial}{\partial x})^\alpha (\frac{\partial}{\partial y})^\alpha f(x, y) \qquad (3.7)$$

$$D^\alpha f(x, y) \approx \frac{1}{h^{2\alpha}} \sum_{k=-\lfloor M/2 \rfloor}^{\lfloor M/2 \rfloor} \sum_{l=-\lfloor N/2 \rfloor}^{\lfloor N/2 \rfloor} p(k, l).f(x - kh, y - lh) \qquad (3.8)$$

where M and N are defined as follows: $x = Mh$ and $y = Nh$ represent the number of past elements of f considered to calculate the fractional differentiated image. $M \times N$ represents the size of the "mask", and $\lfloor x \rfloor$ denotes integer part of x.

$p(k, l) = \omega_k(\alpha) \times \omega_l(\alpha)$ are elements of the matrix P calculated from the coefficients of the Newton's binomial Eq. (3.5) corresponding to the horizontal and vertical components respectively.

The previous equation can be seen as a convolution of the image f with the filter $P_M^{(\alpha)}(x, y)$. Hence, we can write :

$$g(x, y) = D^\alpha f(x, y) = f(x, y) \otimes P_M^{(\alpha)}(x, y) \qquad (3.9)$$

where $\otimes$ is 2D-convolution operator.

Figure (3.1) shows an example of two-dimension differentiated function for different α values. One can remark the amplitude range modification: the range is increased for negative α values whereas it is decreased for positive α values. Consequently, average length of the codes necessary to code the entire image is decreased.

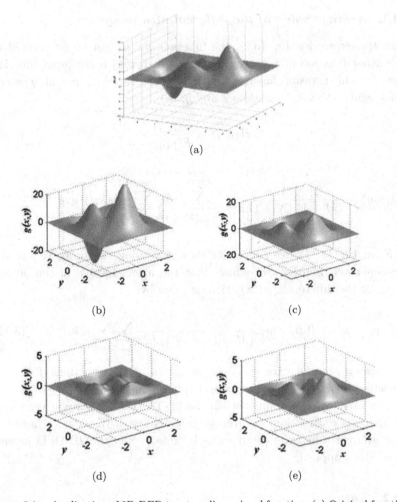

Figure 3.1. Application of 2D-DFD to a two dimensional function. (a) Original function $f(x, y) = 10(x - x^3 - y^5)e^{-x^2-y^2} + 3e^{-(x+1)^2-y^2}$, (b) Fractional differentiated function $g(x, y)$ obtained with 2D-DFD for $\alpha = -0.4$, (c) Fractional differentiated function $g(x, y)$ obtained with 2D-DFD for $\alpha = -0.2$, (d) Fractional differentiated function $g(x, y)$ obtained with 2D-DFD for $\alpha = 0.4$, (e) Fractional differentiated function $g(x, y)$ obtained with 2D-DFD for $\alpha = 0.2$.

3.4. Statistical Properties of the Differentiated Image

We propose to analyze two statistical properties of the differentiated function: average value and entropy function.

3.4.1. *Average value of the differentiated image*

From the expression Eq. (3.9), the function $g(x,y)$ can be interpreted as the output function of a discrete filter, where $f(x,y)$ is the input function (signal). The transfer function, with Laplace variables p and q which correspond to the real variables x and y, is:

$$H(p,q) = \frac{G(p,q)}{F(p,q)} \qquad (3.10)$$

$$H(p,q) = \frac{1}{(M+1).(N+1).h^{2\alpha}} \sum_{k=-\lfloor M/2 \rfloor}^{\lfloor M/2 \rfloor} \sum_{l=-\lfloor N/2 \rfloor}^{\lfloor N/2 \rfloor} p(k,l).\exp^{-h\alpha(pk+ql)}$$

$$(3.11)$$

From Eq. (3.11), we can easily show (by using the properties of the *two-dimension Fourier transform*) that the average value of the output signal, or the differentiated function, is given by:

$$\mu_g = \mu_f.H(0,0) = \mu_f.\frac{1}{(M+1).(N+1).h^{2\alpha}} \sum_{k=0}^{M} \sum_{l=0}^{N} p(k,l) \qquad (3.12)$$

where μ_f and μ_g are the average values of the functions f and g, respectively, H is the two-dimension Laplace transform of $h(x,y)$.

The value of μ_g is infinite when the 2D-DFD order is negative. Then, the image is centred and its average value is saved. In order to have the same average value, the saved value is added when the 2D-DFD inverse transform is applied.

3.4.2. *Entropy*

In this subsection, we show that applying 2D-DFD with a positive order to a given image allows reducing its entropy, through the increase of the non-uniformity of its histogram.

The Shannon entropy of a gray level image (I) is defined by:

$$H(I) = -\sum_{i=0}^{L-1} p_i log_2 p_i \qquad (3.13)$$

where p_i is the probability of the gray level i and L is the total number of gray levels (usually 256 for gray level images).

When applying 2D-DFD to "Lena" image, the curve shown in Figure (3.2) indicates an exponential decrease of the entropy from 7.60 to 4.80. The modifications of the image histogram due to the differentiation are presented in the Figure (3.3), with the value of α varying from 0.1 to 0.5.

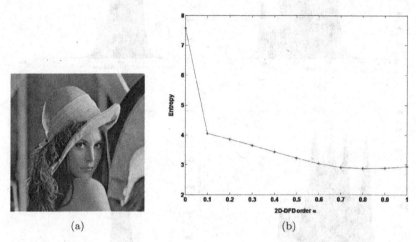

(a)   (b)

Figure 3.2. Entropy reduction. (a) Original Lena image, (b) Entropy variation with different 2D-DFD order values.

This decrease exists for all images and depends on image features. Theoretically, the 2D-DFD is reversible, but in practice this property is not totally verified because of the problem of rounding the pixels values of the differentiated image (from real values to integer values). This problem must be solved to obtain a perfect reversibility. Therefore, the operator is considered as quasi-reversible. The original image can be easily reconstructed by applying the inverse 2D-DFD, which simply corresponds to the application of 2D-DFD with $-\alpha$ (as shown on Figure (3.4)).

The analysis of the sensitivity of the method to the variation of 2D-DFD order (α) showed that the entropy varies significantly when α varies by steps of 0.1.

Based on this result, one can easily integrate this operator in compression schemes, as shown in Figure (3.5). The optimal value of the 2D-DFD order α, that corresponds to the optimum of the entropy, also depends on image features.

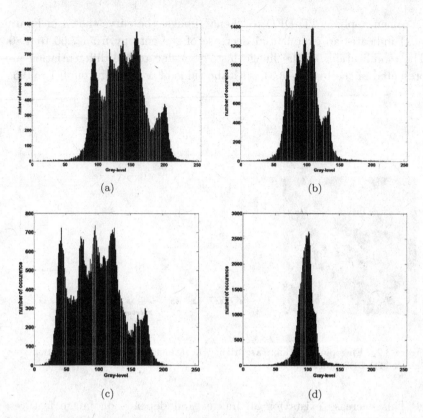

Figure 3.3.   Histogram modification through the application of 2D-DFD. (a) Original
histogram, (b) $\alpha = 0.1$, (c) $\alpha = 0.3$, (d) $\alpha = 0.5$.

3.5. Choice of the Optimal Order

The optimal order is that which minimizes the Shannon entropy given
by Eq. (3.13) and guarantees a good reconstruction. In order to find the
optimal value of the 2D-DFD order, we apply it with different values, from
0.1 to 2, and we select the value that verifies the two mentioned constraints.

In our experiments, a good visual quality (confirmed by an expert)
of the reconstructed image is obtained for the following values of α :
0.6, 0.7 and 0.8, the corresponding entropy values are: 2.844, 2.575
and 2.447 $bits/pixel$. Then, we chose the order $\alpha = 0.7$ and $H =
2.575$ $bits/pixel$. The comparison between the original image and the
reconstructed image is presented on the Figure (3.7).

Figure 3.4. Reversibility of 2D-DFD. (a) Differentiated image histogram with $\alpha = 0.1$, (b) Reconstructed image.

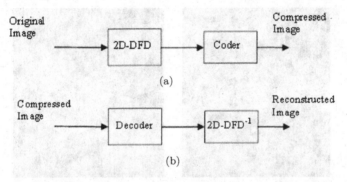

Figure 3.5. Compression and decomposition schemes. (a) Compression scheme, (b) Decompression scheme.

3.6. Conclusion

We have presented in this chapter a two-dimension extension of the fractional differentiation theory. The quasi-reversible operator has been used to reduce the entropy of any given image. This feature makes it particularly appropriate for entropy coding.

In a future work, it will be interesting to evaluate the proposed transformation by integrating it in some well known compression scheme, as JPEG 2000, SPHIT and SPECK, for instance.

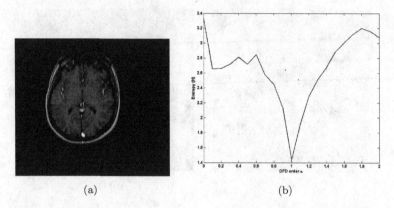

(a)   (b)

Figure 3.6.   Choice of the optimal order. (a) Original MRI image, (b) Variation of the entropy.

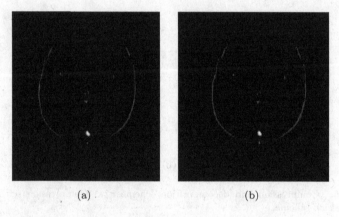

(a)   (b)

Figure 3.7.   Comparison between the original and reconstructed images for $\alpha = 0.7$. (a) Original image, (b) Reconstructed image.

It would be also interesting if one could define the optimal α order value for a given image, before transforming it through the 2D-DFD. This procedure would avoid calculating the entropy of the image for various values of α (the classical way to find the optimum).

References

1. Y. Shi and Q. H. Sun, Image and video compression for multimedia engineering, *CRC Press LLC*, (2000).
2. K. Oldham and J. Spanier, The fractional Calculus, *Academic Press* (1974).
3. I. Prodlubny, Geometric and physical interpretation of fractional integration and fractional differentiation, *Fractional calculus and applied analysis* **5** (4), 367-386, (2002).
4. A. Oustaloup and H. Linars, The CRONE path planning, *Math. and Compu. in Simu.*, **41**, 209-217, (1996).
5. J. L. Battaglia, O. Cois, O., L. Puigsegus, and A. Oustaloup, Solving an inverse heat conduction problem using a non-integer identified model, *Inter. J. of Heat and Mass Trans.*, **44**, 2671-2680, (2001).
6. C. Ramus-Serment, X. Moreau, M. Nouillant, A. Oustaloup and F. Levron, Generalised approach on fractional response of fractal networks, *Chaos, Solutions and fractals*, **14**, 479-488, (2002).
7. B. Mathieu, P. Melchior, A. Oustaloup, and Ch. Ceyral, Fractional differentiation for edge detection, *Signal Processing*, **83**, 2421-2432,(2003).
8. Y. Ferdi, J. P. Herbeuval, A. Charef and B. Boucheham, R wave detection using fractional digital differentiation, *ITBM-RBM*, **24** (5-6), 273-280, (2003).

Chapter 4

Parallel Genetic Algorithm Based Clustering for Object and Background Classification

P. Kanungo*, P. K. Nanda** and A. Ghosh+

*Department of Electronics and Telecommunication Engineering,
Image Analysis and Computer Vision Laboratory,
C. V. Raman College of Engineering, Bhubaneswar 752054, India
+Center for Soft Computing Research, Indian Statistical Institute,
203 B.T Road, Kolkata 700108, India
**ITER, Siksha O Anusandhan University,
Jagamohan Nagar, Khandagiri, Bhubaneswar-751030, India

Separation of object and background in a given scene is vital while addressing the problem of fault diagnosis. This can be viewed as a two class problem and hence an efficient classification strategy can be employed to separate object from background. The literature is rich with classification techniques, nevertheless there are rooms for improvement. In this chapter, we present the two novel strategies devised for classification. This is based on the Parallel Genetic Algorithm (PGA) based clustering. The two schemes have been verified with different examples having two and three classes. The efficacy of the proposed methods has compared with that of Otsu's[7] and Kwon's[9] method.

Contents

4.1 Introduction 70
4.2 Determination of Niches by Clustering 71
4.3 Proposed Methods 73
    4.3.1 Featureless (FL) approach 73
    4.3.2 Featured Based (FB) approach 73
4.4 GA Class Model 74
    4.4.1 Crowding method 75
    4.4.2 Generalized crossover (GC) 76
    4.4.3 GA based clustering 78
    4.4.4 Parallel Genetic Algorithm (PGA) 79
    4.4.5 PGA based clustering 79
    4.4.6 Algorithm 80
4.5 Results and Discussions 82

4.6 Conclusion 87
References 89

4.1. Introduction

Detection and tracking of moving objects in a given scene has been the prime importance in visual surveillance and monitoring. In case of fault diagnosis, often it is required to separate the foreground and background of given scene. There has been consistent effort to classify the background and foreground with moving objects in a given scene. Separation of foreground and background can be viewed as a classification problem. This inturn implies to segment the given image into background and foreground. Thresholding has been one of the potential tools that has been extensively used[1,2] to separate foreground and background.

In this chapter, we address the problem of classification of object and background using the notion of clustering and thresholding. Genetic and Parallel Genetic Algorithm (GA and PGA) based clustering schemes have been proposed to determine the niches of the histogram distribution and these niches are subsequently used to determine the threshold using the histogram distribution. In the following, we present some of the existing thresholding approaches followed by the proposed novel approaches.

It is important in image processing to select an appropriate threshold of gray level for extracting object from the background. Image thresholding is a necessary step in many image analysis and applications.[1-4] In its simplest form, thresholding means to classify the pixels of a given image into two groups (e.g. objects and background), one containing pixels with their gray values above a certain threshold, and the other including those with gray values equal to and below the threshold. This is called bi-level thresholding. In multilevel thresholding, one can select more than one threshold, and use them to divide the whole range of gray values into several sub ranges. Most of the thresholding techniques[5-8] utilize shape information of the histogram of the given image to determine appropriate threshold.

In an ideal case, for images having two classes, the histogram distribution has a deep and sharp valley between two peaks representing objects and background respectively. Therefore, the threshold can be chosen as the bottom of this valley.[4] However, for most real pictures, it is often difficult to detect the valley precisely because; (i) valley could be flat and broad and (ii) the two peaks could be extremely unequal in height, often producing no traceable valley. Rosenfeld et al.[3] proposed the valley sharpening techniques which restricts the histogram to the pixels with large absolute values of derivatives. S. Watanable et al.[5] proposed the difference histogram method, which selects threshold at the gray level with the maximal amount of difference. These methods utilize information concerning neighboring pixels or edges in the original picture to modify the histogram so as to make it suitable for determination of optimal threshold. Another well known method, Otsu's[7] method, deals with the selection of optimal threshold using the discriminant criterion. This is used to maximize interclass variance of gray level while minimizing the intra class variance. This method yields very satisfactory results for two class problems and this method has also been proven to be quite effective for multi class problems. Another class of methods deals directly with the gray level histogram by parametric techniques. The histogram is approximated by a sum of Gaussian distributions in the least square sense, and statistical decision procedures are applied.[8] However, such methods are tedious and computationally involved. Recently, the notion of cluster analysis has been employed for determination of optimal threshold.[9,10] Kwon[9] has taken the histogram of the image and the information on the spatial distribution of the image into account for determination of optimal threshold. Thus, the thresholding problem has reduced to clustering problems that have generated the number of clusters, cluster centers and partition matrix. Arifin et al.[10] have proposed a novel method by taking hierarchical cluster organization into account. They have also proposed measures to improve the merging criterion so as to maximize the distance of cluster means as well as the new merged clusters. A new similarity measure based on the inter class and intra class variance of the clusters is proposed by Arifin et al.[10] Qiao et al.[11] have proposed a variance and intensity contrast based thresholding scheme for segmenting small objects in a given scene.

This chapter is organized as follows. Section 4.2 deals with the notions of clustering that is used to determine the peaks or valleys. The proposed approaches are formulated in Section 4.3. The notions of crowding and GA and PGA based clustering algorithm have been presented in Section 4.4. Different results and discussion on the results are presented in Section 4.5. The concluding remarks are presented in Section 4.6.

4.2. Determination of Niches by Clustering

Histogram distribution provides some first hand information about the image. Selection of threshold from histogram often depends upon the shape of the distribution. If the histogram distribution exhibits clear bimodality separated by a distinct valley, the determination of threshold selection reduces to determination of valley point. Different methods have been proposed[1-4] to determine the valley point. Nevertheless, accurate determination of valley points is not a trivial task because of noise, nonuniform lighting etc. In the following, we describe about the two methods that we propose to determine the valley even in case of noisy as well as overlapping classes of histogram distribution.

We have proposed two methods to determine the optimal threshold for classification. The first one, called Feature Less(FL) approach, exploits the shape information of the discrete histogram distribution of the original image to determine the optimal threshold. This optimal threshold corresponds to the valley of the histogram landscape. In the histogram landscape, each mode is assumed to correspond to one of the classes of the image. For example, histogram having two modes(two peaks and one valley) as shown in Fig. 4.1(a) correspond to two classes in the given image. Therefore, the problem is cast as a classification problem.

Often, because of the non-smooth nature of discrete histogram distribution, the conventional exhaustive method may obtain incorrect threshold leading to poor classification. In case of discrete histogram distribution, exhaustive search for the minimum gray value may lead to pseudo thresholds because the exhaustive search may obtain minimum value at either the initial portion or the final portion of the histogram distribution. Hence, we propose a clustering technique to detect peaks corresponding to different modes of the histogram. Irregularity in the distribution, for example, could be due to the presence of a small kink in one of the peaks of the distribution, thereby misleading one peak as two peaks. In our work, a Parallel Genetic Algorithm (PGA) based clustering technique is proposed to detect the peaks and, in the sequel, the valley between the successive peaks is obtained by exhaustive search method. The peaks or niches are determined by maintaining stable subpopulation at each peaks. This is achieved by the proposed GA and PGA based crowding method that maintains stable subpopulation or clusters of population elements at different peaks. Maintenance of stable subpopulation could be attributed to the maintenance of diversity among the population elements. Thus, the peaks can be determined. The proposed FL approach yields satisfactory results, but the performance is found to deteriorate with overlapping class distributions that results from either the nature of the image or the presence of noise. In such situations, FL approach found incorrect thresholds and hence poor classification. In order to ameliorate the situation, a Feature Based (FB) approach is proposed. In this approach, a feature of the image is determined and the histogram corresponding to the feature is considered as opposed to the histogram of the original image. This feature histogram is used for determination of optimal threshold for the original image. The process of determination of optimal threshold, or in other words valley of the featured histogram, is same as that of the FL approach. PGA based clustering algorithm is used to determine the peaks and thereafter the valley is obtained by the exhaustive search method. The valley, thus obtained, is used as the threshold for the original image. FL and FB methods are validated for two as well as three class images. FB approach is compared with FL, Otsu's[7] and Kwon's[9] approaches and it is found that the FB approach is the best among these four methods.

4.3. Proposed Methods

4.3.1. *Featureless (FL) approach*

The shape of the discrete histogram distribution is considered. For example, for a two class problem as shown in Fig. 4.1(a), an optimal threshold corresponding to the valley needs to be found out. This is obtained as follows. First, the peaks of the histogram distribution are determined by PGA based crowding and then the valley point, in between the two peaks, is determined by exhaustive search method. Similarly for a three class problems, three peaks need to be determined and two thresholds corresponding to two successive valley points may be determined.

4.3.2. *Featured Based (FB) approach*

By and large, the histogram distributions for noisy scenes have overlapping class distributions. In such situations, the proposed FL approach yields approximate results with large percentage of misclassification error. This could be attributed to the overlapping class distributions. In order to minimize the error due to overlapping of the class distributions, a feature based approach is proposed. This approach deals with the histogram distribution corresponding to an image dealing with features only. The feature from the original image is extracted as follows. A window of a given size is considered around a pixel and the distributions of the pixels over the window is assumed to be Gaussian. The first moment of this distribution over the window is considered as the feature and this is governed by the second moment(variance) of the distribution. With Gaussian assumption it is known that the likelihood estimates of the first and second moment over a window size of w is

$$\hat{\mu}_{w_{ij}} = \frac{1}{N_w} \sum_{k=1}^{N_w} x_k \quad and \quad \hat{\sigma}^2_{w_{ij}} = \frac{1}{N_w} \sum_{k=1}^{N_w} \left(x_k - \hat{\mu}_{w_{ij}}\right)^2 \qquad (4.1)$$

The first moment of the pixels is considered as the feature value if the following condition is satisfied.

$$if \quad |x_{ij} - \hat{\mu}_{w_{ij}}| \leq \hat{\sigma}_{w_{ij}}/K \quad then \quad x_{ij} = \hat{\mu}_{w_{ij}} \qquad (4.2)$$

Where K is a positive constant bounded between 1 to 10 to take care of smoothness and also to differentiate edge and non-edge pixels. x_{ij} is the gray value of the $(i,j)^{th}$ pixel, $\hat{\mu}_{w_{ij}}$ is the mean value, $\hat{\sigma}_{w_{ij}}$ is the standard deviation, N_w denotes the number of pixels in the window. The features corresponding to pixels of the whole image are derived and histogram of the feature pixels is considered. The optimal threshold for the original image is obtained from the modified histogram. The modified histogram either reduces the degree of overlapping or removes the overlapping between class distributions. The proposed PGA based clustering algorithm is used to determine the peaks and thereafter the valley is determined by exhaustive search method.

4.4. GA Class Model

Usually, GAs have been extensively used for function optimization and hence determination of global optimal solution. In case of nonlinear multimodal function optimization, the problem of determining the global optimal solution as well as local optimal solutions reduces to determining the niches in the multimodal functions. Thus, the problem boils down to clustering the population elements around the niches of the function. Some effort has been directed in this direction for last couple of years where new strategies and algorithms have been proposed.[14,15]

In case of optimization of nonlinear multimodal function, by and large, GA will yield one of the global optimal solutions. In such a case, each mode or niche of the function will correspond to either one of the global optimal or local optimal solutions. Therefore, Basic Genetic Algorithm (BGA) will fail to produce jointly the global as well as local solutions. When BGA is run for nonlinear multimodal function, finally all the population of elements converge to one of the niches or modes that corresponds to the global

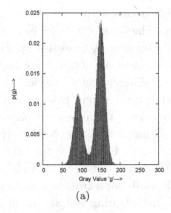 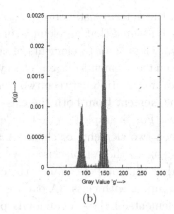

(a)   (b)

Figure 4.1. (a) Normalized histogram of the image, (b) Featured based normalized histogram.

optimum solution. In case of nonlinear multimodal function optimization, determination of all the niches and hence local and global solutions could be achieved by maintaining diversity among the population of elements. Maintenance of population diversity was addressed by D.J.Cavicchio[12] in his doctoral dissertation. He introduced several preselection schemes and one of them was quite successful at preserving population variance. De. Jong[13] in his doctoral dissertation presented technique which he referred to as the "Crowding Factor Model" or more simply "Crowding". Hence GA with crowding notion can be employed to maintain clusters at niches. We consider a histogram distribution having several niches, where each niche corresponds to a one of the classes of a given image. Thus, the problem of determination of niches reduces to determining the different classes of an image. Hence, GA based crowding serves as the class model.

4.4.1. Crowding method

The notion of crowding is inspired by ecological phenomenon where similar individuals in a natural population compete against each other for limited resources. Dissimilar individuals tend to occupy different niches and hence typically they do not compete. This results that in a fixed size population at equilibrium, new members of a particular species replace old members of that pieces. Crowding method attempts to maintain the diversity of the preexisting mixtures. The deterministic crowding that we have used in our algorithm, in terms of number classes, is explained as follows.

In the deterministic crowding, sampling occurs without replacement.[15] We will assume that an element in a given class is closer to an element of its own class than to elements of the other classes. A crossover operation between two elements of same class yields two elements of that class, and the crossover operation between two elements of different class will yield either: (i) one element from both the classes, (ii) or one element from two hybrid classes. For example, for a four class problem, the crossover operation between two elements of class AA and BB may results in elements either belonging to the set of classes AA, BB, or AB, BA. Hence the class AB offspring will compete against the class AB parents, the class BA offspring will compete with class BA parents. Analogously for a two class problem, if two elements of class A randomly paired, the offspring will also be of class A, and the resulting tournament will advance two class A elements to the next generation. The random pairing of two class B elements will similarly result in no net change to the distribution in the next generation. If an element of class A gets paired with an element of class B, one offspring will be from class A, and the other from class B. The class A offspring will compete against class A parent, the class B offspring against the class B parent. The end results will be that one element of the both classes advances to the next generation and hence no net change.

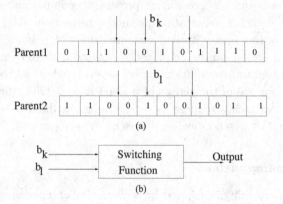

Figure 4.2. Generalized crossover opearator.

4.4.2. *Generalized crossover (GC)*

Generalized Crossover(GC) operator is proposed by Nanda et al.[16,17] and typically, the GC operator when applied to two parents produce one offspring instead of two offsprings as in the basic GA. The operator can be described as follows. Two parents P_1 and P_2 are selected at random and the two crossover points are also selected at random. In between the two crossover points, two bits of the respective positions of the two selected parents are now passed through a switching function to produce one output. This is shown in Fig. 4.2(a) and Fig. 4.2(b). For two variable case, a switching function is selected at random from the 16 possible function and the two bits are impressed as the input and the corresponding output is stored in the same bit position of one of the parents. Analogously, all the bits are generated by selecting the other respective bits from the two parents and passing through the randomly selected switching function. Hence, a stream of bits between the two crossover points is generated that replaces one of the parents to generate one offspring. The motivation is two fold: (i) it helps to examine the diversity of solutions in solution space, (ii) this model is more plausible from the evolutionistic sense that two parents produce one offspring at a time. Same GC operator is applied to the same two parents with the two new randomly chosen crossover points and the necessary switching function is applied to produce one more offspring. As a result of this operation, two offsprings are produced from the two parents by applying the GC operator twice. This process may be repeated to produce M offsprings from N parents in order to maintain the total population of elements constant over generations M is equal to N.

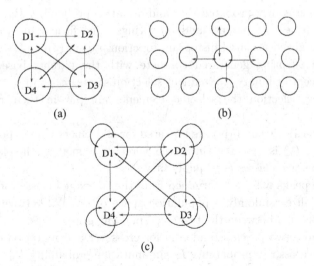

(a)   (b)

(c)

Figure 4.3.   (a) Island model (b) Stepping stone model (c) Proposed interconnection model.

4.4.3. GA based clustering

Once the stable subpopulation is maintained at the peaks of the multimodal function, the problem is to determine the valley between the two successive peaks. The two peaks correspond to two gray levels and in between these two gray values the minimum of the function is found out. The fitness function is defined as follows

$$\text{Fitness function for peaks} \quad f(g) = p(g) \quad g \in [0, L] \tag{4.3}$$

$$\text{Fitness function for valley} \quad f(g) = p(g) \quad g \in [p_1, p_2] \tag{4.4}$$

Where g denotes the gray value, p_1 denotes the first peak's gray value, p_2 denotes the second peak's gray value and $p(g)$ denotes the featured histogram distribution. We have employed basic GA to determine the minimum of the objective function which is the fitness function itself. Our proposed algorithm consists of determining all the peaks of the histogram distribution and in the sequel to find out the minima in between each pair of peaks. The salient steps of the algorithm are:

(i) Initialize randomly a population space of size N_p (each element corresponds to a gray value between 0 and 255) and their classes are determined.

(ii) Choose two parents randomly for crossover and mutation operation with crossover probability P_c and mutation probability P_m. Compute the fitness of parents and off-springs. The fitness function is the normalized featured histogram function $p(g)$ in (3).

(iii) The offspring generated compete with the parents based on the concept of binary tournament selection strategy.

(iv) After selection the selected elements are put in their respective classes.

(v) Step (ii), (iii) and (iv) are repeated for all elements in the population.

(vi) Steps (v) is repeated till the convergence is met i.e. the elements of respective classes are equally fit.

(vii) The peaks will be determined from the converged classes of step (vi)

(viii) Initialize randomly a population space of size N_v between the two peaks (i.e. between the two corresponding gray values).

(ix) Choose two parents randomly for crossover and mutation operation with crossover probability P_c and mutation probability P_m. Compute the fitness of parents and off-springs. The fitness function is the featured normalized histogram function $p(g)$ in (4).

(x) The fittest two elements between the parents and offspring are selected for the next generation in the selection strategy.

(xi) Step (ix), (x) are repeated for all elements in the population.

(xii) Step (xi) is repeated till the convergence is met.

(xiii) The converged value is the gray value corresponding to the valley between the two peaks. The image is then segmented using this value as threshold.

4.4.4. Parallel Genetic Algorithm (PGA)

Genetic algorithms have been extensively used to solve complex nonliner optimization problems. It has been found that hard problems require the population size to be very large. This in turn incurs high computational burden. Thus PGA is motivated to reduce the computational burden.

There are different ways to parallelize GAs. The two widely used PGA are (i) Coarse grained PGA (ii) Finegrained PGA. In course grained PGA, the population is divided into a few subpopulations keeping them relatively isolated from each other. The communication between subpopulations is established by an operator called migration. By this operation, individuals from one deme are transfered to other demes. In coarse grained model, the two population models used for the population structure are (i) Island Model and (ii) Stepping Stone model. In Island model, the whole population elements is partitioned into geographical isolation and the individuals are allowed to migrate from one subpopulation as shown in Fig. 4.3(a). In stepping stone model the notion of partitioning remains same as that of Island model, but the migration is restricted to neighboring subpopulation as shown in Fig. 4.3(b). In fine grained model, the population is partitioned into a large number of subpopulations, each with very less number of population elements. Thus, the ideal case is to have just one individual for each processing elements. This model requires massively parallel computers.

4.4.5. PGA based clustering

In this work, we have used the course grain model with different number of subpopulations. However, the results presented here correspond to a topology having four demes. As seen from Fig. 4.3(a), in course grain topology, the interconnection is among all the demes. In order to accelerate convergence of the algorithms, we have proposed a new notion of self migration and hence a new interconnection topology as shown in Fig. 4.3(c). As observed from Fig. 4.3(c), the self loop introduces the intramigration where the worst fit individuals are replaced by the best individuals while adhering to the good-bad replacement policy.[16,18] The proposed new crossover operator presented in Section 4.2 has been used in PGA algorithm.

4.4.6. Algorithm

The objective of designing parallel GA is two fold: (i) reducing the computational burden and (ii) improving the quality of the solutions. The design of PGA involves choice of multiple populations where the size of the population must be decided judiciously. These populations may remain isolated or they may communicate exchanging individuals. In this parallel scheme, the population is divided into demes and the demes evolve for convergence. After some generations migration is carried out to achieve convergence. This helps in accelerating the convergence and also improves the quality of the solution. We have adopted the good-bad(GB) based migration policy.[16,18] In our problem we considered four demes D1, D2, D3 and D4 and the interaction network model is shown in Fig. 4.3(c). Tournament selection mechanism is applied to all demes. A new crossover operator known as Generalized Crossover (GC) operator[16] has been used in the PGA. The steps of the parallelized crowding scheme are the following.

(1) Initialize randomly a population space of size N_p (each element corresponds to a gray value between 0 and 255) and their classes are determined.

(2) Divide the population space into fixed number of sub-populations and determine the class of individuals in each sub-population.

(3)　(i) In the given sub-population, choose two elements at random for Generalized Crossover (GC) and Mutation operation with crossover probability P_c and mutation probability P_m.

(ii) Evaluate fitness of each parents and offspring. The fitness function is the featured normalized histogram function $p(g)$ in (3).

(iii) The tournament selection mechanism is a binary tournament selection among the two parents and offsprings, the set which contains the individual having highest fitness among the four elements is selected to the set of parents for the next generation.

(iv) Repeat steps i, ii and iii for all the elements in the sub population.

(v) Repeat steps i, ii, iii and iv for a fixed number of generations

(4) Step 3 is repeated for each sub-population.

(5) Migration is allowed from each deme to every other deme. The individuals are migrated based on the selected migration policy. Number of elements to migrate are determined from the selected rate of migration$R_m ig$. The elements migrate with migration probability P_{mig}.

(6) Self Migration is allowed in each deme based on the selected migration policy and selected rate of self-migration $R_s mig$with a probability P_{smig}

(7) Repeat Step 3,4,5 and 6 till convergence is achieved. The algorithm stops when the average fitness of the total population is above pre-selected threshold.

(8) The peaks will be determined from the converged classes of step 7.

(9) Initialize randomly a population space of size N_v between the two peaks (i.e. between the two corresponding gray values).

(10) Use PGA (step 2-7 is repeated till the convergence is achieved) to find the valley between the two peaks. The fitness function is as in (4).

(11) Use the valley points gray value to segment the image.

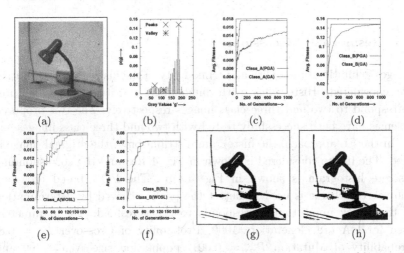

Figure 4.4. (a) Image 1, (b) Histogram with detected peaks and valley, (c) Average fitness vs generation of class "A" PGA and GA, (d) Average fitness vs generation of class "B" PGA and GA, (e) class "A" with self loop (SL) and without self loop (WOSL), (f) class "B" with self loop (SL) and without self loop (WOSL), (g) Segmented image using FL, (h) Segmented image using Otsu's approach.

Table 4.1.   Threshold Values and Misclassification Error for diffrent window size using the FB approach.

Window Size (WS)	Sample Images					
	Image 1		Image 2		Image 3	
	T	ME in %age	T	ME in %age	T	ME %age
3x3	107	0.8942	126	0.5748	106	0.4593
5x5	107	0.8942	129	0.5748	119	0.3403
7x7	110	0.8942	127	0.5748	121	0.3403
9x9	116	0.8286	130	0.5748	112	0.0000
11x11	107	0.8942	129	0.5748	114	0.0000
13x13	104	0.8942	108	1.4148	114	0.0000
15x15	110	0.8942	110	1.2904	118	0.3403

Table 4.2.   Performance evaluation of Otsu's, Kwon's, FL and FB approach for two class images.

Sample images	Threshold Selection Methods							
	Otsu's Approach		Kwon's Approach		FL Approach		FB Approach	
	T	ME %age	T	ME %age	T	ME %age	T	ME %age
Image 1	123	2.8595	122	1.762	114	0.0	116	0.8286
Image 2(SNR 22dB)	121	0.705	119	0.759	119	0.759	111	0.5748
Image 3(SNR 22dB)	126	0.6165	109	0.162	129	0.8240	106	0.2472

Table 4.3.   Performance evaluation of Otsu's, Kwon's, FL and FB approach for three class images.

Sample images	Threshold Selection Methods											
	Otsu's Approach			Kwon's Approach			FL Approach			FB Approach		
	T_1	T_2	ME %age	T_1	T_2	ME %age	T_1	T_2	ME %age	T_1	T_2	ME %age
Image 4	96	155	11.2503	101	197	76.6708	88	171	13.0600	112	167	5.5298
Image 5	100	160	2.3787	125	127	14.9711	99	154	1.5349	115	140	2.9010

4.5. Results and Discussions

Images exhibiting bimodality and trimodality in the histogram distribution are considered. Histograms with bimodality and trimodality features correspond to two and three class images respectively. The two proposed schemes have been successfully tested with two and three class images.

In the FL approach, the histogram distribution of the original image is used. The image considered is shown in Fig. 4.4(a) and the corresponding discrete histogram is shown in Fig. 4.4(b). The PGA based crowding and search scheme is used to detect the peaks followed by determination of the valley point that corresponds to the threshold. The parameters used for GA are Generation=1000, Probability of Crossover P_c = 0.8, Probability of Mutation P_m = 0.001, population size N_p = 400 and N_v = 100. The parameters used for PGA are: Generation=1000, Migration period is 10 generations, Number of demes is 4, Probability of Crossover P_c = 0.8, Probability of Mutation P_m = 0.001, population size N_p = 400 and N_v = 100, Probability of migration P_{mig} = 0.8, Migration rate R_{mig} = 4%,, Probability of self migration P_{smig} = 0.8 and Self migration

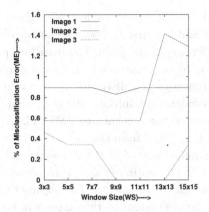

Figure 4.5.   Percentage of misclassification verses window size (Image 1, 2 & 3 are Fig. 4(a), 5(a) & 6(a)).

rate R_{smig} = 2%. The peaks detected by PGA are at 71 and 189 and the corresponding threshold T=114. GA and PGA based algorithms are compared and it is observed that PGA converges much faster than that of GA. This phenomenon is evident from Fig. 4(c) and (d) that corresponds to class A and class B respectively. For example, for class A, PGA converges around 100 generations while GA takes around 1000 generations. In PGA, we have used the island model with interconnection and we have proposed a fully interconnected model by introducing a new notion of self migration(SL). The proposed interconnection model is found to converge faster than that of the model without self migration(WOSL). This may be observed from Fig. 4.4(e) and (f) for both the classes. The threshold value thus obtained is used to segment the image and the segmented image is shown in Fig. 4.4(g). Our result is compared with that of Otsu's in Fig. 4(h) and it can be observed from Fig. 4.4(h) that there are missclassified pixels near the rod and also at the back of the table of the image. This misclassification is absent in case of result obtained by the proposed FL method in Fig. 4.4(g). The percentage of misclassification is determined as follows

$$ME = 1 - \frac{\mid B_O \cap B_T \mid + \mid F_O \cap F_T \mid}{\mid B_O \mid + \mid F_O \mid} \tag{4.5}$$

Where background and foreground are denoted by B_O and F_O for the original image, and by B_T and F_T for the test image. The threshold and the percentage of Misclassification Error(ME) are tabulated in Table 4.1. The FB approach is also validated with two and three class images. The feature pixels are generated as follows. A window of a given size is considered around the pixel x_{ij} and the first moment i.e. average value of the pixels is considered as the feature of the pixel. The distribution of the pixels over a window is assumed to be Gaussian and the selection of the feature is governed by the variance of the distributions as given by (2). Since the feature depends on window size, initially the selection of optimum window size is considered based on the percentage of ME. The ME for three images is shown in Fig. 4.5. It is found from simulation that the percentage of ME is minimum with a window size of 9x9. The corresponding results are also tabulated in Table 4.1. The optimum size, thus found empirically is used as the window size in case of the images. The featured pixels are generated and thus feature image is created. In this approach, the histogram of the featured pixels is used. The image considered in FB approach is shown in Fig. 4.6(a) and the histogram is shown in Fig. 4.6(b). The histogram of featured pixels is shown in Fig. 4.6(c). This featured histogram exhibit clear modes and the almost all gray levels are present. The proposed PGA based crowding algorithm is used to detect the peaks and the peaks are at 73 and 188 and the valley at 116. The detected peaks and valleys are shown in Fig. 4.6(d). The parameters of the PGA is same as that of the FL approach. The convergence of PGA based scheme predominantly depends on the proper choice of the migration policy and the rate of migration. The effect of these two parameters is also studied. Fig. 4.6(i) shows the effect of different migration policies for class A. It is observed that the algorithm converges faster with GB migration policy while with Random-Random (RR) migration policy, the algorithm does not converge. In case of class B of Fig. 4.6(j), the algorithm converges with RR policy but much slow as compared to other policies. Hence, GB migration policy becomes the proper choice for PGA based scheme. The effect of the rate of migration is demonstrated in Fig. 4.6(k) and 4.6(l). The rate of migration among demes has been varied from 2% to 8% and it has been observed that increase in the rate of migration enhances the speed of convergence. But, it is also observed that beyond a threshold value of migration rate the performance deteriorates. The segmented result obtained using the FB approach and Otsu's approach are shown in Fig. 4.6(m) and (n) respectively. It is observed that there are misclassified pixels near base of the rod and back of the table. These are absent in image obtained by the FB approach. This phenomenon is also reflected from the percentage of misclassification error tabulated in Table 4.2.

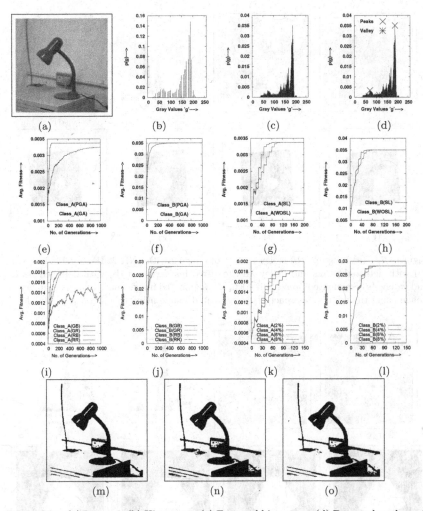

Figure 4.6. (a) Image 1, (b) Histogram, (c) Featured histogram, (d) Detected peaks and valley, (e) Average fitness vs generations of class "A" in case of PGA and GA, (f) Average fitness vs generations of class "B" in case of PGA and GA, (g) and (h) Interconnection models with SL and WOSL for class A and class B, (i) and (j) different migration policies for Class A and Class B, (k) and (l) different migration rate in GB migration policy for Class A and Class B, (m) Segmented image using the FB, (n) Segmented image using Otsu's approach, (o) Segmented image using Kwon's method.

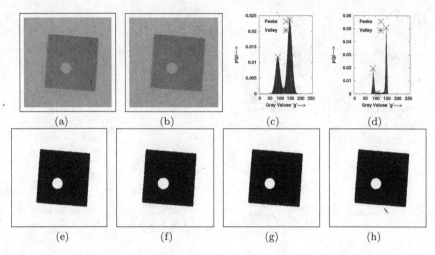

Figure 4.7. (a) Image 2, (b) Noisy version of image 2 with SNR 22dB, (c) Histogram of (b) with detected peaks and valley, (d) Featured histogram of (b) with detected peaks and valley, (e) Segmented image using FL, (f) Segmented image using FB, (g) Segmented image using the Otsu's Approach, (h) Segmented image using the Kwon's Approach.

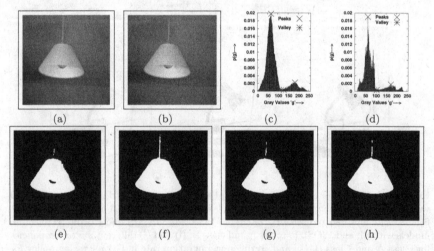

Figure 4.8. (a) Image 3, (b) Noisy version of image 3 with SNR 22dB,(c) Histogram of (b) with detected peaks and valley, (d) Featured histogram of (b) with detected peaks and valley, (e) Segmented image using FL, (f) Segmented image using FB, (g) Segmented image using the Otsu's Approach, (h) Segmented image using the Kwon's Approach

The FB approach has also been tested with noisy images as shown in Fig. 7(a) and Fig. 8(a). Fig. 7(b) is the corresponding histogram which exhibits clear bi-modality. The noisy version of image of Fig. 7(a) having signal to noise ratio (SNR) 22dB is shown in Fig. 7(c). We define SNR as $SNR_{dB} = 10\log_{10}\left(\sum_{ij} x_{ij}^2 / \sum_{ij} n_{ij}^2\right)$. The histogram of the noisy image, as shown in Fig. 4.7(d), shows overlapping of the object and background distributions. The peaks are detected at 92 and 151 and the corresponding threshold is at 119. It is clearly observed from Fig. 4.7(e) that the histogram of the featured pixels shows bi-modality. The peaks and valley are detected at 89,150 and 111 respectively. The segmented images are shown in Fig. 4.7(f),(g) and (h) that corresponds to FL, FB and Otsu's approach. From Table 4.2, it is found that the misclassification error is more in case of Otsu's method. Hence, the FB approach performs better than that of FL and Otus's approach. The efficacy of the FB approach is more evident in the third example as shown in Fig. 4.8. It is observed from the segmented results shown in Fig. 4.8(f),(g) and (h) that FB approach could preserve edges and reduced the number of misclassified pixels. In case of Otsu's approach from Table 4.2, it is observed that the ME is more than two times of that of the FB approach. Thus, the FB approach is more suitable for noisy as well as images having overlapping class distributions.

We have also validated the proposed FL and FB scheme in case of three class images as shown in Fig. 4.9 and 4.10. The percentage of misclassification is presented in Table 3. It may be observed from the segmented results of Fig. 9 and 10 that FB outperforms the FL and Otsu's approach. It is also evident from Table 3 that the percentage of ME is minimum in case of FB approach. Thus, in all the cases the proposed FB approach yielded better results than the FL and Otsu's approach.

4.6. Conclusion

In this chapter, we have presented two schemes, one dealing with the original histogram distributions(FL) and the other dealing with a histogram of featured pixels(FB). The thresholds are found by detecting first the peaks by the proposed PGA based crowding strategy followed by valleys. A new interconnection model is proposed to accelerate the convergence as well as the quality of solution. It is also observed that the proposed model with a new crossover operator yielded better results. The FB proved to be better than the FL and Otsu's approach. Specifically in case of noisy images and overlapping histogram distributions, FB approach could yield segmentation results with less misclassified pixels. We have validated the

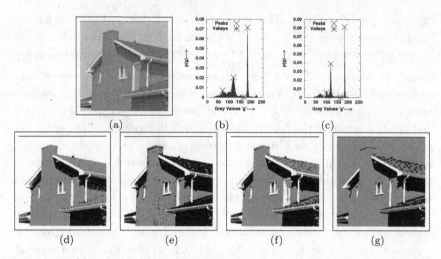

Figure 4.9. (a) Image 4, (b) Histogram with detected peaks and valleys, (c) Featured histogram with peaks and valleys, (d) Segmented image using FL, (e) Segmented image using FB, (f) Segmented image using Otsu's approach, (g) Segmented image using Kwon's approach.

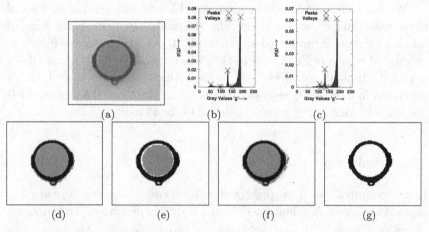

Figure 4.10. (a) Image 5, (b) Histogram with detected Peaks and valleys, (c) Featured histogram with Peaks and Valleys, (d) Segmented image using the FL, (e) Segmented image using FB, (f) Segmented image using Otsu's approach, (g) Segmented image using Kwon's approach.

proposed approaches for two as well as three class images. In all these cases, the FB approach has minimum ME. Current work focus on incorporating new feature to reduce the percentage of misclassified pixels.

Acknowledgments

This research work has been supported by Image Analysis and Computer Vision (IACV) Lab of C. V. Raman College of Engineering, Bhubaneswar, Orissa, India and the collaborative research project with Center for Soft Computing, ISI, Kolkata, India.

References

1. K. S. Fu and J. K. Mui, "A survey on image segmentation", *Pattern Recognition* 13:3-16,1981.
2. P. K. Sahoo, S. Soltani, A. K. C. Wong, "A survey of thrsholding technique", *Computer Vision, Graphics, and Image Processing* 41:133-260, 1988.
3. N. R. Pal, S. K. Pal, "A review on image segmentation techniques", *Pattern Recognition* 26(9):1277-1294,1993.
4. M. Sezgin, B. Sankur, "Survey over image thresholding techniques and quantitative performance evaluation", *Journal of Electronic Imaging* 13(1):146-165 2004.
5. S. Watanable, CYBEST Group, "An automated apparatus for cancer processing", *Comp. Graph. Image Processing* 3:350-358,1974.
6. J. S. Weszka, R. N. Nagel, A. Rosenfeld, "A threshold selection technique", *IEEE Trans. Syst., Man, Cybern.* 23:1322-1326,1974.
7. N. Otsu, "A threshold selection method from gray-level histograms", *IEEE Trans. Syst., Man, Cybern.* SMC-9(1):62-66,1979.
8. J. Kittler, J. Illingwoth, "Minimum error thresholding", *Pattern Recognition* 19(1):41-47,1986.
9. S. H. Kwon, "Threshold selection based on cluster analysis", *Pattern Recognition Letters*,25:1045-1050,2004
10. A. Z. Arifin, A. Asano, "Image segmentation by histogram thresholding using hierarchical cluster analysis", *Pattern Recognition Letters*,27:1515-1521,2006
11. Y. Qiao,Q. Hu, G. Qian, S. Luo, W. L. Nowinski, "Thresholding based on variance and intensity contrast", *Pattern Recognition*,40:596-608,2007
12. D.J.Cavicchio, "Adaptive search using simulated evolution", *Unpublished doctoral dissertation*, University of Michigan, Ann Arbor, 1970.
13. K.A.De. Jong, "An analysis of the behaviour of a class of genetic adaptive systems", *Doctoral dissertation*, University of Michigan, 1975.
14. S. W. Mahfoud, "Simple analytical models of genetic algorithms for multimodal function optimization", *Technical Report*, Illinois Genetic Algorithm Laboratory, IlliGAL report No. 93001, 1993.
15. S. W. Mahfoud, "Cross over interaction among niches", *Proc. of 1st IEEE Conference on Evolutionary Computation, world Congress on Computation Intelligence*, 188-193, 1993.

16. P. K. Nanda, D. P. Muni,P. Kanungo,"Parallelized crowding scheme using a new interconnection model",*International Conference on Fuzzy Systems*, Calcutta, LNAI(2275), Springer-Verlag:436-443,2002.

17. P.K.Nanda, B. Ghosh, T.N. Swain,"Parallel genetic algorithm based unsupervised scheme for extraction of power frequency signals in the steel industry", *IEE Proc. on Vision, Image and Signal Processing*, U.K, vol. 149,no. 4, pp.204-211, August 2002.

18. P. K. Nanda, P. Kanungo,"Parallel genetic algorithm based crowding scheme using neighboring net topology",*Proc. of Sixth International Conference on Information Technology*, Bhubaneswar,583-585,2003.

Chapter 5

Bipolar Fuzzy Spatial Information: First Operations in the Mathematical Morphology Setting

Isabelle Bloch

TELECOM ParisTech (ENST)
Dept. TSI - CNRS UMR 5141 LTCI
46 rue Barrault, 75013 Paris, France
Isabelle.Bloch@enst.fr

Bipolarity has not been much exploited in the spatial domain yet, although it has many features to manage imprecise and incomplete information that could be interesting in this domain. This paper is a first step to address this issue, and we propose to define mathematical morphology operations on bipolar fuzzy sets (or equivalently interval valued fuzzy sets or intuitionistic fuzzy sets).

Contents

5.1   Introduction   92
5.2   Preliminaries   94
5.3   Algebraic Dilation and Erosion of Bipolar Fuzzy Sets   95
5.4   Morphological Erosion of Bipolar Fuzzy Sets   96
5.5   Morphological Dilation of Bipolar Fuzzy Sets   98
    5.5.1   Dilation by duality   98
    5.5.2   Dilation by adjunction   98
    5.5.3   Links between both approaches   99
5.6   Properties and Interpretation   99
5.7   Illustrative Example   102
5.8   Derived Operators   103
    5.8.1   Morphological gradient   104
    5.8.2   Conditional dilation   108
    5.8.3   Opening, closing and derived operators   108
5.9   Conclusion   109
References   109

5.1. Introduction

In many domains, it is important to be able to deal with bipolar information.[1] Positive information represents what is granted to be possible (for instance because it has already been observed or experienced), while negative information represents what is impossible (or forbidden, or surely false). This view is supported by studies in cognitive psychology,[2] which show that two independent types of information (positive and negative) are processed separately in the brain. The intersection of the positive information and the negative information has to be empty in order to achieve consistency of the representation, and their union does not necessarily covers the whole underlying space (i.e. there is no direct duality between both types of information).

This domain has recently motivated work in several directions. In particular, fuzzy and possibilistic formalisms for bipolar information have been proposed.[1] Interestingly enough, they are directly linked to intuitionistic fuzzy sets,[3] interval-valued fuzzy sets[4] and vague sets, as shown by several authors.[5,6]

When dealing with spatial information, in image processing or for spatial reasoning applications, this bipolarity also occurs. For instance, when assessing the position of an object in space, we may have positive information expressed as a set of possible places, and negative information expressed as a set of impossible or forbidden places (for instance because they are occupied by other objects). As another example, let us consider spatial relations. Human beings consider "left" and "right" as opposite relations. But this does not mean that one of them is the negation of the other one. The semantics of "opposite" captures a notion of symmetry (with respect to some axis or plane) rather than a strict complementation. In particular, there may be positions which are considered neither to the right nor to the left of some reference object, thus leaving room for some indetermination.[7] This corresponds to the idea that the union of positive and negative information does not cover all the space. Similar considerations can be provided for other pairs of "opposite" relations, such as "close to" and "far from" for instance.

An example is illustrated in Figure 5.1. It shows an object at some position in the space (the rectangle in this figure). Let us assume that some information about the position of another object is provided: it is to the left of the rectangle and not to the right. The region "to the left of the rectangle" is computed using a fuzzy dilation with a directional fuzzy structuring element providing the semantics of "to the left",[7] thus defining the positive information. The region "to the right of the rectangle" defines the negative information and is computed in a similar way. The membership functions μ_L and μ_R, represent respectively the positive and negative parts of the bipolar fuzzy set. They are not the complement of each other, and we have:$\forall x, \mu_L(x) + \mu_R(x) \leq 1$.

Figure 5.1. Region to the left of the rectangle (positive information, μ_L) and region to the right of the rectangle (negative information, μ_R). The membership degrees vary from 0 (black) to 1 (white).

Another example, for the pair of relations close/far, is illustrated in Figure 5.2. The reference object is the square in the center of the image. The two fuzzy regions are computed using fuzzy dilations, using structuring elements that provide the semantics of "close" and "far".[8] Again, the two membership functions μ_C and μ_F are not the complement of each other and actually define a bipolar fuzzy set, with its positive and negative parts.

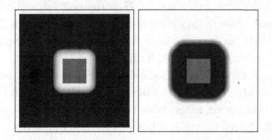

Figure 5.2. Region close to the square (μ_C) and region far from the square (μ_F).

To our knowledge, bipolarity has not been much exploited in the spatial domain. The above considerations are the motivation for the present work, which aims at filling this gap by proposing formal models

to manage spatial bipolar information. Additionally, imprecision has to be
included, since it is an important feature of spatial information, related
either to the objects themselves or to the spatial relations between them.
More specifically, we consider bipolar fuzzy sets, and propose definitions
of mathematical morphology operators (dilation and erosion) on these
representations, extending our preliminary work.[9] To our knowledge, this
is a completely new contribution in the domain of bipolar fuzzy sets. The
choice of mathematical morphology for a first insight into spatial bipolar
fuzzy sets is related to its wide use in image and spatial information
processing,[10,11] its interest for modeling spatial relations in various formal
settings (quantitative, qualitative, or fuzzy),[12] and its strong algebraic
bases,[13] which are suited to extensions to the bipolar case.

In Section 5.2, we recall some definitions on bipolar fuzzy sets. Then
we introduce definitions of algebraic dilations and erosions of bipolar fuzzy
sets in Section 5.3. In the spatial domain, specific forms of these operators,
involving a structuring element, are particularly interesting.[10] They are
called morphological dilation and erosion. Morphological erosion is then
defined in Section 5.4. Two forms of morphological dilations are proposed
in Section 5.5, either based on duality or on adjunction. Properties are
given in Section 5.6, as well as some simple illustrations in Section 5.7.
Finally, some derived operators are introduced in Section 5.8.

5.2. Preliminaries

Let $\mathcal{S}$ be the underlying space (the spatial domain for spatial information
processing). A bipolar fuzzy set on $\mathcal{S}$ is defined by a pair of functions
(μ, ν) such that $\forall x \in \mathcal{S}, \mu(x) + \nu(x) \leq 1$. Note that a bipolar fuzzy
set is equivalent to an intuitionistic fuzzy set.[3] It is also equivalent to an
interval-valued fuzzy set,[4] where the interval at each point x is $[\mu(x), 1 - \nu(x)]$.[5] Although there has been a lot of discussion about terminology in
this domain recently,[5,14] we use the bipolarity terminology in this paper, for
its appropriate semantics, as explained in our motivation. For each point x,
$\mu(x)$ defines the degree to which x belongs to the bipolar fuzzy set (positive
information) and $\nu(x)$ the non-membership degree (negative information).
This formalism allows representing both bipolarity and fuzziness.

Let us consider the set of pairs of numbers (a, b) in $[0, 1]$ such that
$a + b \leq 1$. This set is a complete lattice, for the partial order defined as:[15]

$$(a_1, b_1) \preceq (a_2, b_2) \text{ iff } a_1 \leq a_2 \text{ and } b_1 \geq b_2. \tag{5.1}$$

The greatest element is $(1,0)$ and the smallest element is $(0,1)$. The supremum and infimum are respectively defined as:

$$(a_1, b_1) \vee (a_2, b_2) = (\max(a_1, a_2), \min(b_1, b_2)), \qquad (5.2)$$

$$(a_1, b_1) \wedge (a_2, b_2) = (\min(a_1, a_2), \max(b_1, b_2)). \qquad (5.3)$$

The partial order $\preceq$ induces a partial order on the set of bipolar fuzzy sets:

$$(\mu_1, \nu_1) \preceq (\mu_2, \nu_2) \text{ iff } \forall x \in \mathcal{S}, \mu_1(x) \le \mu_2(x) \text{ and } \nu_1(x) \ge \nu_2(x). \qquad (5.4)$$

Note that this corresponds to the inclusion on intuitionistic fuzzy sets.[3] Similarly the supremum and the infimum are equivalent to the intuitionistic union and intersection.

It follows that, if $\mathcal{B}$ denotes the set of bipolar fuzzy sets on $\mathcal{S}$, $(\mathcal{B}, \preceq)$ is a complete lattice.

5.3. Algebraic Dilation and Erosion of Bipolar Fuzzy Sets

Once we have a complete lattice, it is easy to define algebraic dilations and erosions on this lattice.

Definition 5.1. A dilation is an operator δ from $\mathcal{B}$ into $\mathcal{B}$ that commutes with the supremum:

$$\delta((\mu, \nu) \vee (\mu', \nu')) = \delta((\mu, \nu)) \vee \delta((\mu', \nu')). \qquad (5.5)$$

An erosion is an operator ε from $\mathcal{B}$ into $\mathcal{B}$ that commutes with the infimum:

$$\varepsilon((\mu, \nu) \wedge (\mu', \nu')) = \varepsilon((\mu, \nu)) \wedge \varepsilon((\mu', \nu')). \qquad (5.6)$$

The following result is useful for proving the next results.

Lemma 5.1.

$$(\mu, \nu) \preceq (\mu', \nu') \Leftrightarrow \begin{cases} (\mu, \nu) \vee (\mu', \nu') = (\mu', \nu') \\ (\mu, \nu) \wedge (\mu', \nu') = (\mu, \nu) \end{cases} \qquad (5.7)$$

The following results are directly derived from the properties of complete lattices.[13]

Proposition 5.1. *Algebraic dilations δ and erosions ε on $\mathcal{B}$ satisfy the following properties:*

- δ *and ε are increasing operators;*

- $\delta((0,1)) = (0,1);$
- $\varepsilon((1,0)) = (1,0);$
- *by denoting (μ_x, ν_x) the canonical bipolar fuzzy set associated with (μ, ν) and x such that $(\mu_x, \nu_x)(x) = (\mu(x), \nu(x))$ and $\forall y \in \mathcal{S} \setminus \{x\}, (\mu_x, \nu_x)(y) = (0,1)$, we have $(\mu, \nu) = \bigvee_x (\mu_x, \nu_x)$ and $\delta((\mu, \nu)) = \bigvee_x \delta((\mu_x, \nu_x)).$*

The last result leads to morphological operators in case $\delta((\mu_x, \nu_x))$ has the same "shape" everywhere (and is then a bipolar fuzzy structuring element). This case is detailed in Sections 5.4 and 5.5.

Definition 5.2. A pair of operators (ε, δ) defines an adjunction on $(\mathcal{B}, \preceq)$ iff:

$$\forall (\mu, \nu) \in \mathcal{B}, \forall (\mu', \nu') \in \mathcal{B}, \delta((\mu, \nu)) \preceq (\mu', \nu') \Leftrightarrow (\mu, \nu) \preceq \varepsilon((\mu', \nu')) \quad (5.8)$$

Again we can derive a series of results from the properties of complete lattices and adjunctions.

Proposition 5.2. *If a pair of operators (ε, δ) on $\mathcal{B}$ defines an adjunction, then the following results hold:*

- *δ is a dilation and ε is an erosion, in the sense of Definition 5.1;*
- *$\delta\varepsilon \preceq Id$, where Id denotes the identity mapping on $\mathcal{B}$ (i.e. $Id(\mu, \nu) = (\mu, \nu)$);*
- *$Id \preceq \varepsilon\delta$;*
- *$\delta\varepsilon\delta\varepsilon = \delta\varepsilon$ and $\varepsilon\delta\varepsilon\delta = \varepsilon\delta$, i.e. the compositions of a dilation and an erosion are idempotent operators.*

The following representation result also holds.

Proposition 5.3. *If ε is an increasing operator, it is an algebraic erosion if and only if there exists δ such that (ε, δ) is an adjunction. The operator δ is then an algebraic dilation and can be expressed as:*

$$\delta((\mu, \nu)) = \inf\{(\mu', \nu') \in \mathcal{B} : (\mu, \nu) \preceq \varepsilon((\mu', \nu'))\}. \quad (5.9)$$

A similar representation result holds for erosion.

5.4. Morphological Erosion of Bipolar Fuzzy Sets

We now assume that $\mathcal{S}$ is an affine space (or at least a space on which translations can be defined). The general principle underlying morphological erosions consists in translating the structuring element at every position in space and check if this translated structuring element is included in the original set.[10] This principle has also been used in the main extensions of mathematical morphology to fuzzy sets.[16-21] Similarly, defining morphological erosions of bipolar fuzzy sets, using bipolar fuzzy structuring elements, requires to define a degree of inclusion between bipolar fuzzy sets. Such inclusion degrees have been proposed in the context of intuitionistic fuzzy sets.[22] With our notations, a degree of inclusion of a bipolar fuzzy set (μ', ν') in another bipolar fuzzy set (μ, ν) is defined as:

$$\inf_{x \in S} I((\mu'(x), \nu'(x)), (\mu(x), \nu(x))) \tag{5.10}$$

where I is an implication operator. Two types of implication can be defined,[22,23] one derived from an intuitionistic (or bipolar) t-conorm $\bot$:

$$I_N((a_1, b_1), (a_2, b_2)) = \bot((b_1, a_1), (a_2, b_2)), \tag{5.11}$$

and one derived from a residuation principle from an intuitionistic t-norm $\top$:

$$I_R((a_1, b_1), (a_2, b_2)) = \sup\{(a_3, b_3) : \top((a_1, b_1), (a_3, b_3)) \preceq (a_2, b_2)\} \tag{5.12}$$

where (a_i, b_i) are numbers in $[0, 1]$ such that $a_i + b_i \leq 1$ and (b_i, a_i) is the standard negation of (a_i, b_i).

Two types of t-norms and t-conorms are considered in[22] and will be considered here as well:

(1) operators called t-representable t-norms and t-conorms, which can be expressed using usual t-norms t and t-conorms T:

$$\top((a_1, b_1), (a_2, b_2)) = (t(a_1, a_2), T(b_1, b_2)), \tag{5.13}$$

$$\bot((a_1, b_1), (a_2, b_2)) = (T(a_1, a_2), t(b_1, b_2)). \tag{5.14}$$

(2) Lukasiewicz operators, which are not t-representable:

$$\top_W((a_1, b_1), (a_2, b_2)) = (\max(0, a_1 + a_2 - 1), \min(1, b_1 + 1 - a_2, b_2 + 1 - a_1)), \tag{5.15}$$

$$\bot_W((a_1, b_1), (a_2, b_2)) = (\min(1, a_1 + 1 - b_2, a_2 + 1 - b_1), \max(0, b_1 + b_2 - 1)). \tag{5.16}$$

In these equations, the positive part of $\top_W$ is the usual Lukasiewicz t-norm of a_1 and a_2 (i.e. the positive parts of the input bipolar values). The negative part of $\bot_W$ is the usual Lukasiewicz t-norm of the negative parts

(b_1 and b_2) of the input values. The two types of implication coincide for the Lukasiewicz operators.[15]

Based on these concepts, we can now propose a definition for morphological erosion.

Definition 5.3. Let (μ_B, ν_B) be a bipolar fuzzy structuring element (in $\mathcal{B}$). The erosion of any (μ, ν) in $\mathcal{B}$ by (μ_B, ν_B) is defined from an implication I as:

$$\forall x \in \mathcal{S}, \varepsilon_{(\mu_B, \nu_B)}((\mu, \nu))(x) = \inf_{y \in \mathcal{S}} I((\mu_B(y - x), \nu_B(y - x)), (\mu(y), \nu(y))).$$

(5.17)

5.5. Morphological Dilation of Bipolar Fuzzy Sets

Dilation can be defined based on a duality principle or based on the adjunction property. Both approaches have been developed in the case of fuzzy sets, and the links between them and the conditions for their equivalence have been proved in.[24] Similarly we consider both approaches to define morphological dilation on $\mathcal{B}$.

5.5.1. *Dilation by duality*

The duality principle states that the dilation is equal to the complementation of the erosion, by the same structuring element (if it is symmetrical with respect to the origin of $\mathcal{S}$, otherwise its symmetrical is used), applied to the complementation of the original set. Applying this principle to bipolar fuzzy sets using a complementation c (typically the standard negation $c((a, b)) = (b, a)$) leads to the following definition of morphological bipolar dilation.

Definition 5.4. Let (μ_B, ν_B) be a bipolar fuzzy structuring element. The dilation of any (μ, ν) in $\mathcal{B}$ by (μ_B, ν_B) is defined from erosion by duality as:

$$\delta_{(\mu_B, \nu_B)}((\mu, \nu)) = c[\varepsilon_{(\mu_B, \nu_B)}(c((\mu, \nu)))].$$

(5.18)

5.5.2. *Dilation by adjunction*

Let us now consider the adjunction principle, as in the general algebraic case. An adjunction property can also be expressed between a bipolar t-norm and the corresponding residual implication as follows:

$$\mathsf{T}((a_1, b_1), (a_3, b_3)) \preceq (a_2, b_2) \Leftrightarrow (a_3, b_3) \preceq I_R((a_1, b_1), (a_2, b_2))$$
$$(5.19)$$

with $I_R((a_1, b_1), (a_2, b_2)) = \sup\{(\alpha, \beta) : \alpha + \beta \le 1, \mathsf{T}((a_1, b_1), (\alpha, \beta)) \preceq (a_2, b_2)\}$.

Definition 5.5. Using a residual implication for the erosion for a bipolar t-norm T, the bipolar fuzzy dilation, adjoint of the erosion, is defined as:

$$\delta_{(\mu_B, \nu_B)}((\mu, \nu))(x) = \inf\{(\mu', \nu')(x) : (\mu, \nu)(x) \preceq \varepsilon_{(\mu_B, \nu_B)}((\mu', \nu'))(x)\}$$
$$= \sup_{y \in S} \mathsf{T}((\mu_B(x - y), \nu_B(x - y)), (\mu(y), \nu(y))). \quad (5.20)$$

5.5.3. *Links between both approaches*

It is easy to show that the bipolar Lukasiewicz operators are adjoint, according to Equation 5.19. It has been shown that the adjoint operators are all derived from the Lukasiewicz operator, using a continuous bijective permutation on $[0, 1]$.[22] Hence equivalence between both approaches can be achieved only for this class of operators.

5.6. Properties and Interpretation

Proposition 5.4. *All definitions are consistent: they actually provide bipolar fuzzy sets of $\mathcal{B}$.*

Let us first consider the implication defined from a t-representable bipolar t-conorm. Then the erosion writes:

$$\varepsilon_{(\mu_B, \nu_B)}((\mu, \nu))(x) = \inf_{y \in S} \perp((\nu_B(y - x), \mu_B(y - x)), (\mu(y), \nu(y)))$$
$$= \inf_{y \in S} (T((\nu_B(y - x), \mu(y)), t(\mu_B(y - x), \nu(y)))$$
$$= (\inf_{y \in S} T((\nu_B(y - x), \mu(y)), \sup_{y \in S} t(\mu_B(y - x), \nu(y))).$$
$$(5.21)$$

This resulting bipolar fuzzy set has a membership function which is exactly the fuzzy erosion of μ by the fuzzy structuring element $1 - \nu_B$, according to the original definitions in the fuzzy case.[16] The non-membership function is exactly the dilation of the fuzzy set ν by the fuzzy structuring element μ_B.

Let us now consider the derived dilation, based on the duality principle. Using the standard negation, it writes:

$$\delta_{(\mu_B,\nu_B)}((\mu,\nu))(x) = (\sup_{y\in S} t(\mu_B(x-y),\mu(y)), \inf_{y\in S} T((\nu_B(x-y),\nu(y))).$$

$$(5.22)$$

The first term (membership function) is exactly the fuzzy dilation of μ by μ_B, while the second one (non-membership function) is the fuzzy erosion of ν by $1-\nu_B$, according to the original definitions in the fuzzy case.[16]

This observation has a nice interpretation, which well fits with intuition. Let (μ,ν) represent a spatial bipolar fuzzy set, where μ is a positive information for the location of an object for instance, and ν a negative information for this location. A bipolar structuring element can represent additional imprecision on the location, or additional possible locations. Dilating (μ,ν) by this bipolar structuring element amounts to dilate μ by μ_B, i.e. the positive region is extended by an amount represented by the positive information encoded in the structuring element. On the contrary, the negative information is eroded by the complement of the negative information encoded in the structuring element. This corresponds well to what would be intuitively expected in such situations. A similar interpretation can be provided for the bipolar fuzzy erosion.

From these expressions it is easy to prove the following result.

Proposition 5.5. *In case the bipolar fuzzy sets are usual fuzzy sets (i.e. $\nu = 1-\mu$ and $\nu_B = 1-\mu_B$), the definitions lead to the usual definitions of fuzzy dilations and erosions. Hence they are also compatible with classical morphology in case μ and μ_B are crisp.*

Let us now consider the implication derived from the Lukasiewicz bipolar operators (Equations 5.15 and 5.16). The erosion and dilation write:

$$\forall x \in S, \varepsilon_{(\mu_B,\nu_B)}((\mu,\nu))(x) =$$

$$\inf_{y\in S}(\min(1,\mu(y)+1-\mu_B(y-x),\nu_B(y-x)+1-\nu(y)),\max(0,\nu(y)+\mu_B(y-x)-1)) =$$

$$(\inf_{y\in S}\min(1,\mu(y)+1-\mu_B(y-x),\nu_B(y-x)+1-\nu(y)),\sup_{y\in S}\max(0,\nu(y)+\mu_B(y-x)-1)),$$

$$(5.23)$$

$$\forall x \in S, \delta_{(\mu_B,\nu_B)}((\mu,\nu))(x) =$$

$$(\sup_{y\in S}\max(0,\mu(y)+\mu_B(x-y)-1), \inf_{y\in S}\min(1,\nu(y)+1-\mu_B(x-y),\nu_B(x-y)+1-\mu(y)).$$

$$(5.24)$$

The negative part of the erosion is exactly the fuzzy dilation of ν (negative part of the input bipolar fuzzy set) with the structuring element μ_B (positive part of the bipolar fuzzy structuring element), using the Lukasiewicz t-norm. Similarly, the positive part of the dilation is the fuzzy dilation of μ (positive part of the input) by μ_B (positive part of the bipolar fuzzy structuring element), using the Lukasiewicz t-norm. Hence for both operators, the "dilation" part (i.e. negative part for the erosion and positive part for the dilation) has always a direct interpretation and is the same as the one obtained using t-representable operators, for t being the Lukasiewicz t-norm.

In the case the structuring element is non bipolar (i.e. $\forall x \in \mathcal{S}, \nu_B(x) = 1 - \mu_B(x)$), then the "erosion" part has also a direct interpretation: the positive part of the erosion is the fuzzy erosion of μ by μ_B for the Lukasiewicz t-conorm; the negative part of the dilation is the erosion of ν by μ_B for the Lukasiewicz t-conorm.

Proposition 5.6. *If the bipolar fuzzy sets are usual fuzzy sets (i.e. $\nu = 1-\mu$ and $\nu_B = 1 - \mu_B$), the definitions based on the Lukasiewicz operators are equivalent to the fuzzy erosion defined[16] by the infimum of a t-conorm for the classical Lukasiewicz t-conorm, and to the fuzzy dilation defined by the supremum of a t-norm for the classical Lukasiewicz t-norm, respectively.*

Proposition 5.7. *The proposed definitions of bipolar fuzzy dilations and erosions commute respectively with the supremum and the infinum of the lattice $(\mathcal{B}, \preceq)$.*

Proposition 5.8. *The bipolar fuzzy dilation is extensive (i.e. $(\mu, \nu) \preceq \delta_{(\mu_B,\nu_B)}((\mu,\nu)))$ and the bipolar fuzzy erosion is anti-extensive (i.e. $\varepsilon_{(\mu_B,\nu_B)}((\mu,\nu)) \preceq (\mu,\nu))$ if and only if $(\mu_B,\nu_B)(0) = (1,0)$, where 0 is the origin of the space $\mathcal{S}$ (i.e. the origin completely belongs to the structuring element, without any indetermination).*

Note that this condition is equivalent to the conditions on the structuring element found in classical and fuzzy morphology to have extensive dilations and anti-extensive erosions.[10,16]

Proposition 5.9. *If the dilation is defined from a t-representable t-norm, the following iterativity property holds:*

$$\delta_{(\mu_B,\nu_B)}(\delta_{(\mu'_B,\nu'_B)}((\mu,\nu))) = \delta_{(\delta_{\mu_B}(\mu'_B),1-\delta_{(1-\nu_B)}(1-\nu'_B))}((\mu,\nu)). \qquad (5.25)$$

5.7. Illustrative Example

Let us now illustrate these morphological operations on the simple example shown in Figure 5.1. Let us assume that an additional information, given as a bipolar structuring element, allows us to reduce the positive part and to extend the negative part of the bipolar fuzzy region. This can be formally expressed as a bipolar fuzzy erosion, applied to the bipolar fuzzy set (μ_L, μ_R), using this structuring element. Figure 5.3 illustrates the result in the case of a classical structuring element and in the case of a bipolar one. It can be observed that the region corresponding to the positive information has actually been reduced (via a fuzzy erosion), while the region corresponding to the negative part has been extended (via a fuzzy dilation).

An example of bipolar fuzzy dilation is illustrated in Figure 5.4 for the bipolar fuzzy set close/far of Figure 5.2. The dilation corresponds to a situation where the structuring element represents by how much the positive part of the information can be expanded (positive part of the structuring element), for instance because new positions become possible, and by how much the negative part of the information should be reduced (negative part of the structuring element), for instance because it was too severe. These operations allow modifying the semantics attached to the concepts "close" and "far": in this example, a larger space around the object is considered being close to the object, and the regions that are considered being far from the object are put further away.

When several pieces of information are available, such as information on direction and information on distance, they can be combined using fusion tools, in order to get a spatial region accounting for all available information. This type of approach has been used to guide the recognition of anatomical structures in images, based on medical knowledge expressed as a set of spatial relations between pairs or triplets of structures (e.g. in an ontology), in the fuzzy case.[25–27] This idea can be extended to the bipolar case. As an example, a result of fusion of directional and distance information is illustrated in Figure 5.5. The positive information "to the left" of the reference object (and the negative part "to the right") is combined with the dilated distance information shown in Figure 5.4. The positive parts are combined in a conjunctive way (using a min here) and the negative parts in a disjunctive way (as a max here), according to the semantics of the fusion of bipolar information.[1] This example shows how the search space can be reduced by combining spatial relations to

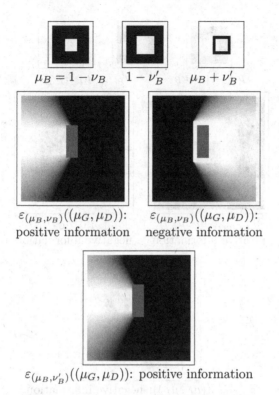

$$\mu_B = 1 - \nu_B \qquad 1 - \nu'_B \qquad \mu_B + \nu'_B$$

$\varepsilon_{(\mu_B, \nu_B)}((\mu_G, \mu_D))$: $\varepsilon_{(\mu_B, \nu_B)}((\mu_G, \mu_D))$:
positive information   negative information

$\varepsilon_{(\mu_B, \nu'_B)}((\mu_G, \mu_D))$: positive information

Figure 5.3. Illustration of a bipolar fuzzy erosion on the example shown in Figure 5.1. A first non bipolar structuring element (μ_B, ν_B) with $\nu_B = 1 - \mu_B$ is used. The results, displayed on the second line, show the reduction of the positive part via an erosion of μ_L with $1 - \nu_B = \mu_B$ and an extension of the negative part via a dilation of μ_L by μ_B. Next, another structuring element, which is truly bipolar, (μ_B, ν'_B) with $\mu_B + \nu'_B \leq 1$ is used. The negative part is the same as in the first case (since μ_B is the same). The positive part undergoes a stronger erosion since $1 - \nu'_B \geq 1 - \nu_B$ (figure in the third line).

reference objects, expressed as bipolar fuzzy sets. This can be considered as an extension to the bipolar case of attention focusing approaches.

5.8. Derived Operators

Once the two basic morphological operators, erosion and dilation, have been defined on bipolar fuzzy sets, a lot of other operators can be derived in a quite straightforward way. We provide a few examples in this section.

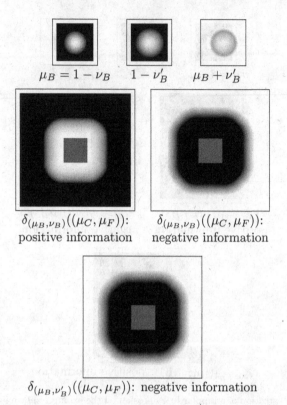

$\mu_B = 1 - \nu_B \qquad 1 - \nu'_B \qquad \mu_B + \nu'_B$

$\delta_{(\mu_B, \nu_B)}((\mu_C, \mu_F))$: \qquad $\delta_{(\mu_B, \nu_B)}((\mu_C, \mu_F))$:

positive information \qquad negative information

$\delta_{(\mu_B, \nu'_B)}((\mu_C, \mu_F))$: negative information

Figure 5.4. Illustration of a bipolar fuzzy dilation on the example shown in Figure 5.2. Results with a non bipolar fuzzy structuring element (μ_B, ν_B) with $\nu_B = 1 - \mu_B$ are illustrated on the second line. They show the extension of the positive part via a dilation of μ_C by μ_B and a reduction of the negative part via an erosion of μ_F by $1 - \nu_B = \mu_B$. Another structuring element (μ_B, ν'_B) is used next, which is bipolar: $\mu_B + \nu'_B \le 1$. The positive part is the same as in the first case (same μ_B). The negative part (displayed in the third line) is more eroded, since $1 - \nu'_B \ge 1 - \nu_B$.

5.8.1. *Morphological gradient*

A direct application of erosion and dilation is the morphological gradient, which extracts boundaries of objects by computing the difference between dilation and erosion.

Definition 5.6. Let (μ, ν) a bipolar fuzzy set. We denote its dilation by a bipolar fuzzy structuring element by (δ^+, δ^-) and its erosion by $(\varepsilon^+, \varepsilon^-)$.

 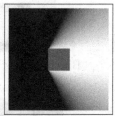

Positive information μ_L Negative information μ_R

 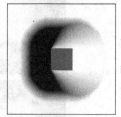

Conjunctive fusion of   Disjunctive fusion of
positive information   negative information

Figure 5.5. Fusion of bipolar information on direction (μ_L, μ_R) and on distance $\delta_{(\mu_B, \nu_B')}((\mu_C, \mu_F))$ of Figure 5.4.

We define the bipolar fuzzy gradient as:

$$\nabla(\mu, \nu) = (\min(\delta^+, \varepsilon^-), \max(\delta^-, \varepsilon^+)) \qquad (5.26)$$

which is the set difference, expressed as the conjunction between (δ^+, δ^-) and the negation $(\varepsilon^-, \varepsilon^+)$ of $(\varepsilon^+, \varepsilon^-)$.

Proposition 5.10. *The bipolar fuzzy gradient has the following properties:*

(1) Definition 5.6 defines a bipolar fuzzy set.
(2) If the dilation and erosion are defined using t-representable bipolar t-norms and t-conorms, we have:

$$\nabla(\mu, \nu) = (\min(\delta_{\mu_B}(\mu), \delta_{\mu_B}(\nu)), \max(\varepsilon_{1-\nu_B}(\nu), \varepsilon_{1-\nu_B}(\mu))). \qquad (5.27)$$

Moreover, if (μ, ν) is not bipolar (i.e. $\nu = 1 - \mu$), then the positive part of the gradient is equal to $\min(\delta_{\mu_B}(\mu), 1 - \varepsilon_{\mu_B}(\mu))$, which is exactly the morphological gradient in the fuzzy case.

An illustration is displayed in Figure 5.6. It illustrates both the imprecision (through the fuzziness of the gradient) and the indetermination (through the indetermination between the positive and the negative parts).

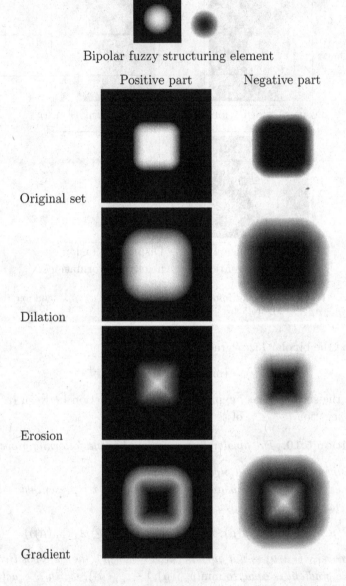

Figure 5.6.   Gradient using a fuzzy bipolar structuring element.

Another example is shown in Figure 5.7. The object is here somewhat more complex, and exhibits two different parts, that can be considered as two connected components to some degree. The positive part of the gradient provides a good account of the boundaries of the union of the two components, which amounts to consider that the region between the two components, which has lower membership degrees, actually belongs to the object. The positive part has the expected interpretation as a granted position and extension of the contours. The negative part shows the level of indetermination in the gradient: the gradient could be larger as well, and it could also include the region between the two components.

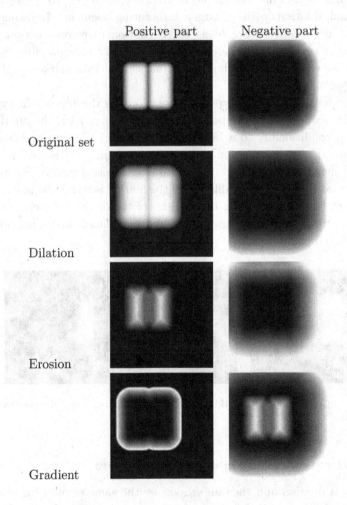

Figure 5.7. Gradient using a fuzzy (non bipolar) structuring element on a more complex object.

5.8.2. Conditional dilation

Another direct application of the basic operators concerns the notion of conditional dilation (respectively conditional erosion).[10] These operations are very useful in mathematical morphology in order to constrain an operation to provide a result restricted to some region of space. In the digital case, a conditional dilation can be expressed using the intersection of the usual dilation with an elementary structuring element and the conditioning set. This operation is iterated in order to provide the conditional dilation with a larger structuring element. Iterating this operation until convergence leads to the notion of reconstruction. This operation is very useful in cases we have a marker of some objects, and we want to recover the whole objects marked by this marker, and only these objects.

The extension of these types of operations to the bipolar fuzzy case is straightforward: given a bipolar fuzzy marker (μ_M, μ_N), the dilation of (μ_M, μ_N), conditionally to a bipolar fuzzy set (μ, ν) is simply defined as the conjunction of the dilation of (μ_M, μ_N) and (μ, ν). It is easy to show that this defines a bipolar fuzzy set. An example is shown in Figure 5.8, showing that the conditional dilation of the marker is restricted to only one component (the one including the marker) of the original object (only the positive parts are shown). Iterating further this dilation would provide the whole marked component.

Figure 5.8.   Conditioning set, marker and conditional dilation (only the positive parts are shown).

5.8.3. Opening, closing and derived operators

Applying a dilation and then an erosion by the same structuring element defines a closing, while applying first an erosion and then a dilation defines an opening. Thanks to the strong algebraic framework introduced in Section 5.3, opening and closing have all required properties: they are idempotent and increasing (hence they define morphological filters), opening is anti-extensive and closing is extensive (whatever the choice of the structuring element).

From these new operators, a lot of other ones can be derived, extending the classical ones to the bipolar case. For instance, several filters can be deduced from opening and closing, such as alternate sequential filter,[10] by applying alternatively opening and closing, with structuring elements of increasing size. Another example is the top-hat transform,[10] which allows extracting bright structures having a given approximative shape, using the difference between the original image and the result of an opening using this shape as a structuring element. Such operators can be directly extended to the bipolar case using the proposed framework.

5.9. Conclusion

New concepts on bipolar fuzzy sets are introduced in this paper, in particular algebraic and morphological dilations and erosions, for which good properties are proved and nice interpretations in terms of bipolarity in spatial reasoning can be derived. Further work aims at exploiting these new operations in concrete problems of spatial reasoning, in particular for handling the bipolarity nature of some spatial relations.

References

1. D. Dubois, S. Kaci, and H. Prade. Bipolarity in Reasoning and Decision, an Introduction. In *International Conference on Information Processing and Management of Uncertainty, IPMU'04*, pp. 959–966, Perugia, Italy, (2004).
2. J. T. Cacioppo, W. L. Gardner, and G. G. Berntson, Beyond Bipolar Conceptualization and Measures: The Case of Attitudes and Evaluative Space, *Personality and Social Psychology Review.* **1**(1), 3–25, (1997).
3. K. T. Atanassov, Intuitionistic Fuzzy Sets, *Fuzzy Sets and Systems.* **20**, 87–96, (1986).
4. L. A. Zadeh, The Concept of a Linguistic Variable and its Application to Approximate Reasoning, *Information Sciences.* **8**, 199–249, (1975).
5. D. Dubois, S. Gottwald, P. Hajek, J. Kacprzyk, and H. Prade, Terminology Difficulties in Fuzzy Set Theory – The Case of "Intuitionistic Fuzzy Sets", *Fuzzy Sets and Systems.* **156**, 485–491, (2005).
6. H. Bustince and P. Burillo, Vague Sets are Intuitionistic Fuzzy Sets, *Fuzzy Sets and Systems.* **79**, 403–405, (1996).

7. I. Bloch, Fuzzy Relative Position between Objects in Image Processing: a Morphological Approach, *IEEE Transactions on Pattern Analysis and Machine Intelligence.* **21**(7), 657–664, (1999).

8. I. Bloch, On Fuzzy Distances and their Use in Image Processing under Imprecision, *Pattern Recognition.* **32**(11), 1873–1895, (1999).

9. I. Bloch. Dilation and Erosion of Spatial Bipolar Fuzzy Sets. In *International Workshop on Fuzzy Logic and Applications WILF 2007*, vol. LNAI 4578, pp. 385–393, Genova, Italy (jul, 2007).

10. J. Serra, *Image Analysis and Mathematical Morphology.* (Academic Press, London, 1982).

11. P. Soille, *Morphological Image Analysis.* (Springer-Verlag, Berlin, 1999).

12. I. Bloch, Spatial Reasoning under Imprecision using Fuzzy Set Theory, Formal Logics and Mathematical Morphology, *International Journal of Approximate Reasoning.* **41**, 77–95, (2006).

13. H. J. A. M. Heijmans and C. Ronse, The Algebraic Basis of Mathematical Morphology – Part I: Dilations and Erosions, *Computer Vision, Graphics and Image Processing.* **50**, 245–295, (1990).

14. K. T. Atanassov, Answer to D. Dubois, S. Gottwald, P. Hajek, J. Kacprzyk and H. Prade's Paper "Terminology Difficulties in Fuzzy Set Theory – The Case of "Intuitionistic Fuzzy Sets"", *Fuzzy Sets and Systems.* **156**, 496–499, (2005).

15. C. Cornelis and E. Kerre. Inclusion Measures in Intuitionistic Fuzzy Sets. In *ECSQARU'03*, vol. LNAI 2711, pp. 345–356, (2003).

16. I. Bloch and H. Maître, Fuzzy Mathematical Morphologies: A Comparative Study, *Pattern Recognition.* **28**(9), 1341–1387, (1995).

17. D. Sinha and E. R. Dougherty, Fuzzification of Set Inclusion: Theory and Applications, *Fuzzy Sets and Systems.* **55**, 15–42, (1993).

18. B. de Baets. Generalized Idempotence in Fuzzy Mathematical Morphology. In eds. E. Kerre and M. Nachtegael, *Fuzzy Techniques in Image Processing*, Studies in Fuzziness and Soft Computing 52, pp. 58–75. Physica Verlag, Springer, (2000).

19. M. Nachtegael and E. E. Kerre. Classical and Fuzzy Approaches towards Mathematical Morphology. In eds. E. E. Kerre and M. Nachtegael, *Fuzzy Techniques in Image Processing*, Studies in Fuzziness and Soft Computing, chapter 1, pp. 3–57. Physica-Verlag, Springer, (2000).

20. T.-Q. Deng and H. Heijmans, Grey-Scale Morphology Based on Fuzzy Logic, *Journal of Mathematical Imaging and Vision.* **16**, 155–171, (2002).

21. P. Maragos, Lattice Image Processing: A Unification of Morphological and Fuzzy Algebraic Systems, *Journal of Mathematical Imaging and Vision.* **22**, 333–353, (2005).

22. G. Deschrijver, C. Cornelis, and E. Kerre, On the Representation of Intuitionistic Fuzzy t-Norms and t-Conorms, *IEEE Transactions on Fuzzy Systems.* **12**(1), 45–61, (2004).

23. C. Cornelis, G. Deschrijver, and E. Kerre, Implication in Intuitionistic Fuzzy and Interval-Valued Fuzzy Set Theory: Construction, Classification,

Application, *International Journal of Approximate Reasoning*. **35**, 55–95, (2004).

24. I. Bloch. Duality vs Adjunction and General Form for Fuzzy Mathematical Morphology. In *WILF*, vol. LNCS 3849, pp. 354–361, Crema, Italy (sep, 2005).

25. I. Bloch, T. Géraud, and H. Maître, Representation and Fusion of Heterogeneous Fuzzy Information in the 3D Space for Model-Based Structural Recognition - Application to 3D Brain Imaging, *Artificial Intelligence*. **148**, 141–175, (2003).

26. O. Colliot, O. Camara, and I. Bloch, Integration of Fuzzy Spatial Relations in Deformable Models - Application to Brain MRI Segmentation, *Pattern Recognition*. **39**, 1401–1414, (2006).

27. C. Hudelot, J. Atif, and I. Bloch, Fuzzy Spatial Relation Ontology for Image Interpretation, *Fuzzy Sets and Systems*. **159**, 1929–1951, (2008).

Chapter 6

Approaches to Intelligent Information Retrieval

Gabriella Pasi

Universit degli Studi di Milano Bicocca
Viale Sarca 336, 20126 Milano, Italy
pasi@disco.unimib.it

In this paper some directions of research in IR are pointed out.
In particular the focus is on the problem of personalization and
context modeling, and on the definition of new paradigms for content
representation.

Contents

6.1 Introduction 113
6.2 Information Retrieval 115
6.3 Personalization and Context Modeling 118
    6.3.1 Content-based information filtering 120
6.4 Recent Approaches to Textual Content Representation 121
6.5 An Approach to Personalized Document Indexing 124
6.6 Conclusions 126
References 126

6.1. Introduction

The advent and the rapid diffusion of the Internet and the expansion of
the World Wide Web have caused a strong resurgence of interest in the
problem of automatically accessing information relevant to specific user's
needs. The amount of information available on the Web has increased to a
point that there are great demands for effective systems that allow an easy
and "intelligent" access to information. By intelligent is here meant the
capability of the system to both manage imperfect (vague and/or uncertain)
information, and to adapt its behaviour to the user context (Bordogna and
Pasi, 2001; Broder, 2007; Pasi, 2003, Zadeh 2004, 2007). Moreover, more

recently, the increasing interest in defining the so called Semantic Web requires the definition of a basic infrastructure more powerful and flexible than the existing one to organise and to give a meaning to the available information, and to allow a better communication between humans and machines, (Davies et al., 2003).

The most used systems for accessing information on the Web are search engines, which are the tip of the iceberg of the research in Information Retrieval (IR), a Computer Science discipline whose roots date to late 60ties (Manning et al., 2008). However, despite of the above mentioned needs most search engines are based on retrieval models defined several years ago, and the query language which most of these systems employ is the Boolean query language, defined as the formal query language of the first Information Retrieval Systems (IRSs). The Boolean query language forces the user to precisely express her/his information needs as a set of unqualified keywords. This query language is neither able to allow the approximate expression of information needs nor to capture the user context: two distinct users formulating the same query (i.e. selecting the same keywords) would obtain the same results in spite of the fact that their choices could be defined to different aims and with a distinct notion of relevance in mind. Moreover in textual Information Retrieval (Information Retrieval of textual documents) the information granules on which the IR systems work are constituted by the terms extracted from or associated with the texts (called the *index terms*). This means that texts are generally represented and managed as bags of unrelated words, thus making the automatic management of texts unaware of their meaning. Moreover, search engines do not have any deduction capability, i.e. the capability to answer a query by a synthesis of information, which resides in various parts of the sparse and often unstructured knowledge base constituted by the Web (Zadeh, 2004, 2007). The central concept in IR is *relevance*; as the result of a query evaluation an IRS produces a numeric estimate of documents relevance to that query. However, only the user who formulates the query can determine the relevance of a document, i.e., the usefulness, pertinence, appropriateness, or utility of that document with respect to her/his needs (formally expressed by a query). Relevance is time, situation, and user specific. The relevance estimate performed by IRSs is strongly based on the so called *aboutness*, i.e. the content matching between a user query and a formal document representation (based on index terms). However, the concept of relevance that users have in mind is influenced by several additional factors that go beyond whether or not a given document is *about* the topics covered in the users' queries. Since relevance depends on many complex factors related to the user, and also to the considered documents and document sources, an effective automatic estimate of the relevance of documents to a query should take into account a multi-dimensional relevance model (Barry, 1994). Search engines make a relevance estimate which is a combination of various factors, among which *aboutness* and web page *popularity*, modeled by link analysis (Brin and Page, 1998; Farahat et al., 2006). However the central role of users is not sufficiently exploited.

To overcome the limitations of current IRSs and search engines, in recent years a great deal of research has been deployed to the main aim of modeling the subjectivity, the uncertainty, the vagueness and the context dependence intrinsic to the process of locating information relevant to specific users' needs. This research trend is also witnessed by the increasing use of the expression "Web Intelligence", which is strongly related to Computational Intelligence: to make a system intelligent means to make it flexible, adaptive and able to learn from experience (Zhong et al., 2003).To this purpose, the application of machine learning and soft computing techniques has been widely experienced in IR as a means to obtain a greater flexibility in designing systems for Information Access that can communicate naturally and learn by the interaction with the user (Avancini et al., 2006; Crestani and Pasi, 2000; Herrera-Viedma et al. 2006, Sebastiani 2002).

In this chapter some hot research topics concerning Textual Information Retrieval are synthetically presented. The aim of this chapter is not to be exhaustive with respect to the several research efforts which are being done in the field of IR. Its aim is just to point out some promising research directions. In section 2 the basic definition of Information Retrieval is given. In section 3 the problem of personalization in the context of IR is introduced. In section 4 the problem of representing the meaning of texts is discussed.

6.2. Information Retrieval

Information Retrieval (IR) aims at defining systems able to provide a fast and effective content-based access to a large amount of stored information usually organized in documents (information items) (Manning et al., 2007). Information can be of any kind: textual, visual, or auditory, although most actual IRSs store and enable the retrieval of only textual information.

A user accesses the IRS by explicitly formulating a query through a set of constraints (generally keywords) that the relevant information items must satisfy. The aim of the IRS is to evaluate the user query and to retrieve all documents which it estimates relevant to that query. This is achieved by comparing the formal representation of the documents with the formal user's query. The activity of IRSs is then based on the solution of a decision-making problem: how to identify the information items that correspond to the users' information preferences (i.e. relevant to their information needs)? What a user expects from an IRS is a list of the relevant documents ordered according to her/his preferences. The IRS acts then as an intermediary in this decision process: it simulates the decision process that the user would personally undertake. The documents constitute the alternatives on which the decision process has to be performed to the aim of identifying the relevant ones.

To achieve this aim an IRS is based on a model which provides a formal representation of both documents and user queries. The Boolean model, the Vector Space model, the probabilistic models and fuzzy models are examples of IR models (Manning et al., 2007).

The main components of an IRS are: a document collection, a query language, and a matching mechanism which estimates the relevance of documents to queries (see Figure 6.1).

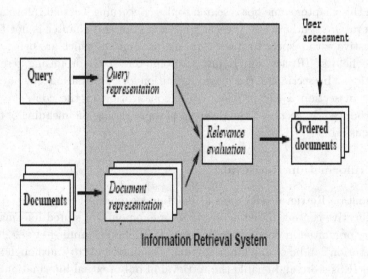

Figure 6.1. Scheme an IRS.

The input of these systems is constituted by a user query; their output is usually an ordered list of selected items, which have been estimated relevant to the information needs expressed in the user query.

Most of the existing IRSs and search engines offer a very simple modelling of IR, which privileges efficiency at the expenses of effectiveness. A crucial aspect affecting the effectiveness of an IRS is related to the characteristics of the query language, which should represent in the more accurate and faithful way the user's information needs. The available query languages are based on keywords specification, and do not allow to express uncertainty and vagueness in specifying the constraints that the relevant information items must satisfy. In real situations, however, users would find much more natural to express their information needs in an uncertain and approximate way. Most importantly the user system interaction is not iterative, but it is based on a unique query formulation to which a unique answer follows (list of retrieved documents).

Another important aspect which affects the effectiveness of IRSs is related to the way in which the documents' information content is represented; the documents' representations are extremely simple, based on keywords extraction and weighting. Moreover the IRSs generally produce a unique representation of documents for all users, not taking into account that each user looks at a document content in a subjective way, by possibly emphasizing some subparts with respect to others. This adaptive view of the document is not usually modelled. Another important aspect is related to the fact that on the Web some standards for the representation of semi-structured information are becoming more and more employed (such as XML); for this reason a great deal of research is devoted to structured Information Retrieval, aimed at exploiting the document structure both to index and inquiry the information they contain (Fuhr et al., 2006).

In recent years a strong deal of research to improve IRSs was devoted to the modelling of the concept of partiality intrinsic in the IR process and to making the systems adaptive, i.e. able to learn the users' concept of relevance. In particular, a set of approaches that has received a strong interest goes under the name of Soft Information Retrieval. These approaches apply some of the so called Soft Computing techniques, among which Fuzzy Set Theory (Crestani and Pasi, 2000; Herrera-Viedma et al., 2007; Pasi, 2006; Sanchez, 2007).

In the following sections the focus is not on specific soft computing or machine learning techniques applied to IR, but on some problems that the research in IR is facing to improve the process of automatically identifying information relevant to specific users needs. In particular, the notion of context modeling is introduced.

6.3. Personalization and Context Modeling

So far, much research in IR has dealt with ad hoc models that were based on shaky theoretical basis and neither did fully capture nor did fully explain the complexity of the IR task and of the IR context. A query is still considered as a fixed and complete representation of a static information need.

For several years the approach of research to improve the effectiveness of IRS was to improve the internal components of the systems while only marginally taking into account external components, such as the user and her/his *personal* point of view. Researchers have recently realised the importance that external components play in this process. A term used to describe these external components is *context*, where context consists of descriptions of the elements involved in search, such as the system, the user, the interaction methods that influence a user's information need, and what may play a role in the estimate of relevance of information items (Dumais et al. 2004; Finkelstein et al. 2001; Foltz and Dumais, 1992; Shen et al. 2005b; Shen et al. 2006; Sugiyama et al., 2004). The user's context may affect how she/he interacts with a retrieval system and how she/he makes decisions about the objects retrieved in a personalized way. IR researchers have come to the conclusion that to improve the effectiveness of content-based searching they need to consider more and more the role of context. In fact, it is now well understood that user context and personalization are critical to the development of the next generation of search technologies (Bierig and Gker, 2006; Broder, 2007; Joachims, 2002). Indeed, a closer inspection of dominant search engines reveals that the major search engines have approached the problem of personalized search. In (Bahrat, 2000), an approach is presented to model search context, intented as queries recently deployed by the user, along with hyperlinks of result pages that the user visited and/or liked in the context of each query. This approach was experimented on several search engines.

Most efforts towards personalized IR are focused on how to capture the user context using, for example, pseudo-relevance feedback via top ranking documents, or implicit relevance feedback via query history, click-through information from query logs, and a range of other factors such as time, location, interaction history. Relevance feedback is an approach proposed in the 70ties as a way to improve retrieval effectiveness (Croft et al., 2001;

Rocchio, 1971; Salton and Buckley, 1990; Wang et al., 2007). After the user submits a query, the IRS does the first run by evaluating the query and ranking documents. Then the relevance feedback system asks the user to explicitly judge the relevance of the retrieved documents, and takes into account the user judgments to expand/modify the original query by thus originating a new query and present newly ranked documents to the user. This process is iteratively applied until the user is satisfied with the retrieved documents. A lot of empirical evaluations show that relevance feedback is an effective way to improve the retrieval effectiveness.

As in many retrieval tasks such as Web search, the user is not willing to provide an explicit feedback to the system, pseudo relevance feedback was later proposed. After the user submits a query, the retrieval system does the first run to rank document and automatically picks a few top ranked document. These top ranked documents are assumed to be relevant by the pseudo relevance feedback engine, and they are used to modify/expand the original query through query expansion to construct a new, more focused query. So while relevance feedback requires user involvement in the relevance judgment process, pseudo feedback does not. Empirical evaluations show that pseudo relevance feedback generally, but not always, can outperform the baseline retrieval. However, pseudo feedback is not as effective as relevance feedback.

Implicit feedback is another approach that totally excludes the user in the feedback process (Kelly and Teevan, 2003; White et al., 2004; Shen et al., 2005a). In interactive information retrieval such as Web search, the user generally has several interactions with the retrieval system. During these interactions, the user gives a lot of hints to the retrieval system, which can help the retrieval system to infer the user's information need better. With implicit feedback the system captures and stores user interaction data such as query and click-through history, and infer the user's information need better through these interaction data (Kelly and Belkin, 2004). Implicit feedback neither asks for the user's explicit relevance judgment nor assumes that top ranked documents of baseline retrieval are relevant. Instead, implicit feedback intelligently infer the user's information need through those hints implicitly provided by the user (Shen et al. 2005a).

Finally, active feedback was proposed in (Shen and Zhai, 2005). Active feedback can be considered as a kind of relevance feedback. But traditional relevance feedback focuses on how to incorporate judged document into the new query (e.g., query term addition and query term re-weighting), while active feedback studies which documents should be presented to the user for relevance judgment in order to maximize the learning benefits of the retrieval system from the user judgment. A general framework was proposed in the paper and several specific algorithms were deduced from the framework.

An important role concerning the modelling of the user's context is played by Information Filtering Systems synthetically described in the next subsection. The integration of approaches to Information Filtering and Information Retrieval has been an important step towards the definition of personalization techniques.

6.3.1. *Content-based information filtering*

Information Filtering is a discipline aimed at defining systems which, on the basis of a prior knowledge of some user interests, generally encoded in a user profile, are able to select and *push* to the user the information relevant to her/his needs. Differently from what happens when using an Information Retrieval system (which requires that the user explicitly specifies some "contextual" information interests through a query), an Information Filtering system applies the selection of relevant items on the basis of a previously defined and usually dynamically updated *user profile*, which represents some user's needs (long term information needs). What is encoded in a user's profile represents a more stable and structured information need with respect to the volatile one expressed by a user query addressed to an Information Retrieval System. Information Filtering systems are typically designed to manage large volumes of dynamically generated information, such as news streams. A typical Information Filtering application repeatedly gathers newly arrived documents for a short period, then compares the representation of the documents with the user profiles and finally pushes the documents estimated relevant to the appropriate users. For example, an email filter eliminates the spam messages from the stream of incoming mail. In this case, the user profile expresses what a user does not want, instead of what he or she wants.

A basic model of a content-based filtering system was proposed in (Belkin and Croft, 1992). The main components of this model are the stream of incoming data, the user profiles, and a matching function that selects the items relevant to the users interest. The user can then evaluate the filtered results by explicitly activating a feedback to modify her/his profile (the representation of user interests). More recent works have split feedback on the user interest into two types, implicit and explicit (Amato et al. 2000). Explicit feedback is where the user must explicitly indicate the relevance or utility of a document or group of documents, such as marking a document as relevant, or providing a rating for the document. Implicit feedback (as already outlined in section 2) is where the actions of the user are recorded, and the view of the user is inferred from those actions. For example, some systems assume that the length of time a document is open will correspond to the interest the user has in the document (i.e. the longer a user reads a document, the more interesting that document will be to him/her). Some classic content based filtering systems include SIFT and Okapi (Bell and Moffat, 1996; Robertson and Walker, 1999; Yan, and Garcia-Molina 1999).

More recently, some content-based IF systems have been defined that, besides estimating the *aboutness* via the matching function, evaluate some additional properties of an incoming document to a user profile, such as their *novelty* (for example NewsJunkie in Gabrilovich et al., 2004). Recently in the context of the European project PENG (PErsonalized News content programminG) a new content-based filtering model has been defined based on a multi-criteria decision making approach (Pasi et al. 2007). In particular, five distinct criteria are measured by the filtering system to an incoming document in order to assess its relevance to a user profile. The core of the model still remains the measure of *aboutness* intended, as outlined before, as an indication of the similarity of the contents of the document to the information needs represented in the user profile. A very new property which has been defined in the new filtering model is the *coverage* of the incoming document contents of the user profile contents. The three additional measures that in our model can contribute to filter incoming documents and to assess their relevance to user's profiles are *novelty* (Gabrilovich et al., 2004; Zhang et al., 2003), *reliability* in the source from which the incoming document originates, and finally *timeliness*.

6.4. Recent Approaches to Textual Content Representation

One of the central problems in the definition of effective IRSs is to formally process a text written in natural language in order to estimate its relevance to a specific user's need. This necessity raises the problem of formally representing the *meaning* of a text, which in turn means to decide which the information granules are and how they can be automatically identified. So far the way to address this quite complex problem in IRSs has oversimplified its natural complexity thus bringing to extremely poor solutions. The indexing process plays a crucial role in determining the effectiveness of an IR system as it generates the formal representation of the contents of the information items (documents' surrogates). The most used automatic indexing procedures are based on term extraction and weighting: the documents are represented by means of a set of index terms with associated weights (the index term weights); an index term weight expresses the degree of significance of the index term as a descriptor of the document information content. The automatic computation of the index term weight is based on the occurrence count of the term in the document and in the whole archive. In this case, a numeric weight is computed for each document d and each term t by means of an indexing function (Manning and Raghavan, 2007; Salton et al., 1984).

As a consequence, also query languages are usually based on (weighted) keywords, thus allowing the matching mechanism to compare two compatible representations. However, keyword-based retrieval models have several limitations; an important one is that they do not take into account the topical structure and content of documents, thus preventing concept-oriented document representation and query formulation.

One of the first approaches that addressed this problem was Latent Semantic Indexing (LSI), which was introduced as a means to detect the latent conceptual structures in texts (Deerwester et al., 1990; Berry et al., 1995). LSI tries to overcome the problems of lexical matching by using statistically derived conceptual indices instead of individual words for retrieval. The basic assumption of LSI is that there is some underlying or latent structure in word usage that is partially obscured by variability in word choice.

More recently, some approaches have been proposed to concept-based Information retrieval. A concept-based representation of both texts and user queries promises important benefits over keyword-based access. One of the addressed benefits is the ability to exploit semantic relationships among concepts in finding relevant documents. Another benefit is the elimination of irrelevant documents by identifying conceptual mismatches. In this context, the use of ontologies is of great importance as it allows the identification of related concepts and their linguistic representatives given a key concept.

The term "*concept-based information retrieval*" does not refer to a strict information retrieval model, approach or paradigm. There has been no proposal of a comprehensive or universally practical concept-based retrieval model. Some approaches have been proposed in the last years, all of which attempt to improve the retrieval effectiveness by exploiting the conceptual or semantic information implied by words into a retrieval methodology. Some approaches make use of a knowledge base and other approaches do not.

By these models, a document is represented as a set of concepts: to this aim a fundamental component is a conceptual structure for mapping concepts to document representations.

Conceptual structures can be general or domain specific and include dictionaries, thesauri and ontologies, and they can be either manually or automatically generated or they may pre-exist (Guarino et al., 1999). In (Gonzalo et al., 1998) an analysis of conceptual structures and their usage to improve retrieval is presented. WordNet and EuroWordNet are examples of (thesaurus-based) ontologies widely employed to improve the effectiveness of IR systems (Miller, 1995).

A conceptual structure can be represented using distinct data structures: trees, semantic networks, conceptual graphs, etc. In (Montes-y-Gomez et al., 2000; Thomopoulos et al., 2003), the use of conceptual graphs for representing documents and queries is discussed. The authors propose a method for measuring the similarity of phrases represented as conceptual graphs. In (Gonzalo et al., 1998), the authors propose an indexing method based on the use of WordNet synsets: the Vector Space Model is employed, by using synsets as indexing space instead of word forms.

In (Chen et al., 1993), a concept based information retrieval approach based on the use of a thesaurus is proposed. In (Kan et al., 2001), an approach to detect the topical structure of a set of documents is presented.

In (Baziz et al., 2007) an approach is presented, based on the representation of both documents and queries by means of trees. Both document and queries are represented by a set of concepts corresponding to nodes in the hierarchical structure of a considered ontology. Each node in the resulting sub-trees corresponds to a disambiguated term from a document/query that matches one concept in the ontology. Sub-trees are obtained by considering only the "subsumption" relation represented by a classical is-a relation (hyperonymy). The idea behind this representation is to complete the document/query description by possibly adding intermediate nodes in order to complete these representations by concepts that do not appear explicitly in a document and/or a query but that deal somewhat with the same topic.

In the next subsection an approach to personalized indexing of documents is presented; this approach proposes to produce a formal document representation in a way which is personalized to users, with the consequence of making the IRS able to produce answer to a query identified by the same keywords.

6.5. An Approach to Personalized Document Indexing

The common way of formally representing documents has the limitation of not taking into account that a term can play a different role within a text, according to the distribution of its occurrences. Let us think for example at an XML document organized in logical sections. For example scientific papers are usually organised into sections like *title*, *authors*, *abstract*, *introduction*, *references*, etc. An occurrence of a term in the *title* has a distinct informative role than an occurrence of the same term in the *references*. Moreover, usual indexing procedures behave as a black box producing the same document representation for all users; this enhances the system's efficiency but implies a severe loss of effectiveness. In fact, when examining a document structured in logical sections the users have their personal views of the document's information content; according to this view in the retrieval phase they would naturally privilege the search in some subparts of the documents' structure, depending on their preferences. This last consideration outlines the fact that the estimate of relevance of a given document could take advantage from an explicit user's indication of her/his interpretation of the document's structure, and supports the idea of *dynamic* and *adaptive* indexing (Bordogna and Pasi, 2005). Adaptive indexing refers to personalized indexing procedures which take into account the users' indications to *interpret* the document contents and to build their synthesis on the basis of this interpretation. It follows that if an archive of semi-structured documents is considered (e.g. XML documents), flexible indexing procedures would make the user able to direct the indexing process by explicitly specifying some constraints on the document structure. This preference specification can be exploited by the matching mechanism to the aim of privileging the search within the most preferred sections of the document, according to the users' indications. The user/system interaction can then generate a personalized document representation, which is distinct for distinct users.

In (Bordogna and Pasi, 2005), a user adaptive indexing model has been proposed, based on a weighted representation of semi-structured documents that can be tuned by users according to their search interests to generate their personal document representation in the retrieval phase. The considered documents may contain multimedia information with different structures. A document is represented as an entity composed of sections (such as *title, authors, introduction, references*, in the case of a scientific paper). The model is constituted by a static component and by an adaptive query-evaluation component; the static component provides an a priori computation of an index term weight for each logical section of the document. The formal representation of a document becomes then a fuzzy binary relation defined on the Cartesian product T × S (where T is the set of index terms and S is the set of identifiers of the documents' sections): with each pair <section, term>, a significance degree in [0,1] is computed, expressing the significance of the term in the document section.

The adaptive component is activated by the user in the phase of query formulation and provides an aggregation strategy of the N index term weights (where N is the number of sections) into an overall index term weight. The aggregation function is defined on the basis of a two level interaction between the system and the user. At the first level the user expresses preferences on the document sections, outlining those that the system should more heavily take into account in evaluating the relevance of a document to a user query. This user preference on the document structure is exploited to enhance the computation of index term weights: the importance of index terms is strictly related to the importance for the user of the logical sections in which they appear.

At the second level, the user can decide which aggregation function has to be applied for producing the overall significance degree (see Figure 6.2). This is done by the specification of a linguistic quantifier such as *at least k*

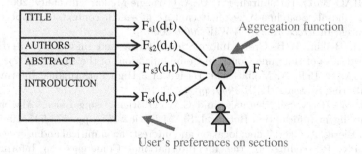

Figure 6.2.   Sketch of the Personalized Indexing Procedure.

and *most*; in the fuzzy indexing model defined in (Bordogna and Pasi, 2005) linguistic quantifiers are formally defined as Ordered Weighted Averaging (OWA) operators (Yager, 1988).

By adopting this document representation the same query can produce different document rankings, depending on the user indications.

It is very important to notice that the elicitation of users' preferences on the structure of a document is a quite new and recent research approach, which can remarkably improve the effectiveness of IRSs.

6.6. Conclusions

In this paper a synthetic overview of some recent research approaches to the design of more effective Information Retrieval Systems has been presented. In particular the important problems of personalization and context modeling have been introduced, as well as some recent approaches to document indexing.

References

1. G. Amato, U. Straccia, C. Thanos, EUROgatherer: a Personalised Gathering and Delivery Service on the Web, in Proc. of the 4th SCI-2000, 2000.
2. H. Avancini, A. Lavelli, F. Sebastiani, R. Zanoli. Automatic Expansion of Domain-Specific Lexicons by Term Categorization, *ACM Transactions on Speech and Language Technology*, 3:1-30, 2006.
3. C.L. Barry, User-defined relevance criteria: an exploratory study. *Journal of the American Society for Information Science.* 45(3), 149-159, 1994.
4. M. Baziz, M. Boughanem, G. Pasi, H. Prade. An Information Retrieval Driven by Ontology: from Query to Document Expansion. In Proceedings of Large-Scale Semantic Access to Content (Text, Image, Video and Sound) (RIAO 2007), Pittsburgh, PA, USA, Carnegie Mellon University, 2007.
5. K. Bharat, Searchpad: Explicit capture of search context to support web search. In *Proceeding of WWW 2000*, 2000.
6. N.J. Belkin, W.B. Croft, Information filtering and Information Retrieval: Two sides of the same Coin?, in Communications of the ACM, 35(12), 1992.
7. T. A. H. Bell, A. Moffat. The Design of a High Performance Information Filtering System. SIGIR 1996, pp.12-20, 1996.
8. M. W. Berry, S.T. Dumais, and G.W. O'Brien, Using Linear Algebra for Intelligent Information Retrieval, SIAM Review 37:4, pp. 573-595, 1995.
9. R. Bierig, A. Gker, Time, location and interest: an empirical and user-centred study. Proceedings of the 1st International Conference on Information Interaction in Context, IIiX 2006, pp. 76-87, Copenhagen, Denmark, October 18-20, 2006,.ACM 2006.

10. P. Buitelaar, D. Steffen, M. Volk, D. Widdows, B. Sacaleanu, S. Vintar, S. Peters, H. Uszkoreit. Evaluation Resources for Concept-based Cross-Lingual IR in the Medical Domain. In Proc. of LREC2004, Lisbon, Portugal, 2004.
11. G. Bordogna, G. Pasi, Modelling Vagueness in Information Retrieval. In *Lectures in Information Retrieval*, M. Agosti, F. Crestani and G. Pasi eds., Springer Verlag, 2001.
12. G. Bordogna, G. Pasi, Personalized Indexing and Retrieval of Heterogeneous Structured Documents, Information Retrieval, Kluwer, Vol. 8, Issue 2, pp. 301-318, April 2005.
13. S. Brin, L. Page, The Anatomy of a Large-Scale Hypertextual Web Search Engine, Computer Networks, Vol.30, issue 1-7, 107-117, 1998.
14. A.Z. Broder. The Next Generation Web Search and the Demise of the Classic IR Model. In Proc. ECIR 2007, 2007.
15. H. Chen, K.J. Lynch, K. Basu, D.T. Ng D. T. Generating, integrating, and activating thesauri for concept-based document retrieval. IEEE EXPERT, Special Series on Artificial Intelligence in Text-based Information Systems, 8(2):25-34, 1993.
16. F. Crestani, and G. Pasi (Eds.) Soft Computing in Information Retrieval: Techniques and Applications, Physica Verlag, Studies in Fuzziness Series, 2000.
17. W. B. Croft, S. Cronen-Townsend, and V. Larvrenko. Relevance feedback and personalization: A language modeling perspective. In Proeedings of Second DELOS Workshop: Personalisation and Recommender Systems in Digital Libraries, 2001.
18. J. Davies, D. Fensel, F. van Harmelen. Towards the Semantic Web: Ontology-Driven Knowledge Management. John Wiley & Sons, 2003.
19. S. Deerwester, S. Dumais, G. Furnas, T. Landauer, and R. Harshman, Indexing by latent semantic analysis, Journal of the American Society for Information Science, 41, pp. 391-407, 1990.
20. S. T. Dumais, E. Cutrell, R. Sarin, and E. Horvitz. Implicit queries (IQ) for contextualized search (demo description). In Proceedings of SIGIR 2004, page 594, 2004.
21. A. Farahat, T. LoFaro, J.C. Miller, G. Rae, L.A. Ward, Authority Rankings from HITS, PageRank, and SALSA: Existence, Uniqueness, and Effect of Initialization, SIAM Journal on Scientific Computing, 27(4) , pp. 1181 - 1201, 2006.
22. L. Finkelstein, E. Gabrilovich, Y. Matias, E. Rivlin, Z. Solan, G. Wolfman, and E. Ruppin. Placing search in context: The concept revisited. In Proceedings of WWW 2002, 2001.
23. P.W. Foltz, and S.T. Dumais, Personalized information delivery: an analysis of information filtering methods, In Communications of the ACM 35, 12, 29-38, 1992.
24. N. Fuhr, M. Lalmas, A. Trotman (Eds.). Comparative Evaluation of XML Information Retrieval Systems, 5th International Workshop of the Initiative for the Evaluation of XML Retrieval, INEX 2006, Dagstuhl Castle, Germany,

December 17-20, 2006, Revised and Selected Papers. Lecture Notes in Computer Science 4518 Springer 2007, 2006.

25. E. Gabrilovich, S. Dumais, and E. Horvitz. NewsJunkie: Providing Personalized Newsfeeds via Analysis of Information Novelty, Proceedings of the Thirteenth International World Wide Web Conference 2004 (WWW 2004), May 2004, New York, NY, 2004.

26. J. Gonzalo, F. Verdejo, I. Chugur, J. Cigarrn J. Indexing with WordNet synsets can improve text retrieval, in Proc. the COLING/ACL '98 Workshop on Usage of WordNet for Natural Language Processing, 1998.

27. N. Guarino, C. Masolo, G. Vetere G. OntoSeek: Content-Based Access to the Web. IEEE Intelligent Systems, pp 70-80, 1999.

28. E. Herrera-Viedma, G. Pasi, F. Crestani (Eds.). Soft Computing in Web Information Retrieval: Models and Applications, Series of Studies in Fuzziness and Soft Computing, Springer Verlag, 2006.

29. T. Joachims. Optimizing search engines using clickthrough data, Proceedings of the eighth ACM SIGKDD international conference on Knowledge discovery and data mining, 133 - 142, 2002.

30. M. Y. Kan, J. L. Klavans, K. R. McKeown . Synthesizing composite topic structure trees for multiple domain specific documents, Tech. Report CUCS-003-01, Columbia University, 2001.

31. D. Kelly and N. J. Belkin. Display time as implicit feedback: Understanding task effects. In Proceedings of SIGIR 2004, 2004.

32. D. Kelly and J. Teevan. Implicit feedback for inferring user preference. SIGIR Forum, 32(2), 2003.

33. C. D. Manning, P. Raghavan and H. Schtze, *Introduction to Information Retrieval*, Cambridge University Press. 2008.

34. G. Miller. Wordnet: A lexical database. Communication of the ACM, 38(11), pp. 39–41, 1995.

35. M. Montes-y-Gómez, A. Lpez-Lpez, and A. Gelbukh. Information retrieval with Conceptual Graph matching. In Proc. DEXA, 11th Int. Conf. on Database and Expert Systems Applications, Greenwich, England. LNCS 1873, Springer-Verlag, pp. 312–321, 2000.

36. D.W. Oard, G. Marchionini, A Conceptual Framework for Text Filtering, technical report EE-TR-96-25 CAR-TR-830 CLIS-TR-96-02 CS-TR-3643, University of Maryland, 1996.

37. G. Pasi, Modelling Users' Preferences in Systems for Information Access, International Journal of Intelligent Systems 18:793-808, 2003.

38. G. Pasi, Fuzzy Sets in Information Retrieval: State of the Art and Research trends, In "Fuzzy Sets and Their Extensions: Representation,Aggregation and Models.Intelligent Systems from Decision Making to Data Mining, Web Intelligence and Computer Vision", (H. Bustince, F. Herrera, J. Montero eds.), series Studies in Fuzziness and Soft Computing, Springer Verlag, 2007.

39. G. Pasi, G. Bordogna, R. Villa, A multi-criteria content-based filtering system. In Proc, ACM SIGIR, 775-776, 2007.

40. S. E. Robertson, S. Walker. Okapi/Keenbow at TREC-8. TREC 1999.

41. J. Rocchio. Relevance feedback information retrieval. In TheSmart Retrieval System-Experiments in Automatic Document Processing, pp. 313–323, Prentice-Hall, Kansas City, MO, 1971.

42. G. Salton and C. Buckley. Improving retrieval performance by retrieval feedback. Journal of the American Society for Information Science, 41(4):288–297, 1990.

43. G. Salton, and M.J. McGill, Introduction to modern information retrieval. McGraw-Hill, 1984.

44. E. Sanchez (editor). Fuzzy Logic and the Semantic Web. Elsevier, 2006.

45. F. Sebastiani Machine learning in automated text categorization. *ACM Computing Surveys*, 34(1):1-47, 2002

46. X. Shen and C. Zhai, Active Feedback in Ad-hoc Information Retrieval, Proceedings of 2005 ACM Conference on Research and Development on Information Retrieval (SIGIR'2005), pp. 59-66, 2005.

47. X. Shen, B. Tan, C Zhai. Context Sensitive Information Retrieval Using Implicit Feedback, Proceedings SIGIR'05, August 15–19, 2005, Salvador, Brazil, 2005a.

48. X. Shen, B. Tan, C. Zhai, Exploiting Personal Search History to Improve Search Accuracy,Proceedings of 2006 ACM Conference on Research and Development on Information Retrieval, Personal Information Management Workshop (PIM'2006), 2006.

49. X. Shen, B. Tan, C. Zhai, UCAIR: Capturing and Exploiting Context for Personalized Search, Proceedings of 2005 ACM Conference on Research and Development on Information Retrieval–Information Retrieval in Context Workshop (IRiX'2005), 2005b.

50. K. Sugiyama, K. Hatano, and M. Yoshikawa. Adaptive web search based on user profile constructed without any effort from users. In Proceedings of WWW 2004, 2004.

51. R. Thomopoulos, P. Buche, O. Haemmerl. Representation of weakly structured imprecise data for fuzzy querying. Fuzzy Sets and Systems, 140, 111-128, 2003

52. X. Wang, H. Fang, C.X. Zhai: Improve retrieval accuracy for difficult queries using negative feedback. Proceedings of CIKM 2007: 991-994, 2007.

53. R. W. White, J. M. Jose, C. J. van Rijsbergen, and I. Ruthven. A simulated study of implicit feedback models.

54. In Proceedings of ECIR 2004, pages 311–326, 2004.

55. R. R. Yager, On ordered weighted averaging aggregation operators in multicriteria decisionmaking, IEEE Transactions on Systems, Man and Cybernetics, v.18 n.1, p.183-190, January/February 1988.

56. T.W. Yan, H. Garcia-Molina. The SIFT information dissemination system. ACM Transactions on Database Systems (TODS), 24(4), pp. 529-565,1999.

57. Y. Zhang, W. Xu, and J. P. Callan. Exploration and exploitation in adaptive filtering based on Bayesian active learning. In *Proceedings of ICML 2003*, 2003.

58. L.A. Zadeh, Web Intelligence, World Knowledge and Fuzzy Logic –The Concept of Web IQ (WIQ), Lecture Notes in Computer Science, Volume

3213/2004, Knowledge-Based Intelligent Information and Engineering Systems, 2004.

59. L.A. Zadeh, Web Intelligence, World Knowledge and Fuzzy Logic, in Forging New Frontiers: Fuzzy Pioneers I, Series Fuzziness and Soft Computing, Volume 217/2007, 2007.

60. N. Zhong, J. Liu, and Y.Y. Yao (eds.) *Web Intelligence*, Springer Monograph (2003).

Chapter 7

Retrieval of On-line Signatures

H. N. Prakash and D. S. Guru

Department of Studies in Computer Science, Manasagangotri,
University of Mysore, Mysore - 570 006, India
prakash_hn@yahoo.com, dsg@compsci.uni-mysore.ac.in

In this chapter, the problem of quick retrieval of online signatures is addressed. On-line signature retrieval is an important issue to be tackled when legal and historical documents are to be catlogued based on signatures[23] and when securing electronic documents based on signatures queries.[24] Here, we present a method archiving and retrieving of online signatures. This methodology retrieves signatures in the database for a given query signature according to the decreasing order of the similarity of the spatial topology of the sampled points with that of the query signature. The similarity is based on orientations of corresponding edges drawn in between sampled points of the signatures. The best hypotheses are retrieved in a simple yet efficient way to speed up the subsequent recognition stage. The runtime of the signature recognition process is reduced, because the scanning of the entire database is narrowed down to matching the query with a few top retrieved hypotheses. The experimentation conducted on a large MCYT_signature database[7] has shown promising results.

Contents

7.1 Introduction 132
    7.1.1 Signature analysis 132
    7.1.2 Related work 132
    7.1.3 Signature retrieval 133
7.2 Retrieval Model 134
    7.2.1 Signature representation 134
    7.2.2 Retrieval 135
7.3 Experimentation 137
7.4 Conclusions 141
References 142

7.1. Introduction

7.1.1. *Signature analysis*

Handwritten signature is one of the earliest biometrics used for general authentication. Its simplicity, ease to capture and the flexibility that it provides for human verification, makes it the most widely used biometric. Automatic human signature analysis is a complex and specific area of handwriting analysis with a high scientific and techical interest.[14] There are two different categories in signatures: Offline (static) signatures and Online (dynamic) signatures. Offline signature is nothing but an image of a signature captured by camera or obtained by scanning a signature which is on a paper or a document. Offline signatures (conventional signatures) are supplemented by other features like azimuth, elevation and pressure in case of online signatures. Online signatures are more robust as they store additional features, other than just signature image. Any signature biometric identification problem[15] has two distinct phases: (i) recognition and (ii) verification. In verification, the query signature is compared with a limited set of signatures of the class whose identity is claimed. Verification is the process in which a query signature is tested to decide it truly belongs to a particular person.[1] In the recognition phase, presence of an identity in the database is ascertained,[19],[1] It involves matching stage that extends to entire dataset/database, which is more time consuming.

7.1.2. *Related work*

7.1.2.1. *Signature verification*

Signature analysis is an active research field[18] with an application like validation of checks and other financial documents. Due to practical significance of signature verification a lot of research has been carried out in the last two decades and many techniques like dynamic time warping,[4] Baysian classifiers,[25] neural networks,[1] support vector machine,[16] Hidden Markov Model[17] have been already recommnded.[6] investigated spatial properties of handwritten images through matrix analysis. For details of progress in online signature verification the readers are refered to a reviw paper.[9]

7.1.2.2. *Signature recognition*

Automatic signature recogntion has receieved less attention compared to signature verification despite the potential applications that could use signature as an identification tool. For example automatic signature recogniion system can be used in validation of identity of an individual who needs an access to secured zone or security sensitive facilities.[20] Other potential applications of signature recognition is in law-enforcement applications which requires identification of perpetrators and in analysis of some historical documents.[15] Some techniques applied in the area of signature recogntion are: application of vector quantization - dynamic time warping scheme for signature recognition,[5] application of active deformable models for approximating the external shape of the signatures,[2221] compare support vector machines and multilayer perceptron for signature recognition.

7.1.3. *Signature retrieval*

Theoritical point of view signature verification is 1:1 matching process while signature recognition is 1:N matching problem hence signature recogition looks more complex. In the work[15] signature recognition and signature verification are treated as two seperate consecutive stages, where succesful verification is highly dependent on succesful recognition. Pavlidis et al. (1998) state that it would be of great value if an intelligent signature identification system be capable of arriving at a decision (recognition and verification) based only on the signature of the user. In this context the signature recognition system is applied as an efficient preprocessing stage for signature verification.

Essentially any signature recognition system can be optimized when the query signature is matched with best hypotheses than the entire database. Hence, in this work we focus on quick retrieval of online signatures for optimizing subsequent robust recognition/verification system. Signature retrieval mechanism that retrieves the best hypotheses from the database attains importance. Efficient retrieval of handwritten signatures is still a challenging work if the signature database is large. Unlike fingerprint, palm print and iris, signatures have significant amount of intra class variations, making the research even more compelling. This approach with the potential application of signature recognition / verification system optimized with efficient signature retrieval mechanism, justify from our point of view the importance of finding the effective automatic solutions to signature recognition problems.

So far the only work on signature retrieval is by Han and Sethi.[14] They work on handwritten signatures and use a set of geometrical and topological features to map a signature onto 2D-strings.[2] However, 2D-strings are not invariant to similarity transformations and any retrieval systems based on them are hindered by many bottlenecks.[11] There are several approaches for perceiving spatial relationships such as nine-directional lower triangular matrix (9DLT),[3] triangular spatial relationship (TSR)[13] and Similarity measure (SIM_R).[12] In order to overcome the said problem, we proposed spatial topology of equitemporal points for online signature retrieval based on SIM_R[10] and a comprehensive work of the same is discussed in this chapter. The methodology retrieves signatures quickly from the database for a given query in the decreasing order of their similarity with the query. Consequently the system can be used as a preprocessing stage which reduces the runtime of the recognition process as scanning of the entire database is narrowed down to contrasting the query with a top few retrieved hypotheses during recognition. Experimentation has been conducted on a MCYT_signature database[7] which consists of 8250 signatures (see Appendix A) and it has shown promising results.

7.2. Retrieval Model

This section of the chapter explains the method of signature representation and subsequently corresponding retrieval techniques.

7.2.1. *Signature representation*

The approach involves sampling of online signature at equitemporal interval for x, y coordinates, to get say n sample points. The first sampled point is labeled as '1' and the second as '2' and so on and so forth until n, the last sampled point. A complete directed graph of n nodes is then envisaged treating the sampled points as vertices where directions originate from the node with smaller label to the one with larger label as shown in Fig.7.1 for $n = 5$. A vector V consisting of the slopes of all the directed edges forms the symbolic representation of a signature and is given by:

$$V = \theta_{12}, \theta_{13}, \cdots, \theta_{1n}, \theta_{23}, \cdots, \theta_{2n}, \theta_{34}, \cdots, \theta_{3n}, \cdots, \theta_{n-1n} \qquad (7.1)$$

Where θ_{ij} is the slope of the edge directed from the node i to the node j, $1 \leq i \leq n - 1, 2 \leq j \leq n$, and $i < j$. Thus the vector V is of size

$n(n-1)/2$. A knowledge base of online signature is created by storing these symbolic representative vectors for each specimen signature of every user.

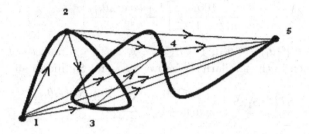

Figure 7.1.   Online signature with nodes and edges.

7.2.2.   *Retrieval*

In this subsection, we present two models for retrieval of online signatures based on query a signature: The one is based on similarity between the orientations of edges and the other one is based on the concept of triangular spatial relationship(TSR).

7.2.2.1.   *Edge orientation based model*

Let S_1 and S_2 be two signatures and V_1 and V_2 be the corresponding vectors representing the slopes of the edges in S_1 and S_2. Now the similarity between S_1 and S_2 is analogous to the similarity between the vectors V_1 and V_2. Let

$$V_1 = \{{}^{s_1}\theta_{12}, {}^{s_1}\theta_{13}, \cdots, {}^{s_1}\theta_{1n}, {}^{s_1}\theta_{23}, {}^{s_1}\theta_{24}, \cdots, {}^{s_1}\theta_{ij}, \cdots, {}^{s_1}\theta_{n-1n}\} \quad (7.2)$$

$$V_2 = \{{}^{s_2}\theta_{12}, {}^{s_2}\theta_{13}, \cdots, {}^{s_2}\theta_{1n}, {}^{s_2}\theta_{23}, {}^{s_2}\theta_{24}, \cdots, {}^{s_2}\theta_{ij}, \cdots, {}^{s_2}\theta_{n-1n}\} \quad (7.3)$$

Let $\Delta V = |V_1 - V_2|$, i.e.

$$\Delta V = \{\Delta\theta_{12}, \Delta\theta_{13}, \cdots, \Delta\theta_{1n}, \Delta\theta_{23}, \Delta\theta_{24}, \cdots, \Delta\theta_{ij}, \cdots, \Delta\theta_{n-1n}\} \quad (7.4)$$

Here, ΔV represents the vector of the absolute differences in the slopes of corresponding edges in signatures S_1 and S_2. Assuming a maximum possible similarity of 100, each edge contributes a value of $100.00/(n)(n-1)/2$ towards the similarity. If the difference in the corresponding edge orientations of the two signatures is zero then the computed similarity value is maximum. When the differences in corresponding edge orientations tend to be away from zero, then the similarity between the two signatures reduces. In this case contribution factor[12] towards similarity from each corresponding edges directed from the node i to the node j in S_1 and S_2 is

$$\frac{100}{n(n-1)/2}\left[\frac{1+cos(\Delta\theta_{ij})}{2}\right] \qquad (7.5)$$

where $\Delta\theta_{ij} = |^{s_1}\theta_{ij} - {}^{s_2}\theta_{ij}|$, $1 \le i \le n-1$, $2 \le j \le n$, and $i < j$.

Consequently the similarity[12] between S_1 and S_2 due to all edges is

$$SIM(S_1, S_2) = \frac{100}{n(n-1)/2}\sum_{ij}\left[\frac{1+cos(\Delta\theta_{ij})}{2}\right] \qquad (7.6)$$

where $1 \le i \le n-1$, $2 \le j \le n$, and $i < j$.

Rotation invariance is achieved by aligning the first edge of the query signature with that of database signature before contrasting. The computation complexity the methodology is $O(n^2)$. During retrieval, the query signature is sampled and slopes of the edges are extracted to form a query vector. The query vector is then contrasted with the representative vectors in the database. Signatures are retrieved according to the similarity ranks and the top K retrievals are selected for further matching for accurate recognition.

7.2.2.2. *TSR based model*

In the edge orientation based model (discussed in the previous subsection), we have considered the orientations of edges between the two corresponding sampled points of query and database signatures. For the sake of comparison with the model, we also consider the orientations of edges among three sampled points, forming triangles as shown in Fig.7.2 for six sampled points. The computation of triangular spatial relationship[11] among all possible triangles is $O(n^3)$ time complexity. Therefore we considered the orientation of edges of only successive triangles of query and database signatures for matching as it is of $O(n)$. We refer this method as successive triangle matching. Triangles formed among sampled points are $\Delta123$, $\Delta234$, $\Delta345$ and $\Delta456$. The corresponding triangles are contrasted sequentially between query and database signatures for similarity computation. In general let $1, 2, 3, \cdots, n$ be equitemporal sampled points of online signature. From n points, we can form $n-2$ triangles by considering three successive points at a time. During matching process, the similarity is computed according to eq.1.6 only between sides of the respective triangles of query and database signatures.

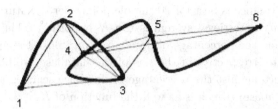

Figure 7.2. Successive triangle matching.

Table 7.1. Query and database signatures combination.

Combination	Number of database signatures	Number of Query signatures
(a)	15	10
(b)	10	15
(c)	5	20

7.3. Experimentation

We have used MCYT dataset for our experimentation as we require large dataset. The dataset of SVC-2004 (signature verification competition) is too small, which is trivial for retrieval purposes. Please refer Appendix A for details of the online signature dataset.

The comparison of retrieval performances of the Edge orientation based model(proposed method) and TSR based model (successive triangle method) is made through a series of extensive experimentation in this section. At the first, retrieval experiments are conducted for different number of sample points n: 10, 20 and 30. Our idea is to study the retrieval system for varying sample points of signatures. For each sampling, keeping 15 signatures in the database, the remaining 10 signatures were considered as queries, out of 25 genuine signatures per class. In total 3300 (*i.e.* 330×10) queries and 4950 (*i.e.* 330 × 15) database signatures comprised the test set for experimentation. The retrieval results are as shown in Fig. 7.3.

The output of the retrieval system is the top K hypotheses. In our experimentations we have set $K = 10$. We define the correct retrieval (CR) for the performance evaluation of retrieval system as

$$CR = (K_c/K_d) \times 100 \qquad (7.7)$$

where K_c is the number of correctly retrieved signatures, K_d is the number of signatures in the database. The experimental results show that the retrieval performance is best for 20 sample points per signature Fig.7.3(b). The output of the retrieval system is top K hypothesis. The value of K is used to define the percentage of database scan. Since the value of K is always absolute irrespective of the size of the database, we have depicted the performance against the percentage of database scan (it is relative to the size of database), which is as well the function of K.

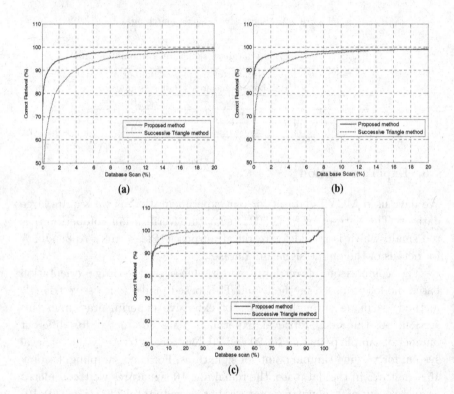

Figure 7.3. Retrieval performance with 15 database signatures and 10 queries per class for different sample points: (a) for 10 sample points (b) for 20 sample points and (c) for 30 sample points.

We have conducted another set of experiments for different numbers of data base signatures for 20 sample points per signatures Fig.7.4. Experiments were carried out for the different numbers (see Table 7.1) of database signatures (out of 25 signatures) for each class and remaining signatures as queries to the system. The system shows the good retrieval performance for 15 database signatures per class Fig.7.4(a). That shows the best performance is obtained for higher number of database signatures. Correct retrieval is 98% for 5% (Top $K = 248$ out of 4950) of database scan and correct retrieval 99% for 10% (Top $K = 495$ out of 4950) of database scan. On summerizing we have obtained best retrieval results for 20 sample points with 15 database signatures (Fig.7.4(a)).

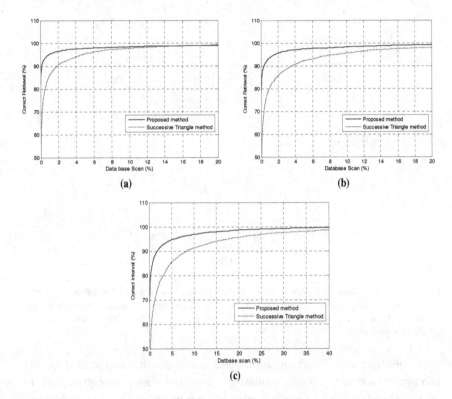

Figure 7.4. Retrieval performance (correct retrieval v/s database scan) with 20 sample points for different number of queries and database signatures: (a) 15 database signatures and 10 queries per class. (b) 10 database signatures and 15 queries per class. (c) 05 database signatures and 20 queries per class.

To evaluate the retrieval performance of the proposed methods for the combination of queries and database signatures as shown in Table 7.1, we compute the precision and recall ratios. For all these experiments, 20 sample points per signature is used. The model based on edge orientation shows better precision compared to the successive triangle matching model based on TSR. The results are shown in Fig.7.5.

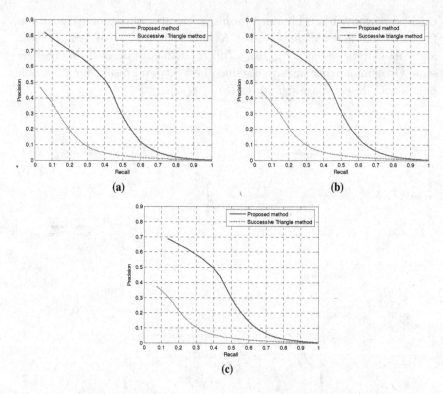

Figure 7.5.   Precision ratio v/s recall ratio for 20 sample points and for different number of queries and database signatures: (a) 15 database signatures and 10 queries per class. (b) 10 database signatures and 15 queries per class. (c) 05 database signatures 20 queries and per class.

Experiments to ascertain the percentage of genuine and skilled forgery acceptance against varying similarity threshold were conducted for the proposed methodology based on edge correspondence. The threshold given in Fig.7.6 is analogous to the percentage of difference in angle $(\Delta\theta_{ij})$ between corresponding edges (and hence spatial similarity). Even for all these experiments 20 sample points per signature is used. The experiments are carried out with five skilled forgeries and five genuine signatures from each class passed as queries to the system. The training set consists of 20 genuine signatures per each class. It can be inferred from Fig.7.6 that for a given threshold of 97 percent, only 2 percent of genuine signatures are rejected and 50 percent of forgeries are rejected. As this is not an authentication scheme, the accepted skilled forgeries can be eliminated later during verification stage.

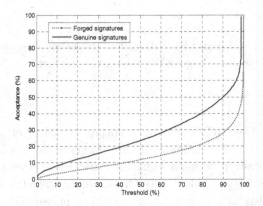

Figure 7.6. Acceptance versus threshold for forgery queries for the proposed method.

7.4. Conclusions

In this chapter we presented two models: one based on edge orientation and another based on triangular spatial relationship for archival and retrieval of online signatures. The results of the experiments conducted on a large dataset for quick retrieval of online signatures are detailed. The retrieval performance of the method based on edge correspondence is compared with the retrieval method based on successive triangle matching. The edge orientation based model is simple, efficient and outperforms the retrieval system based on successive triangle matching model with respect to all parameters (Precision, Recall and Correct Retrieval).

The MCYT_signature dataset used here consists of signatures whose $x - y$ sample length varies from 400 points to around 6000 points. However, our retrieval system is fast as it employs just 20 sample points per signature with promising results in retrieving top K hypotheses. The minimum percentage of database scan required to retrieve relevant signatures for all queries is supposed to be fixed experimentally. This is essentially a K-nearest neighbor problem and K best hypotheses should be retrieved. An attempt has been made in the work of Ghosh[8] in this regard where the parameter K is fixed without experimentation. Hence, the decision of arriving at the optimal percentage of database scan where all the authentic queries find a match can be fixed up analytically.

Acknowledgment

Authors thank Dr. Julian Firrez Auguilar, Biometric Research Lab-AVTS, Madrid, Spain for providing MCYT_signature dataset.

Appendix

The dataset: The MCYT_signature corpus[7] consists of 50 signatures; 25 are genuine and remaining 25 are forgeries for each of the 330 individuals. Totally it forms a signature database of 8250 (i.e. 330 × 25) genuine and 8250 (i.e. 330 × 25) forged online signatures. The online signature consists of x-y co-ordinate positions, pressure(P), azimuth(AZ) and elevation(EL) signals. An x-y plot of an online signature is shown in Fig. A.1, along with pressure, azimuth and elevation information plots.

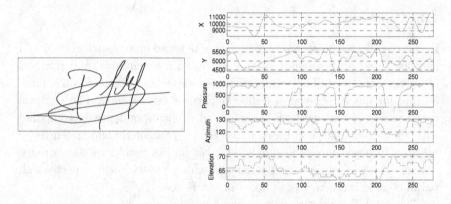

Figure A.1.   Sample online signature from MCYT_signature corpus.

References

1. Bajaj R. and Chaudhury S., (1997), "Signature using Multiple neural Classifiers", *Pattern Recognition*, vol. 30, pp. 1-7.
2. Chang S. K. and Li Y, (1998), "Representation of multi resolution symbolic and binary pictures using 2D-H strings", *Proceedings of the IEEE Workshop on Languages for Automata*, Maryland, pp. 190-195.
3. Chang C. C., (1991), "Spatial match retrieval of symbolic pictures", *Information Science and Engineering*, vol. 7(3), pp. 405-422.
4. Fang P., Zhang Cheng Wu, Fei Shen, Yun Jian Ge and Bing Fang, (2005), "Improved DTW algorithm for signature verification based on writing forces", *International Conference on Intelligent Computing (ICIC 2005),part, LNCS 3644, Spriger-verlag Berlin Heidelberg,,* pp.631-640.

5. Faundez-Zanuy M., (2007), "Online signature recognition based on VQ-DTW", *Pattern Recognition*, vol. 40(3), pp. 981-992.

6. Found B., Rogers D. and Schmittat R., (1998), "Matrix Analysis : A technique to investigate the spatial properties of handwritten images", *Journal of Forensic Document Examination*, vol. 11, pp. 54-74.

7. Garcia J. Ortega,J. Fierrez, D. Simon, J. gozalez, M.Faundez- Zanuy, V. Espinosa, A. Satue I. Hermaez, J-J. Igarza, C.Vivaracho,D. Escudero and Q-I. Mora, (2003), "MCYT baseline corpus: a multimodal biometric database", *IEEE Proc.-Vision Signal Process*" vol. 150, pp. 395-401.

8. Ghosh A. k.,(2006), "An optimum choice of k in nearest neighbor classification", *Computational Statistics and Data Analysis*, vol. 50(11), pp. 3113-3123.

9. Gupta G and McCabe A.,(1997), "Review of dynamic handwritten signature verification", *Technical Report, James Cook University, Townsville, Australia*.

10. Guru D. S., H. N. Prakash and T. N. Vikram,(2007), "Spatial topology of equitemporal points on signature for retrieval" Second international conference, *in proc. intl. conf. Pattern Recognition and Machine Intelligence, PReMI-2007*. Kolkata, India. ,LNCS 4815, pp.128-135.

11. Guru D. S., Punitha P and Nagabhushan P.,(2003), "Archival and retrieval of symbolic images: An invariant scheme based on triangular spatial relationship", *Pattern Recognition Letters*, vol. 24(14), pp. 2397-2408.

12. Gudivada V. N and Raghavan V. V.,(1995), "Design and evaluation of algorithms for image retrieval by spatial similarity", *ACM Transactions on Information Systems*, vol. 13(2), pp. 115-144.

13. Guru D. S and Nagabhushan P.,(2001), "Triangular spatial relationship: A new approach for spatial knowledge representation", *Pattern Recognition Letters*, vol. 22(9), pp. 999-1006.

14. Han Ke and Sethi I. K.,(1995), "Handwritten signature retrieval and identification", *Pattern Recognition Letters*, vol. 17, pp. 83-90.

15. Ismail M.A., and Gad S.,(2000), "Off-line Arabic signature verification", *Pattern Recognition*, vol.33, pp. 1727-1740.

16. Ji Hong-Wei and Zhong-Hua Quan,(2005), "Signature verification using wavelet transform and support vector machine", *International Conference on Intelligent Computing (ICIC 2005), LNCS 3644*, pp. 671-678.

17. Kashi R., .Hu.W.L. Nelson, W. Turin, (1998), "A Hidden Markov Model approach to online handwritten signature verification", *International Journal of Document Analysis and Recognition (IJDAR)* , vol. 1, pp. 102-109.

18. Leclerc and plomondon, (1997), "Automatic signature verification: the state of the art", *International Journal of Pattern recognition and Artificial Intelligence*, vol. 8, pp. 643-660.

19. Lee S and Pan J. C.,(1992), "Off-line tracing and representation of signatures", *IEEE Transaction Systems man and Cybernetics*, vol.22, pp. 755-771.

20. Lee S., and Pan J.C.,(1992), " Offline tracing and representation of signatures", *IEEE Transactions, Systems Man and Cybernetics*, vol. 22, pp.

755-771.

21. Martinez E. F., Sanchez A. and Velez J.,(2006), "Support vector machines versus Multilayer perceptrons for efficient off-line signature recognition", *Artificial Intelligence*, vol. 19, pp. 693-704.

22. Pavlidis I.,Papanikolopouls N. P. and Mavuduru R., (1998), "Signature identification through the use of deformable structures", *Signal processing*, vol. 71, pp. 187-201.

23. Surgur N. Srihari, Shravya Shetty, Siyun Chen, Harish Srinivasan, Chen Huang,GAdy Agam and Ophir Frieder (2006), "Document image retrieval using signature as queries", *Proceedings of the second international conference on Document Image Analysis for Libraries*, vol. 00, PP. 198-203.

24. signpus:-*http://www.signplus.com/en/products*.

25. Xiao X. and Graham Leedham, (2002), "Signature verification using a modified Bayesian network", *Pattern Recognition*, vol. 35, pp. 983-995.

Chapter 8

A Two Stage Recognition Scheme for Offline Handwritten Devanagari Words

Bikash Shaw* and Swapan Kr. Parui

*Computer Vision & Pattern Recognition Unit, Indian Statistical Institute,
203, B.T. Road, Kolkata, India, 700108
bikash_t@isical.ac.in and swapan@isical.ac.in*

A two stage recognition scheme is proposed for recognition of handwritten Devanagari words. 50 different Indian town names are taken as the lexicon for the experiment. The first stage of recognition is based on HMM classifier using view based shape features. On the basis of the confusion matrix obtained from the validation set, it is observed that 49 groups can be constructed from the 50 columns of the confusion matrix. Further classification within each group has resulted in a better classification accuracy. The second stage classification is based on a 32x32 fine-to-coarse representation of a word image obtained by wavelet transforms using modified Bayes discriminant function.

Keywords: Hidden Markov Model (HMM), Handwritten Word Recognition, Devanagari Script, Stroke Primitives, EM Algorithm.

Contents

8.1 Introduction 146
8.2 Devanagari Script 148
8.3 Handwritten Devanagari Word Database 148
8.4 Recognition Scheme Stage I 150
    8.4.1 Pre-processing and feature extraction 150
    8.4.2 HMM classifier for handwritten word recognition 153
    8.4.3 Proposed HMM classifier 154
    8.4.4 Experimental results for stage I 156
8.5 Recognition Scheme Stage II 158
    8.5.1 Grouping scheme 158
    8.5.2 Wavelet features 161
    8.5.3 Modified Bayes classifier 162

---

*Corresponding Author.

8.6 Conclusion 163
References 163

8.1. Introduction

Handwriting recognition is one of the challenging problems in Pattern Recognition. The main reason for the difficulty in this task is the large variation in handwriting style. Handwriting recognition systems can be broadly categorized into two classes: Offline and Online. This categorization is done on the basis of data represented to the system. For the first category, the data presented to the system are the pixels of a static image. This image is obtained by a scanner or CCD camera, after a user has completed writing. That is, handwriting is digitized at a later time after writing whereas, for the second category, handwriting is digitized right at the time of writing. For this, a tablet and stylus is used to capture and digitize the strokes of writing. Offline systems have to cope with large varieties of pen-type, overlapping wide strokes and lack of ordering information for the strokes. Online systems have the time ordering of strokes, pen up/down information and stroke positions.

The problem of handwriting recognition has been studied for several decades[1] and many reports on handwriting recognition in the scripts of developed nations are available in the literature. However, only a few works on handwriting recognition in Indian scripts have been reported.[2-4] The present paper deals with recognition of offline handwritten Devanagari words. Works on recognition of handwritten Devanagari characters/ numerals exist.[5,6] However, only one work on handwritten Devanagari word recognition[7] has been reported and the present work is an extension to this.

There are two approaches to handwritten word recognition: local or analytical approach held at the character level[8] and global approach held at the word level.[9] The first approach involves the segmentation issue, i.e., the words are first segmented into characters or pseudo-characters, and the characters or pseudo-characters are then recognized individually. Since word segmentation is itself a challenging problem, the success of the recognition module depends much on the segmentation performance. The second approach treats the word itself as a single entity and it goes for recognition without doing any explicit segmentation. However, this approach is restricted to applications with a small lexicon. In our present work for word recognition, we apply the second approach.

We have developed a handwritten word image database for Devanagari script for the present study since no such database was available. The training and test results of the proposed approach reported here are obtained on the basis of this database.

We propose in the present paper a two stage recognition approach to handwritten Devanagari word recognition. In Stage I, we use a directional view based feature vector. This feature vector is largely independent of script and can tolerate a slant of about +/- 5 degrees. It is also independent of pen stroke width and image size. Then, for recognition, we construct a hidden Markov model (HMM) on the basis of the directional view based feature vector.

An HMM is capable of making use of both the statistical and structural information present in handwritten images. This is why HMMs have been used in several handwritten character recognition tasks in recent years.[10] The proposed HMM here has the property that its states are not defined a priori, but are determined automatically based on a database of handwritten word images. A handwritten word is assumed to be a sequence of certain stroke primitives. These are in fact the states of the proposed HMM and are found using a mixture of Gaussian distributions. One HMM is constructed for each word. To classify an unknown word image, its class conditional probability for each HMM is computed.

On the basis of the confusion matrix of the validation set of Stage I, we identify groups of classes within each of which the amount of confusion is significant. In Stage II, a classifier is built for each such group of classes. For an unknown word image, Stage I identifies the group which the image belongs to and Stage II identifies the class within this group.

In Stage II, wavelet transform[11] is used to obtain a 32x32 resolution representation of an input word image. Wavelets have been studied thoroughly during the last decade[12] and its applicability in various image processing problems are being explored. The 32x32 resolution is fed into the modified Bayes discriminant function[13] classifier for classification. This classifier is insensitive to a great extent to the estimation error of the covariance matrix because it employs only the dominant eigenvectors. It is more robust and requires less computation time than the ordinary quadratic classifier.

The next section describes Devanagari script followed by Devanagari word image database in Section 8.3. Section 8.4 describes our recogition scheme for Stage I and the subsections in this section illustrate each step in detail. The recognition scheme for Stage II is described in Section 8.5. Conclusions are given in Section 11.6.

0	आसनसोल	10	हुगली	20	इटावा	30	फरिदाबाद	40	लुधियाना
1	औरंगाबाद	11	मैसूर	21	राणाघाट	31	डेहरीओनसोन	41	पोरबंदर
2	कांकीनाड़ा	12	छपरा	22	साहिबगंज	32	गिरिडीह	42	तिसतातोरसा
3	कपूरथला	13	मेरठ	23	अंडमान	33	एटा	43	विराटि
4	खजूराहो	14	ऊटी	24	भरतपुर	34	उलबेड़िया	44	काकूरगाछी
5	ऋषिकेश	15	झरिया	25	हावड़ा	35	डानकुनी	45	देवघर
6	नैनीताल	16	अहमदाबाद	26	जोधपुर	36	सेवड़ाफुलि	46	चित्रकूट
7	चौरंगी	17	महेषतला	27	पानागढ़	37	थाने	47	कोचीन
8	त्रिवेणी	18	एलौरा	28	विजयवाड़ा	38	वैशाली	48	चंदौसी
9	वाराणसी	19	लक्ष्मनपुर	29	क्षत्रपतीनगर	39	देहरादून	49	तंजौर

Figure 8.1. Class number and the Devanagari words forming the lexicon set.

8.2. Devanagari Script

Devanagari script came into existence at around AD 1200 derived from the Brahmi Script. It follows left to right fashion for writing. The Devanagari alphabet is used for writing Hindi, the official language of India & Fiji, Sanskrit, the primary South Asian classical language, Marathi, the state language of the Indian state of Maharashtra, Nepali, the official language of the Kingdom of Nepal. It is closely related to most of the scripts in use today in South Asia, Southeast Asia and Tibet. Devanagari is a form of alphabet called an abugida, as each consonant has an inherent vowel (A) that can be changed with different vowel signs.

Hindi, an Indo-European language derived from Devanagari script is one of the 22 official languages of India and is used, along with English, for Central government administrative purposes. Hindi is the 2nd most popular language by number of native speakers. There are 370 million native speakers of Hindi and 120 million speakers who speaks and knows Hindi as a second language.[Data Source: Ethnologue: Languages of the world, 15th ed.(2005) & Wikipedia.org].

8.3. Handwritten Devanagari Word Database

Handwritten English benchmark word databases exist for the research community and CEDAR word database[14] is one of them. But, there does not exist any benchmark word database for any Indic script except

Bangla. Here, we have attempted to create such a database for handwritten Devanagari words. We have designed a special kind of form to collect the data. The form contains 50 boxes within which a writer is to write.

The writers were from different strata of society. They were school/ college students, business men, housewives and professionals. Each writer was asked to fill a form where the word corresponding to each town name is written once. No restrictions were imposed on the writing style and no handwritten models were provided in order to obtain a database of natural handwriting styles. These handwritten documents were then scanned at 300 dots-per-inch resolution, in 256 levels of gray. For our experiments, we have considered 50 different names of Indian towns as the lexicon set (Fig. 8.1). Thus, the number of word classes here is 50. The whole database of handwritten word images is randomly split into three data sets: a training set with 7000 word images (i.e., 140 word images per class), a test set with 3000 word images (i.e., 60 word images per class) and a validation set with 3000 word images (i.e., 60 word images per class).

	Aman -ullah 17yrsM XII Std		Dinesh Sharma 17yrsM XII Std		Pappu Gupta 17yrsM XII Std
	Laxmi Yadav 27yrsF House Wife		Usha Tiwari 14yrsF VII Std		Sarita Rai 18yrsF XII Std
	Baiju Burman 20yrsM BA1st yr.		Vikram Paswan 19yrsM BA1st yr.		Manoj Singh 18yrsM IX Std
	Biswajit Saha 48yrsM Business		K. L. Shaw 54yrsM Lawyer		Mohsin Khan 14yrsM VIII Std

Figure 8.2. Several handwritten samples of the town name "Tribeni", printed form shown in Fig. 8.1 (class number 8).

A few samples from one town name of our database written by different people are shown in Fig. 8.2., illustrating variation in handwriting style.

8.4. Recognition Scheme Stage I

A hidden Markov model (HMM) is designed for recognition in Stage
I. In this stage, first a word image is preprocessed and then the strokes
are extracted from the word image followed by computation of stroke
features. These stroke features are then fed into the HMM classifier for
training and recognition.

8.4.1. *Pre-processing and feature extraction*

Variation in handwriting style makes the handwriting recognition problem
quite difficult. So to reduce the effect of writing variability related to
different writing styles, we take some preprocessing steps. The feature
extraction module exploits the global approach for extracting features
without explicitly going for word segmentation.

8.4.1.1. *Preprocessing*

Generally, for handwriting recognition, the preprocessing stage includes
image smoothing, skew and slant correction, image height and pen stroke
width correction. For smoothing, the input gray level image is first
median filtered and then binarized by Otsu's[15] thresholding method. The
binarized image is again smoothed using median filtering. No skew and
slant correction is done here. However, our feature extraction method is
insensitive to skew/slant within +/-5 degrees. No image height and pen
stroke width correction is done since the extracted features are invariant
under image height and the extracted strokes are always one-pixel thick
irrespective of the stroke width.

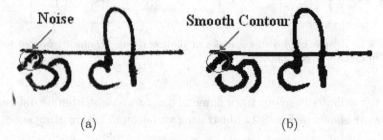

(a)   (b)

Figure 8.3.   (a) An input word image for the word Ooty. (b) Final image obtained after
thresholding and smoothing.

A sample image from the present database and the same after thresholding and smoothing are shown respectively in Figs. 8.3(a) and 8.3(b).

(a) (b)

Figure 8.4. A sample image of Devanagari word Ooty, Dark and gray pixels indicate (a) E and A images respectively, (b) S and A images respectively.

8.4.1.2. *Extraction of strokes*

Let A be a binarized word image. We now describe the process of extraction of vertical and horizontal strokes that are present in A. Let E be a binary image consisting of object pixels in A whose right or east neighbour is in the background. That is, the object pixels of A that are visible from the east (Fig. 8.4(a)) form E. Similarly, S is defined as the binary image consisting of object pixels in A whose bottom or south neighbour is in the background Fig. 8.4(b).

The connected components in E represent strokes that are vertical while the connected components in S represent strokes that are horizontal. Each horizontal or vertical stroke is a digital curve. Shapes of these strokes are processed for extraction of features. Very short curves are not considered. The vertical and horizontal strokes that are present in the word image in Fig. 8.3(b) are shown in Figs. 8.5 and 8.6.

8.4.1.3. *Extraction of features*

One of the major factors for the success of any handwritten recognition module is its feature extraction process. The features should be selected in such a way that it reduces the intra-class variability and increases the inter-class discriminability in the feature space. From each stroke in E and S, 8 scalar features are extracted. These features indicate the shape, size and position of the stroke with respect to the word image. A stroke C in

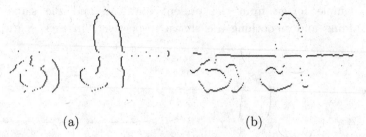

(a)   (b)

Figure 8.5.   (a) E image consisting of vertical strokes obtained from the image in Fig. 8.3(b), (b) S image consisting of horizontal strokes obtained from the image in Fig. 8.3(b).

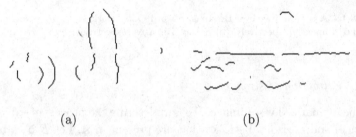

(a)   (b)

Figure 8.6.   (a) Final E image after removal of very short vertical strokes from the image in Fig. 8.5(a), (b) Final S image after removal of very short horizontal strokes from the image in Fig. 8.5(b).

E is traced from bottom upward. Suppose the bottom most and the top most pixel positions in C are P_0 and P_5 respectively. The four points $P_1, \ldots, P_4$ on C are found such that the curve distances between P_{i-1} and P_i $(i = 1, \ldots, 5)$ are equal.[16]   Let α_i, $i = 1, \ldots, 5$ be the angles that the lines $\overrightarrow{P_{i-1}P_i}$ make with the x-axis. Since the stroke here is vertical, $45^0 \leq \alpha_i \leq 135^0$. α_i's are features that are invariant under scaling and represent only the shape. The position features of C are given by $\overline{X}, \overline{Y}$ which are the x and y-coordinates of the centre of gravity of the pixel positions in C. $\overline{X}$ is also useful in arranging the strokes present in an image from left to right. Let L be the length of the stroke C. The 3 features $\overline{X}, \overline{Y}$ and L are normalized with respect to the image height. Thus, the feature vector becomes $(\alpha_1, \alpha_2, \alpha_3, \alpha_4, \alpha_5, \overline{X}, \overline{Y}, L)$.

The features extracted from a horizontal stroke C in S are similar. Here C is traced from west to east. The feature vector of a horizontal stroke C is defined as $(\beta_1, \beta_2, \beta_3, \beta_4, \beta_5, \overline{X}, \overline{Y}, L)$ where $-45^0 \leq \beta_i \leq 45^0$, $\overline{X}, \overline{Y}$ and L are defined in the same way as before.[16]

8.4.2. HMM classifier for handwritten word recognition

8.4.2.1. Hidden Markov models

The basic theory of HMM was published in a series of classic papers by Baum and his colleagues in the late 1960s and early 1970s.[17] HMM is a model in which the observation is a probabilistic function of the state. That is, the resulting model is a doubly embedded stochastic process with an underlying stochastic process that is not observable (it is hidden), but can only be observed through another set of stochastic processes that produce the sequence of observations.

Depending upon the transitions there are two types of HMM : an HMM allowing for transitions from any emitting state to any other emitting state is called an ergodic HMM or a fully connected HMM. The other extreme, an HMM where the transitions only go from one state to itself or to a unique follower, is called a left-right HMM or Bakis Model.

Depending on the observation vectors, HMMs can be classified as discrete, continuous and autoregressive. If the observations are characterized as discrete symbols chosen from a finite alphabet, and within each state of this model, a discrete probability density function is used then it is termed as discrete HMM, whereas if the observations are drawn from continuous density functions then the HMM is called continuous. The HMM is termed autoregressive if the observation vectors are drawn form an autoregressive process.

Generally observations are quantized as discrete signals so that a discrete HMM can be used. However, in some applications, there might be serious degradation after such quantization of continuous signals or vectors. It is advantageous to use HMMs with continuous observation densities in such cases.

8.4.2.2. Literature review of HMM classifiers for word recognition

Hidden Markov Models have been successfully applied in the field of Offline and Online Handwriting recognition. Gillies[18] was the first to use an implicit-segmentation based HMM using left-to-right discrete Hidden Markov Model for cursive word recognition. A semi continuous HMM to recognize cursive words produced by cooperative writers was modeled by Bunke et al.[19] They designed 10 dimensional features and used Baum-Welch algorithm for training. Chen et al.[20] used a continuous density variable duration HMM (CDVDHMM) for unconstrained handwritten word recognition. 35 features based on geometrical features and topological features were used to represent the character symbol in the feature space.

Mohammed & Gader[21] proposed a segmentation free handwritten word recognition technique using continuous density HMMs. They incorporated transition features. Senior & Robinson[22] used a discrete HMM for finding the best word in the lexicon. El-Yacoubi et al.[23] considered two sets of features — (i) a set of global features, namely, loops, ascenders and descenders and (ii) bidimensional dominant transition numbers. They have used discrete HMMs for recognition. Xue and Govindaraju[24] applied transition emitting-HMMs and state emitting-HMMs to accommodate structural features and their continuous attributes.

8.4.3. *Proposed HMM classifier*

An HMM with the state space $S = \{s_1, \ldots, s_N\}$ and observation sequence $Q = q_1, \ldots, q_T$ is defined as $\gamma = (\pi, A, B)$ where the initial state distribution is given by $\pi = \{\pi_i\}$, $\pi_i = \text{Prob}\,(q_1 = s_i)$, the state transition probability distribution by $A = \{a_{ij}(t)\}$ where $a_{ij}(t) = \text{Prob}\,(q_{t+1} = s_j/q_t = s_i)$ and the observation symbol probability distributions by $B = \{b_i\}$ where $b_i(O_t)$ is the distribution for state i and O_t is the observation at instant t. The HMM here is non-homogeneous.

The problem now is how to efficiently compute $P(\boldsymbol{O}/\gamma)$, the probability of an observation sequence $\boldsymbol{O} = O_1, \ldots, O_T$ given a model $\gamma = (\pi, A, B)$. For a classifier of m classes of patterns, we have m separate HMMs denoted by γ_j, $j = 1, \ldots, m$. Let an input pattern $\boldsymbol{X}$ of an unknown class have an observation sequence $\boldsymbol{O}$. The probability $P(\boldsymbol{O}/\gamma_j)$ is computed for each model γ_j and $\boldsymbol{X}$ is assigned to class c whose model shows the highest probability. That is,

$$c = \arg \max_{1 \leq j \leq m} P(\boldsymbol{O}/\gamma_j) \tag{8.1}$$

For a given γ, $P(\boldsymbol{O}/\gamma)$ is computed using the well known forward and backward algorithms.[17] Note that the observation sequence $\boldsymbol{O} = O_1, \ldots, O_T$ in our problem is the sequence of feature vectors of the strokes (arranged from left to right) that are present in a handwritten word image. T is the number of strokes in the image. The states here are certain feature primitives (or more specifically, individual 8-dimensional Gaussian distributions in the feature space) that are found below using EM (Expectation Maximization) algorithm.

8.4.3.1. *HMM parameters*

A feature vector $\boldsymbol{\theta} = (\theta_1, \theta_2, \theta_3, \theta_4, \theta_5, \overline{X}, \overline{Y}, L)$ can come either from a vertical or from a horizontal stroke. It is assumed that the features follow a multivariate Gaussian mixture distribution. In other words, $\boldsymbol{\theta} = (\theta_1, \theta_2, \theta_3, \theta_4, \theta_5, \overline{X}, \overline{Y}, L)$ has a distribution $g(\boldsymbol{\theta})$ which is a mixture of K 8-dimensional Gaussian distributions, namely,

$$g(\boldsymbol{\theta}) = \sum_{k=1}^{K} P_k f_k(\boldsymbol{\theta}) \tag{8.2}$$

where

$$f_k(\boldsymbol{\theta}) = \frac{exp\{-0.5(\boldsymbol{\theta} - \boldsymbol{\mu}_k)^T \Sigma_k^{-1}(\boldsymbol{\theta} - \boldsymbol{\mu}_k)\}}{\{(2\pi)^{8/2} |\Sigma_k|^{1/2}\}} \tag{8.3}$$

and P_k is the prior probability of the k-th component. The unknown parameters of the mixture distribution, namely, $P_k, \boldsymbol{\mu}_k, \Sigma_k$ ($k = 1, \ldots, K$), are estimated using the EM (Expectation Maximization) algorithm[25,26] that maximizes the log likelihood of the training vectors $\{\boldsymbol{\theta}_i, i = 1, \ldots, n\}$ coming from the distribution given by $g(\boldsymbol{\theta})$.

The state space of the proposed HMM consists of states which are characterized by the probability density functions $f_k(\boldsymbol{\theta})$ ($k = 1, \ldots, K$). It is assumed that the vertical and horizontal strokes in the word image database are distributed around K different prototype strokes. These are called stroke primitives corresponding to the mean shape vectors $\boldsymbol{\mu}_1, \boldsymbol{\mu}_2, \ldots, \boldsymbol{\mu}_k$. These K stroke primitives constitute the state space. Thus, the states here are not defined a priori but are determined adaptively on the basis of the training set of word images.

To determine the optimum value of K, we use the Bayesian information criterion (BIC) which is defined as $BIC(K) = -2LL + m log(n)$, for a Gaussian mixture model with K components, LL is the log likelihood value, m is the number of independent parameters to be estimated, n is the number of observations. For several K values, the $BIC(K)$ values are computed. The first local minimum indicates the optimum K value.

8.4.3.2. *Estimation of HMM parameters*

In our implementation, $N = K$ and the observation symbol probability distribution $b_i(O_t)$ is, in fact, the Gaussian distribution $f_i(\boldsymbol{\theta}) = N(\boldsymbol{\mu}_i, \Sigma_i)$.

Thus

$$b_i(O_t) = \frac{exp\{-0.5(O_t - \boldsymbol{\mu}_i)^T \Sigma_i^{-1}(O_t - \boldsymbol{\mu}_i)\}}{\{(2\pi)^{8/2}|\Sigma_i|^{1/2}\}} \qquad (8.4)$$

The parameters produced by EM algorithm are $P_1, P_2, \ldots, P_N$, $\boldsymbol{\mu}_1, \boldsymbol{\mu}_2, \ldots, \boldsymbol{\mu}_N, \Sigma_1, \Sigma_2, \ldots, \Sigma_N$. Let, in a training word image, the strokes be arranged from left to right on the basis of $\overline{X}$ to generate the observation sequence $O_1, O_2, \ldots, O_T$. For each O_t, compute

$$h_i(O_t) = P_i b_i(O_t) / \{\sum_{j=1}^{N} P_j b_j(O_t)\} \qquad (8.5)$$

and O_t is assigned to state k where

$$k = \arg \max_{1 \leq i \leq N} h_i(O_t). \qquad (8.6)$$

This assignment to respective states is done for all L observation sequences (L is the number of training images). Let the state sequence thus generated from an observation sequence $O_1, O_2, \ldots, O_T$ be $Q = q_1, \ldots, q_T$. From these L state sequences, the estimates of the initial state distribution probabilities are computed as ($1 \leq i \leq N$)

$$\pi_i = \frac{number\ of\ occurrences\ of\ \{q_1 = s_i\}}{L} \qquad (8.7)$$

The state transition probability estimates $a_{i,j}(t)$ are computed as ($1 \leq i, j \leq N$, $1 \leq t \leq T - 1$)

$$a_{i,j}(t) = \frac{number\ of\ occurrences\ of\ \{q_t = s_i\ \&\ q_{t+1} = s_j\}}{total\ number\ of\ occurrences\ of\ \{q_t = s_i\}} \qquad (8.8)$$

The above HMM parameter estimates are fine-tuned using re-estimation by Baum-Welch forward-backward algorithm.

8.4.4. *Experimental results for stage I*

The proposed scheme has been tested on the database of handwritten Devanagari word images described in Section 8.3. The results of our study are reported below. To the best of our knowledge, there does not exist any other standard database of handwritten Devanagari word images. The training, test and validation datasets here consist of 7000, 3000 and 3000 handwritten word images respectively. Using these word images, 156906 horizontal and 137250 vertical strokes have been extracted from the training

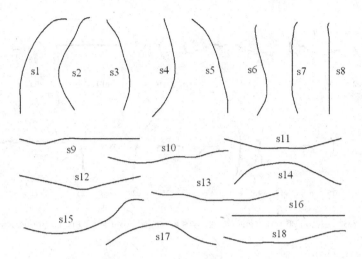

Figure 8.7.   Stroke Primitives for vertical and horizontal strokes for Devanagari word Ooty.

set, 67245 horizontal and 58821 vertical strokes have been extracted from the validation set while 66543 horizontal and 59282 vertical strokes have been extracted from the test set.

The parameters of an HMM for each of the 50 word classes are determined using the method described above. For example, for word class **Ooty**, the optimum K value is found to be 18 based on Bayesian information criterion. The curves corresponding to these 18 mean vectors μ_k are shown in Fig. 8.7. These represent the 18 HMM states for **Ooty**. For the image shown in Figs. 8.6(a) and 8.6(b), there are 26 strokes which are shown in Fig. 8.8. The strokes arranged in terms of $\overline{X}$ from left to right are e1, e2, e3,..., e26 which form the observation sequence. The most likely states of these 26 strokes individually are s15, s4, s13, s17, s7, s15, s17, s6, s4, s16, s17, s15, s3, s15, s2, s14, s15, s4, s1, s14, s16, s3, s18, s6, s16 and s3 respectively which is the state sequence. On the basis these state sequences obtained from the training word images, the estimates of the initial state distribution and the state transition probabilities are obtained.

For an unknown word image, the observation sequence O is found and the probability $P(O/\gamma_j)$ is computed for $j = 0,\ldots,49$. The image is classified as class c where

$$c = \arg \max_{0 \leq j \leq 49} P(O/\gamma_j) \qquad (8.9)$$

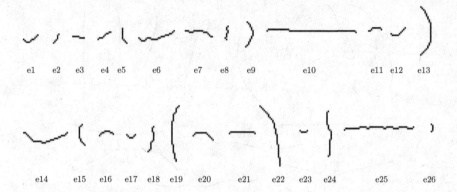

Figure 8.8.   e1 to e26 represent the strokes arranged from left to right (along X-axis).

We have achieved 82.89% correct recognition rate on the validation set and 87.71% on the training set. The recognition accuracy for each word class on the validation set is shown in Table 8.1.

8.5. Recognition Scheme Stage II

On careful observation of the confusion matrix obtained from the validation set, it is seen that there are several groups of word classes within each of which the percentage of misclassification is very high. To take care of these misclassifications, a second stage of classification is designed so that the overall accuracy is improved. The grouping scheme is based on the column entries of the confusion matrix and is described below. A 32x32 fine-to-coarse resolution based on wavelet transform of a word image is used as the feature vector for the second stage. A modified Bayes discriminant function[13] is used for classification within each group.

8.5.1. Grouping scheme

A group of word classes is formed from each column of the confusion matrix. For each column, we select the smallest subset of word classes which incurs an error rate ε or less. The groups generated in this manner are in general overlapping because one word class may belong to more than one such group.

Let a_{ij} be the confusion matrix obtained on the basis of the validation set. In other words, a_{ij} is the number of validation samples coming from

Table 8.1.   Recognition accuracy for each word class at Stage I.

Class	Accuracy	Class	Accuracy
Class 0	93.47	Class 25	69.82
Class 1	80.81	Class 26	65.25
Class 2	67.01	Class 27	89.89
Class 3	94.28	Class 28	79.97
Class 4	69.40	Class 29	80.47
Class 5	84.97	Class 30	70.97
Class 6	84.68	Class 31	94.88
Class 7	69.47	Class 32	80.47
Class 8	89.32	Class 33	87.59
Class 9	93.07	Class 34	88.61
Class 10	78.14	Class 35	73.27
Class 11	80.65	Class 36	84.33
Class 12	95.80	Class 37	83.17
Class 13	73.17	Class 38	77.47
Class 14	87.84	Class 39	86.84
Class 15	88.47	Class 40	75.60
Class 16	94.65	Class 41	82.16
Class 17	74.97	Class 42	74.89
Class 18	71.56	Class 43	93.17
Class 19	94.60	Class 44	60.21
Class 20	89.58	Class 45	92.11
Class 21	96.38	Class 46	73.47
Class 22	90.52	Class 47	74.58
Class 23	91.75	Class 48	92.66
Class 24	82.67	Class 49	95.71
		Average	82.89

i^{th} class that are classified in j^{th} class. We assume ε to be the target error rate in the first stage. Let $N_j = \sum_{i=0}^{49} a_{ij}$ and Thr_j be an integer such that $\sum_{a_{ij} \leq Thr_j} a_{ij} = \varepsilon * N_j$. However, for the discrete nature of a_{ij}, the equality may not hold for any Thr_j and, therefore, we take the largest value of Thr_j such that $\sum_{a_{ij} \leq Thr_j} a_{ij} \leq \varepsilon * N_j$. Now, the jth group G_j $(j = 0, 1, \ldots, 49)$ is defined as $\{i : a_{ij} > Thr_j\}$. For example, the 6th column (i.e for $j = 5$) in the confusion matrix after removing the 0 entries is $[3, 44, 1, 4, 2, 1, 3, 1, 2]^T$ and the corresponding class identities are given by $[2, 5, 8, 14, 15, 18, 29, 31, 34]^T$ where $N_5 = 61$. Suppose $\varepsilon = 0.05$. Note that $\sum_{a_{i5} \leq 1} a_{i5} < \varepsilon * N_5$ and $\sum_{a_{i5} \leq 2} a_{i5} > \varepsilon * N_5$. Thus, $Thr_5 = 1$ and $G_5 = \{2, 5, 14, 15, 29, 34\}$.

Table 8.2.   Groups of classes.

Group Name	Elements of Group[a]
Group 0	{ 0, 1, 2, 4, 5, 6, 7, 8, 9, 13, 16, 17, 18, 22, 23, 24, 26, 28, 29, 30, 31, 32, 34, 35, 36, 37, 38, 39, 40, 41, 42, 43, 44, 45, 47 }
Group 1	{ 1, 6, 7, 26, 30, 37, 38, 39 }
Group 2	{ 2, 6, 40, 47 }
Group 3	{ 3, 12, 16, 19, 21, 24, 25 }
Group 4	{ 4, 9, 10, 18, 47 }
Group 5	{ 2, 5, 14, 15, 29, 34 }
Group 6	{ 2, 6, 7, 11 ,17, 37, 41 }
Group 7	{ 7, 14 }
Group 8	{ 8, 45, 46 }
Group 9	{ 4, 9, 37, 40, 41, 46, 47 }
Group 10	{ 10, 14 }
Group 11	{ 11, 13, 26, 49 }
Group 12	{ 10, 12, 14, 18, 20, 25, 26, 27, 33, 41, 47 }
Group 13	{11, 13 }
Group 14	{ 2, 7, 10, 11, 14, 15, 18, 37, 40, 43 }
Group 15	{ 0, 1, 2, 4, 5, 6, 12, 16, 17, 19, 20, 21, 22, 23, 24, 25, 27, 28, 29, 30, 32, 33, 34, 35, 36, 44, 47 }
Group 16	{ 13, 17 }
Group 17	{ 14, 18, 40 }
Group 18	{ 4, 9, 12, 16, 19, 24, 25, 27, 28, 29, 30, 36, 42, 44, 47 }
Group 19	{ 10, 12, 20, 25, 33, 48 }
Group 20	{ 3, 12, 16, 20, 21, 24, 25, 27, 33, 44 }
Group 21	{ 1, 2, 5, 15, 17, 18, 22, 29, 30, 38, 39, 40, 43, 44 }
Group 22	{ 4, 7, 10, 13, 14, 15, 17, 18, 23, 26, 32, 35, 40, 41, 42, 44, 46, 47 }
Group 23	{ 3, 19, 20, 24, 25, 26, 44 }
Group 24	{ 12, 25 }
Group 25	{ 11, 26, 39 }
Group 26	{ 21, 27 }
Group 27	{ 8, 28, 38, 39, 42, 46, 49 }
Group 28	{ 2, 4, 6, 17, 22, 29, 40 }
Group 29	{ 1, 18, 22, 28, 30, 32, 39, 44 }
Group 30	{ 0, 1, 2; 5, 6, 16, 31, 32, 36, 38. 42, 45, 47 }
Group 31	{ 8, 32, 37, 39, 46, 47 }
Group 32	{ 20, 25, 33 }
Group 33	{ 2, 4, 5, 7, 10, 14, 18, 34 }
Group 34	{ 4, 10, 23, 34, 35, 36, 47 }
Group 35	{ 4, 6, 10, 26, 28, 32, 35, 36, 41, 42, 46, 47 }
Group 36	{ 7, 8, 15, 18, 32, 35, 37, 40, 41 }
Group 37	{ 8, 28, 30, 32, 38, 46 }
Group 38	{ 1, 11, 13, 17, 26, 28, 37, 39, 42, 44, 46, 48, 49 }
Group 39	{ 14, 40 }
Group 40	{ 6, 9, 10, 13, 37, 41, 46, 48 }
Group 41	{ 4, 11, 26, 36, 39, 42, 48 }
Group 42	{ 2, 5, 7, 10, 15, 17, 18, 23, 26, 30, 34, 38, 41, 42, 43 }
Group 43	{ 4, 11, 13, 15, 32, 37, 39, 42, 44, 46, 47 }
Group 44	{ 1, 6, 8, 13, 17, 22, 28, 29, 31, 32, 36, 38, 39, 41, 42, 45, 46, 49 }
Group 45	{ 8, 46, 49 }
Group 46	{ 2, 4, 9, 32, 34, 34, 35, 36, 47 }
Group 47	{ 11, 13, 20, 26, 39, 41, 42, 48 }
Group 48	{ 26, 28, 39, 42, 46, 49}

[a]The numbers in braces represent the class identity for a word class.

It is to be noted here that the size of a group or the number of word classes in a group will vary between 1 and the number of word classes.

Since the number of word classes in the present problem is 50, the confusion matrix has 50 columns. From these 50 columns, 50 groups are constructed using the above algorithm. However, it is observed that both columns 11 and 15 (i.e. for j = 10 and 14) give rise to the same group of classes, namely, {10,14}. These two groups are merged to obtain 49 groups of classes which are shown in Table 8.2. For these 49 groups, 49 different classifiers are designed in the second stage. Let us suppose that a sample s is classified in a class belonging to group G_c in the first stage. In the second stage the sample is fed to the classifier designed for G_c. The output of the second stage classification will be the recognized or output class for the sample s. This scheme provides a sample a chance of getting correctly classified in the second stage even if it is misclassified in the first stage.

8.5.2. *Wavelet features*

The input word image is first binarized using Otsu's thresholding technique and the bounding box (smallest rectangle) enclosing the binarized image is determined. The input gray image within the bounding box is then normalized to the size 64x64. Wavelet decomposition algorithm[11] is applied to the normalized image to obtain a 32x32 smooth approximation of the original image. The highpass filter used for convolution is given by four coefficients (l_0, l_1, l_2, l_3) where

$$l_0 = \frac{1 + \sqrt{3}}{4\sqrt{2}}, \quad l_1 = \frac{3 + \sqrt{3}}{4\sqrt{2}}, \quad l_2 = \frac{3 - \sqrt{3}}{4\sqrt{2}}, \quad l_3 = \frac{1 - \sqrt{3}}{4\sqrt{2}}$$

A word image before and after decomposition is shown in Fig. 8.9. The decomposed image of size 32x32 forms the input vector for classification in the second stage.

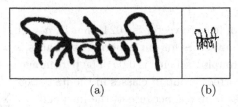

(a)   (b)

Figure 8.9.   (a) Original image for word "Tribeni", (b) Decomposed image obtained by Wavelet transform at resolution 32 x 32.

8.5.3. *Modified Bayes classifier*

The modified Bayes classifier[27] which also constructs quadratic decision boundaries, are more robust and require less computation time and storage than the ordinary quadratic classifier. A modified version of the Bayes discriminant function (modified Bayes discriminant function) as proposed by Kimura et al.[13] is defined by

$$g(\mathbf{X}) = (N + N_0 + 1) \ln \left\{ 1 + \frac{1}{N_0 \sigma^2} \{ \|\mathbf{X} - \mathbf{M}\|^2 \right.$$

$$\left. - \sum_{i=1}^{k} \frac{\lambda_i}{\lambda_i + (N_0/N)\sigma^2} [\phi_i^T (\mathbf{X} - \mathbf{M})]^2 \} \right\}$$

$$+ \sum_{i=1}^{k} \ln \left(\lambda_i + \frac{N_0}{N} \sigma^2 \right) \qquad (8.10)$$

where $\mathbf{X}$ is the feature vector of size n, N is the number of the training samples, $\mathbf{M}$ is the mean vector, ϕ_i and λ_i are the ith eigenvalue and eigenvector of the covariance matrix, and k is the number of dominant eigenvectors $(k < n)$. For the sake of simplicity, the subscript denoting the class is omitted. The feature vector $\mathbf{X}$ is classified in the class which minimizes equation 8.10. In our experiment, the value of σ^2 is calculated by averaging the variance of all features over all categories, and the value of N_0 is determined experimentally to maximize the classifier performance.

The modified Bayes discriminant function is insensitive to a great extent to the estimation error of the covariance matrix because it employs only k dominant eigenvectors.[28] The required computation time and storage is $O(kn)$. The modified Bayes discriminant function is derived from the optimum discriminant function for Gaussian distribution with an unknown covariance matrix by employing a Bayesian approach.[29] The Bayesian approach requires an initial estimate Σ_0 of the covariance matrix and its confidence constant N_0.

Here the size of feature vector is 1024, that is, $n = 1024$. We have taken 100 dominant eigenvectors for our experiment, that is, $k = 100$. The value of ε used in our grouping scheme is 0.05. The percentage of test samples not classified in the correct group of classes in the first stage of classification is 3.28%. This is less than 5% because of the inequality $\sum_{a_{ij} \leq Thr_j} a_{ij} \leq \varepsilon * N_j$ used in the grouping scheme. We have achieved 85.57% correct recognition rate on the test set and 91.25% on the training set.

8.6. Conclusion

In this paper, we have proposed a two stage recognition scheme for recognition of handwritten Devanagari words. In the first stage we have developed an HMM based recognition scheme. From the confusion matrix obtained from the validation set, 49 different groups of classes have been identified. Then a fresh classification within the group was performed using modified Bayes discriminant function. The results of our approach are promising for a small Lexicon size. It indicates that it is possible to scale our system to larger lexicon sets. Our system is based on global approach which extracts global features thus reducing the overhead of segmentation. In future we will try with other classifiers and combinations of classifiers at both stages of classification. We plan to identify features in the second stage which will be more discriminatory than Wavelet features used in the present study. These features can even be group specific because the nature of dissimilarity between classes within one group may be different from that within another group.

References

1. R. Plamondon, S. N. Srihari, On-line and off-line handwriting recognition:A comprehensive survey, *IEEE. Trans. Patt. Anal. & Mach. Intel.*, **22(1)**, pp. 63–84, (2000).
2. A. F. R. Rahman, R. Rahman, M. C. Fairhurst, Recognition of handwritten Bengali characters: a novel multistage approach. *Pattern Recognition*, **35**, pp. 997–1006 (2002).
3. U. Bhattacharya, T. K. Das, A. Datta, S. K. Parui, B. B. Chaudhuri, A hybrid scheme for handprinted numeral recognition based on a self-organizing network and MLP classifiers. *Int. J. Patt. Recog. & Art. Intell.*, **16(7)**, pp. 845-864, (2002).
4. U. Bhattacharya, B. B. Chaudhuri, A majority voting scheme for multiresolution recognition of handprinted numerals, *Proc. of the 7th ICDAR*, Edinburgh, Scotland **I**, pp. 16–20, (2003).
5. K. R. Ramakrishnan, S. H. Srinivasan, S. Bhagavathy, The independent components of characters are 'Strokes', *Proc. of the 5th ICDAR*, pp. 414–417, (1999).
6. G. S. Lehal, N. Bhatt, A recognition system for Devnagri and English handwritten numerals, In Eds. T. Tan, Y. Shi and W. Gao, *Advances in Multimodal Interfaces.- ICMI 2001*, pp. 442–449, LNCS-1948, (2000).
7. Swapan K. Parui and Bikash Shaw, Offline Handwritten Devanagari Word Recognition: An HMM Based Approach, In Eds. Ashish Ghosh, Rajat K. De, Sankar K. Pal, *Pattern Recognition and Machine Intelligence (PReMI-2007)*, pp. 528–535, LNCS 4815, Springer-Verlag , (2007).

8. G. Kim, *Recognition of offline handwritten words and its extension to phrase recognition*, PhD Thesis, University of New York at Buffalo, USA, (1996).

9. D. Guillevic, *Unconstrained Handwriting Recognition Applied to the Processing of Bank Cheques*, Thesis of Doctor's Degree in the Department of Computer Science at Concordia University, Canada, (1995).

10. H. Park, S. Lee, Off-line recognition of large-set handwritten characters with multiple hidden Markov models, *Pattern Recognition*, **29**, pp. 231–244, (1996).

11. I. Daubechies, The wavelet transform, time-frequency localization and signal analysis, *IEEE Transactions on Information Theory*, **36(5)**, pp. 961–1005, (1990).

12. A. Graps, An introduction to wavelets, *IEEE Computational Science and Engineering*, **2(2)**, pp. 50–61, (1995).

13. F. Kimura, T. Wakabayashi, S. Tsuruoka and Y. Miyake, Improvement of Handwritten Japanese Character Recognition using Weighted Direction Code Histogram, *Pattern Recognition*, **30(8)**, pp. 1329–1337, (1997).

14. J. J. Hull, A Database for Handwritten Text Recognition Research, *IEEE. Trans. Patt. Anal. & Mach. Intel.*, **16(5)**, pp. 550–554, (1994).

15. N. Otsu, A threshold selection method from gray-level histograms, *IEEE Trans. on Systems, Man, and Cybernetics* **9**, pp. 62-66, (1979).

16. U. Bhattacharya, S. K. Parui, B. Shaw, K. Bhattacharya, Neural Combination of ANN and HMM for Handwritten Devnagari Numeral Recognition, *Proc. of 10th-IWFHR*, pp. 613–618, (2006).

17. L. R. Rabiner, A tutorial on hidden Markov models and selected applications in speech recognition, *Proceedings of the IEEE.*, **77(2)**, pp. 257–286, (1989).

18. A. M. Gillies, Cursive Word Recognition Using Hidden Markov Models, *Proc. Fifth U.S. Postal Service Advanced Technology Conf.*, Washington, D.C., pp. 557–562, (1992).

19. H. Bunke, M. Roth, and E. Schukat-Talamazzini, Off-Line Cursive Handwriting Recognition Using Hidden Markov Models *Pattern Recognition*, **28(9)**, pp. 1399–1413, (1995).

20. M. Chen , A. Kundu , and S. N. Srihari, Variable Duration Hidden Markov Model and Morphological Segmentation for Handwritten Word Recognition, *IEEE. Trans. Image Processing.* **4(12)**, pp. 1675–1687, (1995).

21. M. Mohammed and P. Gader, Handwritten Word Recognition Using Segmentation-Free Hidden Markov Modeling and Segmentation-Based Dynamic Programming Techniques, *IEEE. Trans. Patt. Anal. & Mach. Intel.*, **18(5)**, pp. 548–554, (1996).

22. A. Senior and A. Robinson, An Off-Line Cursive Handwriting Recognition System, *IEEE. Trans. Patt. Anal. & Mach. Intel.*, **20(3)**, pp. 309–321, (1998).

23. A. El-Yacoubi, M. Gilloux, R. Sabourin, and C. Y. Suen, An HMM-Based Approach for Off-Line Unconstrained Handwritten Word Modeling and Recognition, *IEEE. Trans. Patt. Anal. & Mach. Intel.*, **21(8)**, pp. 752–760, (1999).

24. H. Xue and V. Govindaraju, Hidden Markov Models Combining Discrete Symbols and Continuous Attributes in Handwriting Recognition, *IEEE. Trans. Patt. Anal. & Mach. Intel.*, **28(3)**, pp. 458–462, (2006).
25. K. Fukunaga: *Introduction to Statistical Pattern Recognition*, Academic Press, San Diego, 2nd Edition, (1990).
26. S. K. Parui, U. Bhattacharya, B. Shaw, D. Poddar, A Novel Hidden Markov Models for Recognition of Bangla Characters, *Proc. of 3rd-WCVGIP*, pp. 174–179, (2006).
27. F. Kimura and M. Shridhar, Handwritten numeral recognition based on multiple algorithms, *Pattern Recognition*, **24(10)**, pp. 969–983, (1991).
28. F. Kimura, K. Takashina, S. Tsuruoka and Y. Miyake, Modified quadratic discriminant functions and the application to Chinese character recognition, *IEEE Trans. Pattern Analysis Mach. Intell.*, **9(1)**, pp. 149–153, (1987).
29. D. G. Keehn, A note on learning for Gaussian properties, *IEEE Trans. Inform. Theory IT*, **11(1)**, pp. 126–132, (1965).

Chapter 9

Fall Detection from a Video in the Presence of Multiple Persons

Vinay Vishwakarma, Shamik Sural* and Chittaranjan Mandal

School of Information Technology,
Indian Institute of Technology, Kharagpur, India,
*shamik@sit.iitkgp.ernet.in

In this chapter, we present a model based approach for human fall detection. Initially, we propose a simple fall model for detecting fall in a video containing a single human being. A video is segmented to identify foreground objects and the fall model is applied to detect frames where a fall potentially occurs. It can determine fall situations quite accurately when only one person is present in the video. Next, we improve our method so that it can detect a human fall in the presence of single as well as multiple persons in a video. It consists of three parts: foreground detection, modeling of human shapes using ellipsoids, and finally use of the fall model. A finite state machine (FSM) implementation in conjunction with the fall model helps to monitor people and their activities in a video. Results illustrate that the fall model is efficient and robust enough to accurately detect a falling person in the presence of single as well as multiple persons in a video.

Contents

9.1 Introduction 168
9.2 Related Work 168
9.3 Detecting Fall in a Video Containing a Single Person 172
   9.3.1 Human detection 172
   9.3.2 Fall model 173
   9.3.3 Experimental results 176
9.4 Detecting Fall in a Video Containing Multiple Humans 180
   9.4.1 Foreground detection 181
   9.4.2 Modeling of human shapes using ellipsoids 181
   9.4.3 Enhanced fall model 184
   9.4.4 Experimental results 187
9.5 Conclusion and Future Work 188
References 191

9.1. Introduction

Human fall detection in video is a challenging problem especially when multiple persons are present in the scene. It has importance in video surveillance, health care, human safety and security, and old-age home environments. A study on fall victims reveals[1] that 67% of those who had fallen and remained unattended for more than 72 hours, suffered premature death, compared to only 12% who were attended within an hour. Therefore, timely detection of human fall is important to avoid any serious consequences. A fall detection system would help us to address this problem by reducing the time between the fall and the arrival of required assistance.

We first propose an approach for human fall detection in a video containing a single person, initial results of which have been presented in.[2] An adaptive background subtraction method based on Gaussian Mixture Model (GMM) is applied to detect a human in the video foreground and mark him with his minimum-bounding box. The extracted features from the bounding box are used as input for the fall model to analyze, detect and confirm a fall. We next improve our approach to detect a falling person in a crowd. A foreground object detection method based on a general Bayesian framework is used to extract humans. Individuals are detected from the foreground by locating their head and modeling them into ellipsoids. The enhanced fall model uses a set of extracted features from the ellipsoids to detect and confirm a human fall. A finite state machine (FSM) is implemented in conjunction with the fall model for classifying people's pose in a video.

The organization of this chapter is as follows. Section 9.2 reviews related work in the area of fall detection and posture classification. Section 9.3 describes our approach for detecting fall in a video containing one human being. Section 9.4 extends it to the detection of fall in a video having multiple humans. Finally, conclusion and future work are given in Section 9.5.

9.2. Related Work

Existing fall detection methods can be broadly classified into the following three categories:

(1) Acoustics based Fall Detection

(2) Wearable Sensor based Fall Detection
(3) Video based Fall Detection

In acoustics based fall detection, human activities are measured using vibration on the floor. Fall is detected by analyzing the frequency component of vibration caused by the impact. In wearable sensor based fall detection, falls are detected by using a device attached to the subject. These devices generally use a combination of accelerometers and tilt sensors to automatically detect a fall event. In video based fall detection, human activity is captured in a video and analyzed using image processing techniques. Since video cameras have been widely used for surveillance as well as in home and health care, we use this approach in our method. Related work only on video based fall detection is surveyed here.

Contemporary research in surveillance domain includes event detection, posture classification and activity summarization for a single as well as multiple persons in video. Since the main topic of this chapter is human fall detection, we skip basic techniques proposed in the field of object detection, human shape modeling as well as head detection, and instead emphasize only on fall detection and posture analysis.

A number of approaches have been recently proposed for human fall detection using finite state machine, Hidden Markov Model (HMM) and neural network classifier. Tao et al.[3] use aspect ratio of a person as an observation feature for an on-line hypothesis-testing algorithm in conjunction with a two-state finite state machine to infer fall incident detection. They further extended their work[4] in order to determine a possible fall-down event using a three-state FSM. Cucchiara et al.[5] use a classifier for identification of people and estimation of their pose. It is based on probabilistic classification of the vertical and horizontal projection histograms of the person's blob with a four-state finite state machine for detecting events. In another work,[6] they use the person's projection histogram in every frame and compare it with probabilistic projection maps stored for each posture during the training phase. The posture so obtained is used for further validation using tracking information for classification. A posture state-transition graph is constructed in order to determine four main human postures namely, standing, sitting, laying and crawling.

Toreyin et al.[7] suggest a method for fall detection by constructing a Hidden Markov Model from both audio and video data. They use wavelet transform of the extracted aspect ratio as input feature for the HMM. Cucchiara and Vezzani[8] use probabilistic posture maps and integrate it with Hidden Markov Model to compute an instant posture. In[9] , Anderson et al. extract a set of features from silhouette and use them for temporal pattern recognition. They train an HMM to recognize future performance of these known activities. Application of Pseudo 2-D Hidden Markov Model is suggested in[10] for representing and recognizing human postures based on its 2-D elastic matching property. They compute the probabilities of observation sequences corresponding to each model by Doubly Embedded Viterbi optimization and classify human blob as the human posture with the highest likelihood.   Thome and Miguet[11] use an observation vector that corresponds to the angle between principal axes of the silhouette and the vertical axis for analyzing and recognizing complex activity of elderly people with Hierarchical Hidden Markov Model.

In order to better solve the posture classification problem, Takahashi and Sugakawa[12] use horizontal and vertical projection histograms of the silhouette as feature vectors which is an input to a self-organizing map based classifier. In[13] , authors extract shape features of an object and use them for human posture recognition using active contours and a radial basis function neural network. It classifies human posture into standing, bending and squatting positions. Juang and Chang[14] apply discrete fourier transform to horizontal and vertical projected histograms of the silhouette. They use magnitudes of significant fourier transform coefficients together with the silhouette length-width ratio as features for a neural fuzzy classifier.

A number of approaches have been recently proposed for posture analysis and fall detection using aspect ratio as feature[3,4,7,9,15] . Some of the approaches based on projection histogram are discussed in[5,6,12,13,14,16,17] It is also possible to detect a human fall based on human silhouette analysis[9,12,14,16,17] . Wang[16] proposes blob metrics using multiple appearance representations and activity profiling based on frame-by-frame posture classification. He uses three blob metrics namely, Inner-Distance Shape Context (IDSC), ellipse parameters and normalized projection histogram. Different distance metrics are used to measure similarity between the test and the associated postures using majority voting. Panini and Cucchiara[17] suggest the use of histogram projections from each moving person to classify his postures by adding a machine learning phase in order to generate probability maps. They define a statistical classifier that compares the probability maps and the histogram profiles for posture detection. Systems using human skeleton analysis have been reported in[18].[19] In,[18] Hsu et al. use two features - skeleton for a coarse search and centroid context for a finer classification of postures. In,[19] authors estimate human pose on the basis of a geometrical analysis conducted over a set of features related to the extracted skeletons.

In addition to the approaches introduced above, some of the existing systems use camera in the ceiling to overcome object occlusions[15],[20].[21] In,[15] authors have validated the aspect ratio with the user's personal information such as weight and height to detect a human fall for omni-video clips. Nait-Charif and McKenna[20] extract a person's trajectory using 5-D ellipse parameters in each sequence. An associated threshold on person's speed is used to label the inactivity zone and human fall. They[21] have developed a contextual model to produce human-readable summaries of activity and detect unusual inactivity in abnormal zones for a supportive home environment.

Results reported in the above mentioned references indicate that most of the existing fall detection systems work well when a single person is in the scene. Human fall detection in the presence of a crowd is a challenging problem. To the best of our knowledge, there iş no reported work related to human fall detection from a video in the presence of multiple persons. However, some of the authors have reported work on event detection and classification in a crowd situation[22].[23] In,[22] Bodor et al. developed a position and velocity path characteristic for each pedestrian using Kalman filter based prediction of future state and a set of conditions to generate a warning signal. In,[23] authors use projections of the eigenvectors in a sub-space spanned by the normal crowd scene as an input feature and apply spectral clustering to find the optimal number of models to represent normal motion patterns. Their classification of normal and abnormal events is based on the comparison of the current observation's likelihood given by the bank of models and the detection threshold.

In contrast to the aforementioned studies, we propose a comprehensive methodology oriented towards human fall detection in the presence of single as well as multiple humans in a video. As a first step, we present a method for fall detection in the presence of single human in a video. The method consists of two parts: human detection and use of a fall model. In the second step, we present an approach for fall detection in the presence of multiple humans in a video. The approach consists of three parts: foreground detection, modeling of human shapes using ellipsoids and finally use of an enhanced fall model. The fall model uses a set of extracted features to analyze, detect and confirm a fall situation. A finite state machine implementation in conjunction with the fall model helps to monitor people and their activities.

9.3. Detecting Fall in a Video Containing a Single Person

In this section, we present an approach for human fall detection in videos containing only a single person. It consists of two stages namely, human detection and use of a fall model.

9.3.1. *Human detection*

An adaptive background subtraction method using Gaussian Mixture Model[24] is applied to accurately detect a human in a given video sequence. The Gaussian is defined as $x \sim N(\mu, \sigma^2)$ which shows normal distribution of x corresponding to μ and σ^2. In a particular scene, the distribution of recently observed values of every pixel is characterized by a mixture of Gaussians. Evaluation of Gaussians is done by using a simple heuristic to hypothesize pixels which represent a part of the background process. The probability that a certain pixel has intensity value X at the time t is estimated by $P(X_t)$. The probability of observing the current pixel value is

$$P(X_t) \doteq \sum_{i=1}^{k} w_{i,t} * \eta(X_t, \mu_{i,t}, \Sigma_{i,t}) \tag{9.1}$$

where

$$\eta(X_t, \mu_{i,t}, \Sigma_{i,t}) = \frac{1}{((2\pi)^{\frac{n}{2}} |\Sigma|^{\frac{n}{2}})} * e^{\frac{1}{2}(X_t - \mu_t)^T \Sigma^{-1}(X_t - \mu_t)} \tag{9.2}$$

$$\omega_{i,t} = (1 - \alpha)\omega_{i,t-1} + \alpha(M_{k,t}) \tag{9.3}$$

Here $\omega_{i,t}$ is an estimate of the weight, m is the mean, α is the learning rate, and $M_{k,t}$ is 1 for the model which matches and 0 for the rest.

The background is estimated by specifying the Gaussian distributions which have the most supporting evidence and the least variance. A background pixel has a lower variance than a moving object's pixel. Therefore, initially the Gaussians are ordered in decreasing order of the value of $\frac{\omega}{\alpha}$ to represent a background process. We start the background process with the lowest variance by applying a threshold T, where

$$B = argmin_b(\sum_{k=1}^{b} \omega_k \geq T) \tag{9.4}$$

All pixels X_t which match any of these components are marked as background while remaining pixels are defined as foreground. To identify and analyze each connected set of pixels, we apply connected component analysis, which enables us to mark the rectangular bounding box over an object.

9.3.1.1. *Feature extraction*

We extract a set of features from each object and its bounding box, namely aspect ratio, horizontal (G_x) and vertical (G_y) gradient values and fall angle (θ) to use them further in the fall model.

The aspect ratio of a person is an elementary yet efficient feature to distinguish between normal standing pose such as walking and other abnormal poses such as falling. In Fig. 9.1 (a), we compare the aspect ratio of an object in diverse human poses.

When a fall commences, a drastic variation occurs in either X or Y direction. We compute and compare the gradient values G_x and G_y for every pixel of an object in different human poses as shown in Fig. 9.1 (b).

Fall angle is the angle of a vertical line through the centroid of an object with respect to the horizontal axis of the bounding box. Centroid (C_x, C_y) is the center of mass co-ordinates of an object. In Fig. 9.1 (c), we show fall angles of an object in different poses such as walking and falling.

9.3.2. *Fall model*

Our proposed method for human fall detection is comprised of two stages: fall detection and fall confirmation. We consider a fall model which helps to identify these two stages in a video. Aspect ratio of an object and its horizontal and vertical gradient values are the attributes used for fall detection. On the other hand, fall angle with respect to the horizontal axis of its bounding box is used for fall confirmation. We use rule-based decisions to detect and confirm a fall situation. To classify a human in different poses, we use a finite state machine in conjunction with the fall model.

9.3.2.1. *Fall detection step*

(1) Aspect ratio of human body changes during fall. When a person falls, the height (h) and width (w) of its bounding box varies extremely.

(2) When a person is walking or standing, the horizontal gradient value is less than the vertical gradient value ($G_x < G_y$) and when a person is falling, the horizontal gradient value is greater than the vertical gradient value ($G_x > G_y$).

(3) For every feature, we assign a binary value. If the extracted feature satisfies the rules, we assign binary value 1, otherwise 0.

(4) We apply OR operation on the feature values. If we get the resultant binary value as 1 then we detect the person as falling, otherwise not.

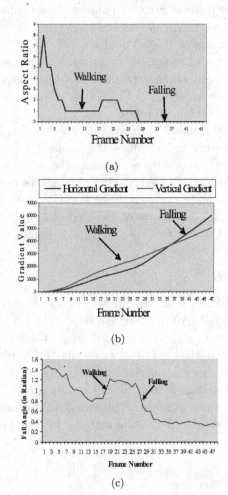

Figure 9.1. Comparison of feature values of an object in different poses taken from a video.

9.3.2.2. *Fall confirmation step*

When an individual is standing, we presume that he is in an upright position and the angle of a vertical line through the centroid with respect to horizontal axis of the bounding box should be approximately $\frac{\pi}{2}$. When a person is walking, the θ value varies from $\frac{\pi}{4}$ to $\frac{\pi}{2}$ (depending on their style and speed of walking) and when a person is falling, the angle is always less than $\frac{\pi}{4}$.

In every frame where a fall has been detected, we execute the fall confirmation step. We calculate the fall angle θ and if θ value is less than $\frac{\pi}{4}$, we confirm that the person is falling. Similarly, we take next few frames and analyze their features by applying the fall model to be assured of a fall situation.

A decision tree capturing the rules for fall detection and fall confirmation is given in Fig. 9.2, where each node denotes a test on an attribute and each branch represents an outcome of the test.

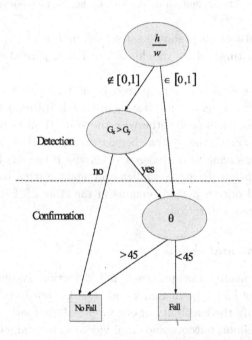

Figure 9.2.   A decision tree for fall detection and fall confirmation.

9.3.2.3. *State transition*

To classify people's poses, we construct a two-state FSM in conjunction with fall detection and fall confirmation step of the fall model. In this FSM, we take two states 'Walk' and 'Fall' respectively, as shown in Fig. 9.3.

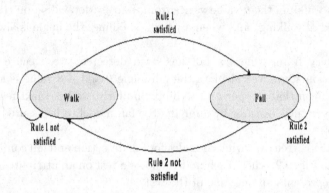

Figure 9.3.   A finite state machine for human fall detection.

Rule 1: Feature values should satisfy fall detection step of the model.

Rule 2: Feature values should satisfy fall confirmation step of the model.

Initially, we assume that the person is in 'Walk' state. When current state is 'Walk', the system begins testing of Rule 1. If Rule 1 is not satisfied, the state remains unchanged; otherwise the state transits to 'Fall'. When current state is 'Fall', the system begins testing of Rule 2. If Rule 2 is satisfied, the state remains unchanged; otherwise it transits back to 'Walk' state - a case when a person has fallen and again started to walk. Alarms will be triggered once a person remains in the state of 'Fall' for a period longer than a pre-set duration.

9.3.3. *Experimental results*

We have implemented our proposed fall detection system using C as the programming language in Linux and tested extensively with different datasets. To verify the feasibility of our proposed approach, we have taken 45 video clips (indoor, outdoor and omni-video) as test target. A handycam (SONY DCR-HC40E MiniDV PAL Handycam Camcorder) was used to capture indoor and outdoor video clips. All videos are taken in fluorescent light. Under such lighting condition, shadows are not well formed and their presence has not turned out to be significant. Video clips contain different possible types of human fall (sideways, forward and backward) as well as no fall situations.

The performance can be measured in terms of true positives (TP) - fall incidents identified correctly as fall incidents, false positives (FP) - non-fall incidents identified as fall incidents, false negatives (FN) - fall incidents missed by the system and true negatives (TN) - non-fall incidents for which system also did not raise an alarm. We only calculate TP and FP values (in %). Using these notions, the mathematical expression of accuracy, sensitivity and specificity[15] can be formulated as follows:

$$\text{Accuracy}(A) = (TP+TN)/(TP+TN+FP+FN)$$
$$\text{Sensitivity} = TP/(TP+FN)$$
$$\text{Specificity} = TN/(TN+FP)$$

Here FN = 100 - TP and TN = 100 - FP.

Table 9.1.   Recognition results of our approach.

Video Type	Scene Type	Total Frame	Fall Type	TP(%)	FP(%)
Indoor	Single	93	Forward	100	0
Indoor	Single	216	Backward	100	0
Indoor	Single	286	Sideway	100	0
Indoor	Single	100	No Fall	N.A.	0
Outdoor	Single	87	Forward	100	0
Outdoor	Single	141	Backward	100	0
Indoor	Multiple	175	Sideway	84	37
Outdoor	Multiple	624	Sideway	54	2
Omni-video	single	376	Forward	90	3
Omni-video	Multiple	1007	Forward	36	16

In Table 9.1, we show results of indoor, outdoor and omni-video clips containing all possible types of human fall. For a video containing a single person, we achieve high TP and low FP as recognition results because of the two-step fall model. Every fall situation is first detected and then confirmed by the model. For a video containing multiple persons, we get low TP and high FP because of the bounding box representation of blob. This bounding box representation may not identify individuals appropriately if the blobs are overlapped or occluded.

In order to compare our method with other fall detection systems, we show separate results - one for omni-video and another for indoor video in

a tabular format. For omni-video clips, we compare our method with the
fall detection system proposed by Miaou et al.[15] as shown in Table 9.2. For
indoor video clips, we compare our method with the fall detection system of
Tao et al.[3] as shown in Table 9.3. For this purpose, the camera was placed
on a table at a horizontal viewing angle with a distance of approximately
7 meters. We evaluate and compare the performance of our fall detection
model with a system using only aspect ratio as shown in Table 9.4. Results
of aspect ratio as a feature parameter are shown in parenthesis. In Fig. 9.4,
we show some successful images of human fall from videos processed by our
approach. Some unsuccessful images of human fall from videos are shown
in Fig. 9.5.

Table 9.2.   Comparison of methods for omni-video clips.

Approach	Accuracy(%)	Sensitivity(%)	Specificity(%)
With personal information, Miaou et al.[15]	81	90	86
Without personal information, Miaou et al.[15]	70	78	60
Proposed approach	94	90	96

Table 9.3.   Comparison of methods for indoor video clips.

Approaches	Video type	Sideways(%)	Forward(%)	Backward(%)
Tao et al.[3]	Indoor	92	82	41
Proposed approach	Indoor	100	100	100

Table 9.4.   Detection performance of our fall detection method.

Video Content	Scene Content	Accuracy(%)	Specificity(%)	Sensitivity(%)
Indoor	Single	100 (95)	100 (97)	100 (90)
Outdoor	Single	100 (93)	100 (90)	100 (95)
Indoor	Multiple	74 (62)	84 (50)	62 (73)
Outdoor	Multiple	79 (64)	97 (85)	54 (37)
Omni-video	Single	94 (89)	96 (92)	90 (81)
Omni-video	Multiple	51 (40)	83 (49)	36 (29)

From the tables, it is seen that the proposed method can accurately
detect most of the possible types of fall in different types of video. To the
best of our knowledge, this is the first successful attempt for fall detection
taking different types of video clips and all possible types of human fall

together. For single person, detection accuracy is almost 100%. For multiple persons in the scene, however, this approach does not perform quite well and achieves about 75-80% accuracy when regular camera is used. Since it is not meant for omni-camera applications, performance is not satisfactory.

Figure 9.4.   Successful image frames of fall detected by our approach.

(a)

(b)

(c)

Figure 9.5.   Image frames of fall undetected by our approach.

9.4. Detecting Fall in a Video Containing Multiple Humans

Human fall detection is challenging especially in a crowded situation. The method discussed in the last section can accurately detect a fall for single person in a video but fails, if the person is in a crowd. We improve our method in order to detect a fall among multiple humans in a video.

This fall detection method consists of three parts: foreground detection, modeling of human shapes using ellipsoids and use of an enhanced fall model. The Gaussian Mixture Model based adaptive background subtraction method is not able to segment people accurately in a video containing complex background[25] . We use a general Bayesian framework which can integrate multiple features to model the background for foreground object detection. We detect individuals from the foreground by first locating their head and then modeling them into ellipsoids. The fall model uses a set of extracted features from ellipsoids to detect and confirm a fall.

9.4.1. *Foreground detection*

The foremost task is to accurately detect humans in a video sequence. We use an algorithm for foreground object detection with the formulation of background and foreground classification based on Bayes decision theory.[26]

Initially, we detect change and no-change pixels of the current image frame by using background subtraction and temporal difference. We define the changed pixel as a motion pixel belonging to a moving object and the unchanged pixel as a non-motion pixel belonging to a stationary object. By using the Bayes decision rule, we classify the pixels associated with stationary or moving objects as part of background or foreground based on the learnt statistics of color and color co-occurrence feature vectors respectively. We combine the classification results from both stationary and moving parts and segment the connected foreground regions. Finally, the feature statistics of color, color co-occurrence and the background model is updated.

9.4.2. *Modeling of human shapes using ellipsoids*

We analyze the foreground blobs using a simple heuristic to hypothesize an ellipsoidal representation of individuals. The objectives of modeling human shapes are as follows:

(1) To determine whether a silhouette contains a single or multiple humans.
(2) To locate individuals in the silhouette.
(3) To generate an ellipsoid as a coarse model of human representation.

In an ideal situation, each blob corresponds to a single moving object. A bounding box representation of blob is efficient and suitable for real-time applications. In a crowded scene, however, a single blob may contain multiple humans due to their physical proximity or a single human may contain multiple blobs due to low color contrast. Therefore, blob analysis using the bounding box is not suitable for a video containing multiple people.[27] Hence, we use an ellipsoid representation for an individual.

In a crowd, the head of a human has the least possibility of getting occluded.[27] We detect individuals in the foreground blob by first locating their head points which is an effective way to segment overlapping people. The process is described below and shown step by step graphically in Fig. 9.6.

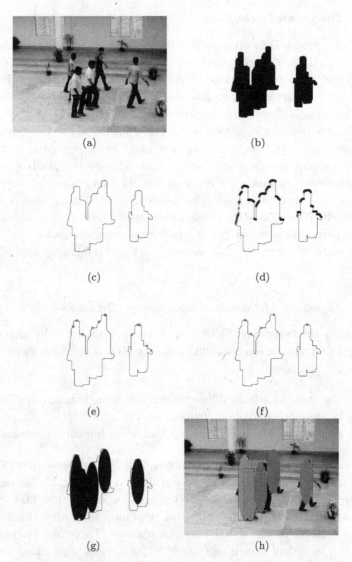

Figure 9.6.   Steps for modeling of human shapes using ellipsoids.

We take an input image frame containing multiple persons (Fig. 9.6a) and detect foreground objects (9.6b). An optimal edge detection algorithm (Canny) is applied on it to get a binary edge map which, in turn, is used to extract contours or silhouettes of the foreground blobs (9.6c). We take vertical projection of silhouettes to get a set of pixels (9.6d). Next, we divide the contour into a set of fragments according to the average size or width of a human. The highest contour point that belongs to a fragment is defined as a peak (9.6e). A peak can be a head point if it has a sufficient number of foreground pixels below it (9.6f). For every head point, we determine its potential height by finding the first point that maps to a contour pixel along the vertical direction within the range as determined by the minimum and the maximum human height. The maximum value is taken as the human height and the height of different humans in the scene is obtained. We generate ellipsoids using the position and the height for each head point (9.6g). Finally, we determine the minimum bounding box of an ellipsoid to denote its position (9.6h).

9.4.2.1. *Feature extraction*

We define a 5-D feature vector for every ellipsoid to represent its state. At time t, the state of an ellipsoid is estimated by $e_t = (x_t, y_t, a, b, \theta_t)$, where (x_t, y_t) is the ellipse center, a and b are the lengths of major and minor axes and θ_t is the rotation angle. This representation of an ellipsoid is sufficient for supporting recognition of human pose. We extract three features from each ellipsoid using its 5-D feature vector. The extracted features are aspect ratio, rotation angle, and position.

Aspect ratio is an effective feature for distinguishing between normal and abnormal human pose. It is defined as the ratio of length and width of ellipsoid's bounding rectangle. In Fig. 9.7, we show the aspect ratio variation of an object in different human states such as walking and falling.

Rotation angle (θ) is the angle of rotation of the y axis with respect to the ellipse major axis. When a person is standing, we assume that he is in an upright position and the angle of y axis to the ellipse major axis is approximately 0. We take a clockwise rotation of the y-axis to the ellipse major axis. A major change occurs in the rotation angle in the case of a falling person. In Fig. 9.8, we show variation of the rotation angle in different human poses.

The position of an ellipsoid varies if the corresponding person has movement. When a person falls down, his position remains static over a

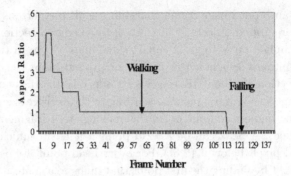

Figure 9.7. Variation of aspect ratio of an object in different human poses.

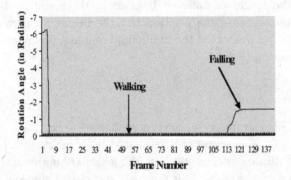

Figure 9.8. Rotation angle variation of an object in different human poses.

sequence of frames. Thus, by comparing features of the current state with its previous state, we can confirm 'Fall' of an individual. Here, we denote the center of an ellipse (x_t, y_t) as its position.

9.4.3. *Enhanced fall model*

An enhanced fall model consists of two steps: fall detection and fall confirmation. We use aspect ratio and rotation angle for the fall detection step. For fall confirmation, we take position of the current state of an ellipsoid and compare with its previous state. A rule-based decision is applied to detect and confirm a fall. An FSM implementation is used in conjunction with the fall model to analyze people's activities and for classifying their postures.

9.4.3.1. *Fall detection step*

(1) The aspect ratio of an ellipse changes during a fall. When a person falls, the height and width of its bounding box vary drastically.

(2) When a person is walking, the rotation angle varies from either $\frac{-7\pi}{4}$ to $\frac{-\pi}{4}$ or $\frac{-3\pi}{4}$ to $\frac{-5\pi}{4}$. When a person is falling, the θ value varies from either $\frac{-\pi}{4}$ to $\frac{-3\pi}{4}$ or from $\frac{-5\pi}{4}$ to $\frac{-7\pi}{4}$.

(3) For every feature, we assign a binary value. If the extracted feature satisfies the rules, we assign a value 1, otherwise 0.

(4) We apply AND operation on the feature values. If we get the resultant binary value as 1 then we consider that the person as falling.

9.4.3.2. *Fall confirmation step*

We take each ellipsoid and compare position parameter of the current state with its previous state. For a walking person, we find a change whereas for a falling person, there is no-change in this parameter of the ellipsoid.

For every frame where a fall has been detected, we apply the fall confirmation step. We take the position parameter of the current state and compare with its previous state. If the value does not change over a sequence of frames, we confirm that the person has fallen and consider the fall as dangerous. If the value of feature parameter changes over a sequence of frames, we consider the fall as temporary. Therefore, we take the next few frames and analyze their features using the fall model to confirm a fall situation and raise an alarm.

A decision tree capturing the enhanced rules for fall detection and fall confirmation is given in Fig. 9.9, where each node denotes a test on an attribute and each branch represents an outcome of the test.

9.4.3.3. *State transition*

We use a three-state FSM in conjunction with our fall model. The implementation of an FSM helps us to classify human in diferent poses. The three states are Walk, Fall and Confirm as shown in Fig. 9.10. In the beginning, we presume that the human is in 'Walk' state. We use the following rules to detect and confirm the fall.

Rule 1: Feature values should satisfy the fall detection step.

Rule 2: Feature values should satisfy the fall confirmation step.

When current state is 'Walk', the system begins testing of Rule 1. If rule 1 is satisfied, the state transits to 'Fall' state; otherwise the state remains

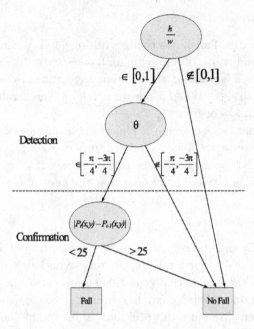

Figure 9.9. A decision tree for fall detection and fall confirmation using the enhanced model.

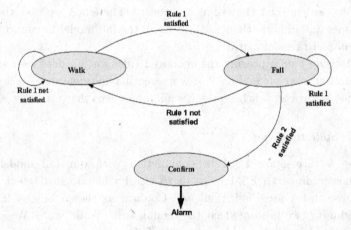

Figure 9.10. An improved finite state machine for human fall detection.

unchanged. When current state is 'Fall', the system begins testing of Rule 1 and Rule 2. If Rule 1 is satisfied, the state remains unchanged; otherwise it transits back to 'Walk' state - a case when a person has fallen and again started to walk. If Rule 2 is satisfied, the state transits to 'Confirm' state; otherwise the state remains unchanged, which is the case when a person has fallen permanently and the system has raised an emergency alarm for assistance.

9.4.4. *Experimental results*

We present results of our method using the refined model. The enhanced approach works effectively despite the difficulties of occlusion, complex background and low color contrast in video.

Table 9.5. Recognition results of our approach.

Video Type	Scene Type	Total Frame	Fall Type	TP(%)	FP(%)
Simple Indoor	Multiple	291	Sideways	100	0
Complex Indoor	Multiple	350	Backward	92	1.5
Complex Indoor	Multiple	376	No Fall	N.A.	0
Simple Outdoor	Multiple	311	Backward	95	0.5
Complex Outdoor	Multiple	429	Sideways	88	1
Simple Indoor	Single	93	Forward	100	0
Simple Outdoor	Single	141	Backward	100	0

In Table 9.5, we show recognition results of our approach. We have taken simple as well as complex types of indoor and outdoor video clip. A simple type video contains a static background with less occlusions whereas a complex type video contains a dynamic background with high occlusions. We achieve high TP for the simple type of video clips and slightly lower TP for complex types of video clips. When a fall situation occurs in the early part of video, the falling person is likely to be more occluded by walking persons present in the scene. Therefore, we get low TP. After a fall situation occurs in the later part of a video, the falling person is likely to be less occluded by walking persons present in the scene. Therefore, we achieve high TP.

In Table 9.6, we show detection performance of our approach. We achieve higher accuracy and specificity in comparison to sensitivity. For complex indoor, simple outdoor and complex outdoor video clips, we get higher accuracy and specificity but lower sensitivity because of low FP and high FN. The improved fall model is effective and detects only true fall

Table 9.6.   Detection performance of our approach.

Video Content	Scene Content	Accuracy(%)	Sensitivity(%)	Specificity(%)
Simple Indoor	Multiple	100	100	100
Complex Indoor	Multiple	95	92	98
Simple Outdoor	Multiple	99	94	99
Complex Outdoor	Multiple	95	88	98
Simple Indoor	Single	100	100	100
Simple Outdoor	Single	100	100	100

incidents. FP is very low as we consider both aspect ratio and rotation angle features together to detect a fall in the detection step and verify the fall in the confirmation step using position feature parameter. For a simple indoor video clip, we achieve almost 100% accuracy, sensitivity and specificity.

This is the first successful attempt for fall detection in a video containing multiple persons. In Fig. 9.11, we show some images of human fall in a crowd which are correctly detected by this fall detection method. Our approach is effective and can detect almost all possible types of human fall even in a crowd. However, the method failed to detect a human fall when the falling person is fully or partially occluded by a walking person in the scene. This is a limitation of our approach, but could be resolved by improving the human shape model. Some cases of human fall which were not detected by this method are shown in Fig. 9.12.

9.5. Conclusion and Future Work

We have presented two methods for detection of human fall. In the first part, we have described a fall detection method for single person in a video. The method consists of two stages: human detection using adaptive background subtraction method based on Gaussian Mixture Model and use of a fall model. The fall model considers a set of extracted features to analyze, detect and confirm a fall. It is simple as well as effective and is able to detect all possible types of human fall in indoor, outdoor and omni-video clips. However, it is not good at detecting a fall in the presence of multiple humans. In the second part, we have proposed an improved fall detection method, which detects human fall even in a crowd. It consists of three parts: foreground detection, modeling of human shapes as ellipsoids and use of an improved fall model. We segment individuals from the foreground and map them into ellipsoids. The model uses a set of extracted features to

Figure 9.11.   Successful results of our approach.

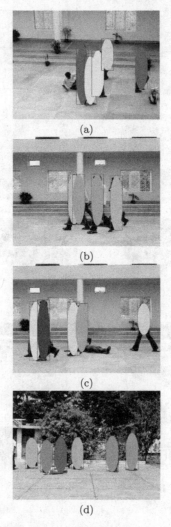

(a)

(b)

(c)

(d)

Figure 9.12.   Unsuccessful results of our approach.

detect and confirm a fall. A finite state machine has been implemented in conjunction with the fall model for classifying people's pose and monitoring their activities. Experimental results show that the proposed approach is able to detect a human fall accurately even in a complex situation. Our method works well in defused lighting conditions such as fluorescent tube lights, which are most commonly used for indoor and outdoor lighting.

In future, we plan to improve our method so that it can handle all forms of occlusions in a video. By enhancing our human shape model, we can make the fall detection system more robust. We also plan to introduce a fuzzy set based classifier instead of the finite state machine implementation. The method can be extended easily for posture classification, activity summarization and behavior analysis.

References

1. F. Marquis-Faulkes, S. J. McKenna, and A. F. Gregor, Gathering the requirements for a fall monitor using drama and video with older people, *Technology and Disability.* **17**, 227–236, (2005).
2. V. Vishwakarma, C. R. Mandal, and S. Sural. Automatic detection of human fall in video. In *Proc. of the Second International Conference on Pattern Recognition and Machine Intelligence, Lecture Notes in Computer Science (LNCS-4815), Springer Verlag,* pp. 616–623, (2007).
3. J. Tao, M. Turjo, M. Wong, M. Wang, and Y. Tan. Fall incidents detection for intelligent video surveillance. In *Fifth International Conference on Information, Communication and Signal Processing,* pp. 1590–1594, (2005).
4. J. Tao, M. Turjo, M. Wong, M. Wang, and Y. Tan. Quickest change detection for health-care video surveillance. In *IEEE International Symposium on Circuits and Systems (ISCAS),* pp. 505–508, (2006).
5. R. Cucchiara, C. Grana, A. Prati, and R. Vezzani. Computer vision techniques for pda accessibility of in-house video surveillance. In *ACM Multimedia 2003 - First ACM International Workshop on Video Surveillance, Berkeley (CA), USA,* pp. 87–97, (2003).
6. R. Cucchiara, C. Grana, A. Prati, and R. Vezzani, Probabilistic posture classification for human-behavior analysis, *IEEE Transactions on System, Man and Cybernetics - Part A : Systems and Humans.* **35**(1), 42–54, (2005).
7. B. Ugur Toreyin, Y. Dedeoglu, and A. Enis Centin. HMM based falling person detection using both audio and video. In *ICCV Workshop on HCI, Lecture Notes in Computer Science, Springer Verlag, Bejing, China,* pp. 211–220, (2005).
8. R. Cucchiara and R. Vezzani. Assessing temporal coherence for posture classification with large occlusions. In *IEEE Workshop on Motion and Video Computing (WACV/MOTION'05),* pp. 269–274, (2005).
9. D. Anderson, J. M. Keller, M. Skubic, X. Chen, and Z. He. Recognizing falls from silhouettes. In *28th IEEE EMBS Annual International Conference, New York City, USA,* pp. 6388–6391, (2006).
10. L. H. W. Aloysius, G. Dong, H. Zhiyong, and T. Tan. Human posture recognition in video sequence using pseudo 2-d hidden markov models. In *8th International Conference on Control, Automation, Robotics and Vision, Kunming, China,* pp. 712–716, (2004).

11. N. Thome and S. Miguet. A HHMM-based approach for robust fall detection. In *Nineth International Conference on Control, Automation, Robotics and Vision (IEEE ICARCV)*, pp. 1–8, (2006).

12. K. Takahashi and S. Sugakawa. Remarks on human posture classification using self-organizing map. In *IEEE International Conference on Systems, Man and Cybernetics*, vol. 3, pp. 2623–2628, (2004).

13. F. Buccolieri, C. Distante, and A. Leone. Human posture recognition using active contours and radial basis function neural network. In *IEEE Conference on Advanced Video and Signal Based Surveillance (AVSS)*, pp. 213–218, (2005).

14. C. Juang and C. M. Chang, Human body posture classification by a neural fuzzy network and home care system applications, *IEEE Transactions on Systems, Man and Cybernetics - Part A : Systems and Humans*. (2007).

15. S. Miaou, P. Sung, and C. Huang. A customized human fall detection system using omni-camera images and personal information. In *First Distributed Diagnosis and Home Health Care (D2H2) Conference, Arlington, Virginia, USA*, pp. 39–42, (2006).

16. L. Wang. From blob metrics to posture classification to activity profiling. In *The 18th International Conference on Pattern Recognition (ICPR'06)*, pp. 736–739, (2006).

17. L. Panini and R. Cucchiara. A machine learning approach for human posture detection in domestics applications. In *The 12th International Conference on Image Analysis and Processing (ICIAP' 03)*, pp. 103–108, (2003).

18. Y. Hsu, J. Hsieh, H. Kao, and H. Y. M. Liao. Human behavior analysis using deformable traingulations. In *IEEE 7th Workshop on Multimedia signal Processing*, pp. 1–4, (2005).

19. C. Castiello, T. D. Orazio, A. M. Fanelli, P. Spagnolo, and M. A. Torsello. A model-free approach for posture classification. In *IEEE Conference on Advanced Video and Signal Based Surveillance (AVSS)*, pp. 276–281, (2005).

20. H. Nait-Charif and S. J. McKenna. Activity summarisation and fall detection in a supportive home environments. In *The 17th International Conference on Pattern Recognition (ICPR)*, vol. 4, pp. 323–326, (2004).

21. S. J. McKenna and H. Nait-Charif, Summarising contextual activity and detecting unusual inactivity in a supportive home environment, *Pattern Analysis Application.* **7**(14), 386–401, (2005).

22. R. Bodor, B. Jackson, and N. Papanikolopoulos. Vision-based human tracking and activity recognition. In *The 11th Mediterranean Conference on Control and Automation, Rhodes, Greece*, (2003).

23. E. L. Andrade, R. Fisher, and S. Blunsden. Detection of emergency events in crowded scenes. In *The Institution of Engineering and Technology Conference on Crime and Security*, pp. 528–533, (2006).

24. C. Stauffer and W. E. L. Grimson. Adaptive background mixture model for real time tracking. In *IEEE Conference on Computer Vision and Pattern Recognition (CVPR'99)*, pp. 246–252, (1999).

25. L. Li, W. Huang, I. Y. H. Gu, and Q. Tian. Foreground object detection from video containing complex background. In *Eleventh ACM International Conference on Multimedia*, pp. 2–10, (2003).
26. L. Li, W. Huang, I. Y. H. Gu, and Q. Tian, Statistical modeling of complex backgrounds for foreground object detection, *IEEE Transactions on Image Processing*. **13**(11), 1459–1472, (2004).
27. T. Zhao and R. Nevatia, Tracking multiple humans in complex situations, *IEEE Transactions on Pattern Analysis and Machine Intelligence*. **26**(9), 1208–1221, (2004).

Chapter 10

Fusion of GIS and SAR Statistical Features for Earthquake Damage Mapping at the Block Scale

G. Trianni, G. Lisini, P. Gamba and F. Dell'Acqua

University of Pavia, Department of Electronics,
Via A. Ferrata, 1, 27100 Pavia, Italy
p.gamba@ele.unipv.it

This work shows that multitemporal SAR data allows to map earthquake damage in urban areas with an acceptable accuracy, provided that ancillary information defining urban blocks be available. A statistical analysis of the parameters of the models representing backscattered intensity or coherence values for each block may be used to discriminate between damaged and undamaged areas and, to some extent, to evaluate the damage. A comparison with a recently proposed supervised segmentation approach shows that similar results may be achieved by means of this simpler unsupervised methodology in some cases, while in other situations the supervised approach shows superior performances.

Contents

10.1 Introduction 195
10.2 Damage Mapping Processing Chain 197
10.3 Damage Mapping Results 200
10.4 Conclusions 205
References 205

10.1. Introduction

At some stages in the disaster management cycle the sheer availability of information, any kind of it, is more important than its absolute accuracy. This is the case for image interpretation tools meant to support immediate manual characterization of a scene via aerial or satellite imagery. For this reason, simple algorithms for fast data mining and analysis are welcome in applications related to disaster and, generally speaking, to civil protection management.

195

The use of remotely sensed imagery in such situations has been steadily growing in the past years, but these efficient and fast algorithms, although not highly accurate, are still lacking in a number of applications.

Thus, on the one hand several projects and web sites make data and maps publicly available, like UNOSAT (http://www.unosat.org) and RESPOND (http://www.respond-int.org). On the other hand, these maps are usually nothing more than geometrically and radiometrically corrected data, with geographical information overlaid. Interpretation is left to the human expert, a visual approach is assumed and thus the maps are intended solely to help the experts understand -on their own- what has happened in the observed area; legends are usually provided which guide the interpretation of the maps. However, the training of the interpreter is not easy, and the problem is worsened by the fact that organizations such as the International Charter on "Space and Major Disasters" (Allenbach et al., 2005) are forced to consider a wide range of sources, so that visual interpretation of diverse data may require multiple skills. This is the reason why the use of SAR data is unlikely in a first phase, although these may happen to be the only available data in case of poor weather condition.

In recent literature, however, some works have already appeared suggesting that multi-temporal SAR data may provide, at a proper temporal and spatial scale, interesting information about disasters, particularly earthquakes and floods. As for the earthquakes are concerned, most of these works employ to a large extent data coming from ground surveys, not only to validate but often also to initiate the process of information extraction. Subsequently, these approaches are really valuable for correlating damage patterns with ground displacements and soil properties (Yonezawa and Takeuchi, 2001, and Matsuoka and Yamazaki, 2005), or to provide very precise 3D changes of the earth crusts (Stramondo et al., 2005), but offer limited validity for damage assessment, and especially for rapid mapping of areas affected by disasters. Other approaches combine SAR data with multi-spectral images (Stramondo et al., 2006). This is surely interesting, but we would like here to restrict the scope of this work to radar data only. There are indeed statistical analyses of SAR data for damage analysis (Mansouri et al., 2005), but they suffer from problems in interpretation, which needs to be guided in order to provide useful information to the viewer. The aim of this work is to make the interpretation process as automatic as possible, and to reduce the time elapsed from data acquisition to information delivery.

Therefore, we cannot rely on the sole use of classification and change detection methodologies that, even for the best ones available so far in technical literature, are still far from providing satisfying and immediately useful results for the final user. Instead, the integrated use of these methods and ancillary data, either already available, or easily extracted by manual interpretation of maps and/or optical images, may focus the imprecise results of multitemporal SAR analysis toward more detailed results, producing maps that are accurate enough for the proposed applications.

10.2. Damage Mapping Processing Chain

The goal of this work is indeed to show that a first, limited accuracy damage mapping in earthquake-stricken areas can be obtained using multitemporal SAR data via a statistical characterization of the backscattered field. To this aim, simple neighborhood of each tested pixel may be considered. The definition of this neighborhood is questionable, and its width/scale must be adaptively changed. This is particularly true in urban environments, usually neither homogeneous nor continuously changing. In this situation one may clearly see the advantage of integrating ancillary data, when available. In fact, they might provide hints or directly indicate homogenous land use areas. By integrating the corresponding information in the extraction flow, it will become more focused and precise, as we will show in the result section.

The basic steps of the proposed algorithm are:

(1) the evaluation of the best approximating statistical function for the SAR feature under test;
(2) the extraction of the statistically significant parameters for the area of interest, possibly using ancillary data to improve the effectiveness of the analysis;
(3) the comparison of the pre- and post-event parameters for efficient characterization of the changes and quick and semi-automated extraction of the damage assessment.

While all these steps have a general validity for any change detection problem involving radar data, we stress here that urban areas are considered, and earthquakes are the focus of this research. This is essential to understand some of the choices detailed in the following paragraphs.

According to the first step described above, we need first to evaluate the best statistical approach useful for characterizing urban areas at the block level. Indeed, using up-to-date SAR technology from satellite platforms out of their commissioning phase, the spatial ground resolution currently achievable is around 6 m (ALOS PALSAR and RADARSAT-1 Fine beam mode), which does not enable statistical analysis at a more detailed level than that of blocks. The technical literature lists, among the proposed distributions, the lognormal and Weibull ones (see [7], for instance). They have been compared for urban areas and polarimetric SAR in [8] and found as reliable and effective. The lognormal distribution is computer according to the formula:

$$p(x) = \frac{1}{x\sqrt{2\pi c}} \exp\left[-\frac{(\ln x - b)^2}{2c}\right] \tag{10.1}$$

The b parameter is connected to the scale of the distribution, while c rules the shape. Weibull distributions are instead characterized by the following formula:

$$p(x) = \frac{cx^{c-1}}{b^c} \exp\left[-\left(\frac{x}{b}\right)^c\right] \tag{10.2}$$

where b e c have identical meaning as for the lognormal distribution.

Weibull distributions are commonly used for the analysis of radar images, when the intensity is selected as the analysis feature. Lognormal distributions have been used in urban areas, since they better adapt to abrupt changes in intensity due to concentrations of strong backscatterers, which is commonplace for densely built-up areas.

The steps in the procedure for the statistical evaluation of a given portion of a given image are therefore:

(1) the computation of parameters b and c, initially set to the mean β and variance V of the logarithm of the amplitude SAR data;
(2) the minimization of the Root Mean Square Error (RMSE) between the original normalized histogram and a lognormal distribution, starting from the above mentioned initial guess;
(3) the computation of the b and c factor, again minimizing the RMSE, for the best fitting Weibull distribution.

An example of the results of this procedure applied to an homogeneous land use block in an urban area is shown in fig. 10.1, where the original histogram and the three approximating distributions are shown and maybe compared. Apparently, there is no clear preference for a given distribution model against the other one; 20 areas in 3 different images have given similar results, thus confirming this consideration.

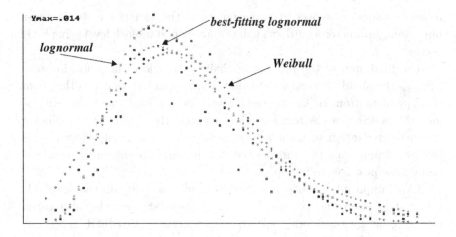

Figure 10.1. Statistical analysis of a test area: points define the actual amplitude value histogram, while the tallest curve is the lognormal distribution base on mean and variance values computed from it, the middle curve the best fitting (in the mean square error sense)lognormal distribution, and the lowest curve is the best fitting Weibull distribution.

A closer look to RMSE values made us prefer the lognormal distribution. Even the initial guess for the distribution parameters reduces the RMSE value below the limit reachable after optimization with a Weibull distribution. On the other hand, the latter shows a more stable set of parameters for images referring to the same situation. This is also true for the initial guess of the lognormal distribution. Since these values are very easy to compute, they are the best candidates for a quick and effective model-based change analysis.

To this aim, it is mandatory to understand if and how the damage produced by the earthquake changes these parameters. Visually, the effects of the earthquake on amplitude SAR images result in a reduction of the contrast between urbanized and rural areas accompanied by a sudden change in the pixel variance. According to what we expect, this change is more valuable in densely built-up areas, with a greater concentration of strong backscatterers against a generally very dark background represented by road pixels.

The statistical analysis of block-based histogram shows in hard-hit areas- a remarkable reduction of the mean amplitude value and, as a consequence of the increased variance, a reduction in the peak of the distributions. Therefore, multitemporal analysis confirms the single date analysis, in that the proposed distributions confirm themselves as suitable representations; moreover, it again points to the variance V as the most important parameter for urban change detection at a block level using SAR images.

The final step of the processing chain is therefore the definition of a suitable threshold for change detection. We may expect that this threshold be dependent from to the particular test site at hand, and this will be indeed discussed in the result section; though, the capability of reducing the characterization to a single parameter is an interesting result of this research. In any case this threshold should be carefully chosen, to avoid too many false positives to popup.

SAR amplitude values are however only a part of the available information, and the complex nature of the data may be also taken into account by considering the coherence between two SAR images. A procedure very similar to the one described in the preceding paragraphs shows that a normal distribution is capable of modeling pre-pre and pre-post coherence data at a block level in urban areas. Moreover, variance values and their changes are an interesting way to characterize damage patterns in these same areas.

10.3. Damage Mapping Results

The test sites for the proposed procedure are the towns of Bam, Iran and the town of Golcuk, Turkey. To analyze the Bam area, a sequence of three acquisitions by the ASAR sensor is considered. In particular, data were recorded on 11th June, 2003, 3rd December, 2003 and 7th January, 2004. Due to the public availability of many results of interpretation work on aerial or satellite images of the area by the ZKI (ZKI, 2006), UNOSAT and RESPOND, ancillary data were reconstructed and are thus considered as available. Similarly, for the Golcuk area, where the earthquake happened in September 1999, ERS-1 and ERS-2 images are available, recorded on 12th and 13th August, before the event, and on 16th September, after the event. Ancillary data were collected using the information extracted from the web sites of various emergency relief agencies.

Following the procedure outlined in the previous section, a complete analysis of the Bam area was first obtained. The threshold for detecting damaged blocks was fixed during a preliminary analysis. Fig. 10.2(a) shows the histograms of percent change in the amplitude variance for undamaged (leftmost curve) versus damaged (righmost curve) blocks in some sample test areas. The vertical axis represents the number of blocks which show a percentage change in variance between the adjacent numbers reported in the horizontal axis. There is some overlap, but 10% is in fact the threshold between the two subsets: blocks with a variance change greater than 10% are assumed to be damaged areas. This criterion will be used in the following valuation of the overall Bam area. Similarly, fig. 10.2(b) shows the percent change for coherence variance of the same test blocks, with the further discrimination between slightly damaged and heavily damaged blocks. This figure shows that a 15% threshold is a good guess for coherence-based statistical discrimination of heavily damaged versus slightly damaged or non-damaged blocks.

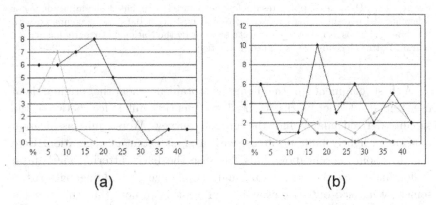

(a)   (b)

Figure 10.2.   Histograms of the percent change in amplitude (a) or coherence (b) for no damage (light grey), low damage (black) and high damage (mid grey).

Fig. 10.3 shows results elaborating amplitude (left) and coherence (right) information, compared with in situ analysis carried out by the National Cartographic service of Iran (http://www.ngdir.ir/, section "Earthquake database") for the same blocks. Due to the very simple target of this research, the figure shows just two categories: damaged (diagonal pattern) versus non-damaged (dotted pattern) blocks, while the available ground truth further discriminates between slightly (horizontal pattern) and heavily damaged (vertical pattern) blocks.

As a matter of fact, there is a very good similarity between the damage patterns obtained by means of amplitude-based (a) and coherence-based (b) statistical analysis at the block level. Moreover, both patterns are remarkably similar to the damage patterns in fig. 10.3(c). Coherence-based results are slightly more accurate (28 out of 36 lightly damaged areas instead of 24).

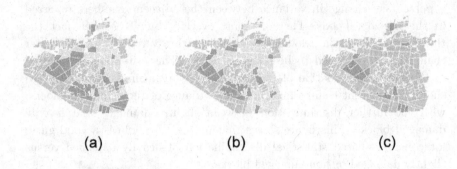

Figure 10.3.   Damage mapping results for the Bam test site, based on amplitude (a) or coherence (b) percent change between pre- and post-event data, to be compared with (c), damaged areas as measured by in situ analysis by the National Cartographic Service of Iran. Pattern legends are explained in the text.

A first comment to the figure is obtained when the original land use legend of the blocks is used to identify difference between the satellite-derived maps and the ground survey. Worst misclassification appears in lightly built up areas, with a great extent of vegetation. Here the threshold chosen above fails, because the backscattering mechanism is dominated by the vegetation, and the change in building patterns is somehow masked out. However, it is interesting to note that this is not a problem of SAR data alone. The same discrepancy between satellite-based damage maps and in situ measurements is observable in the map provided by UNOSAT using SPOT optical data a few days after the earthquake (SERTIT 2004).The results for the second test site, the town of Golcuk, show a very similar behavior. This is peculiar because the change detection thresholds were maintained to the same levels, even if the land use in Golcuk, as well as the damage mechanisms, were very different. In fact, the damage maps are shown in fig. 10.4 (pattern legend is identical to the one for fig. 10.3) and report a total of 30 detected blocks out of 35 for amplitude and 25 for coherence-based analysis. Please note that in this situation an even more precise characterization of the building damage is possible, by further subdividing the ranges of percentage change of the statistical parameters of interest, as shown in fig. 10.4(c), where two additional thresholds, 50% and 80%, were considered.

Moreover, for the Golcuk area a comparison has been carried out, between these results and those obtained from the recently proposed supervised procedure by the same authors of this work (Gamba et al., 2006).

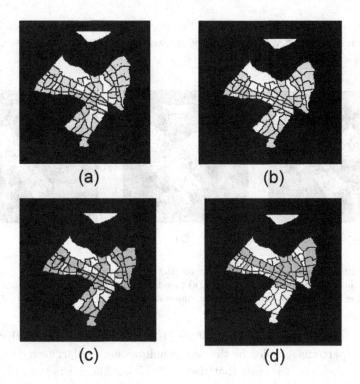

Figure 10.4. Damage mapping results for the Golcuk test site, based on amplitude (a) or coherence (b) percent change between pre- and post-event data, to be compared with (d), ground truth for damaged areas. The map in (c) shows that a finer subdivision of amplitude variance changes may provide an even better damage pattern recognition, with more classes of damages.

The advantage of the algorithm in the present work is its unsupervised nature, while the advantage of the supervised procedure, based on a non-parametric classifier, is its ability to take into account both amplitude and coherence information as a whole. In Gamba et al. (2006) the technique was applied to the Bam test area, but it proved to be useful for the second test site of this work as well. The damage maps using three different combination of the original multitemporal SAR data and other information layers which may be computed from them for the Golcuk area are shown in fig. 10.5, were the same block boundaries used in this work have been considered to produce a per-parcel damage analysis. The features used for this classification are the pre- and post-event intensity, the coherence information and finally the "backscattering coefficient" as defined in Matsuoka (2005), basically the difference between the decimal logarithms of the average pixel values computed in two corresponding, sliding windows over the two figures.

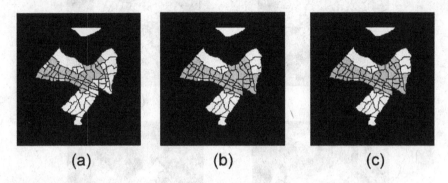

Figure 10.5. Damage mapping results for the Golcuk test site, based on pre- and post-event intensity (a), the same as in (a) plus the Matsuoka backscattering coefficient (b) or the same as in (b) plus coherence information (c).

The qualitative comparison of fig. 10.4 and fig. 10.5 shows that the damage patterns revealed by the two techniques are similar, even if in some parts of the map it is clear that they suffer from different misclassification errors. In particular, the supervised procedure is more capable of detecting the damage, but is it somehow overestimates the damage levels. On the contrary, the statistical analysis shows amore imprecise characterization of the damages, especially for the low damage level. This suggests that a further step in this research may be the definition of a methodology to fuse at the information level the maps available by the two approaches.

A Further comment is that there is a larger misclassification in the Southern part of the urban area. An inspection of Golcuk Municipality Website(http://www.golcuk.bel.tr/en/, section "city map", category "newhousing parcels") has revealed significant development plans for the southern part of the town, which may have already been in progress between the two pre-and post-event images, resulting in significant backscattering changes. This may have "forged" a modification in the features similar to those arising from a collapse of the buildings, in an area where no significant, actual damage was reported (see ground truth in fig. 1.4d) This in turn may have been the cause of the confusion with damage classes observed in the southern part of the town. Another interesting point is that coherence and amplitude-based analysis provide similar overall accuracy, but some distinctions are to be made. The inclusion of coherence produces a limited improvement in the overall accuracy, which is a result of a substantially better classification of the slightly damaged areas contrasted by worse classification of the two other categories. In other words the coherence appears to be the best contributing feature to distinguish slightly damaged areas Finally, the supervised approach is somehow superior, having the intrinsic possibility to exploit the whole complex radar measurements. The introduction of a decision fusion step even for the unsupervised procedure proposed in this paper would be, as noted above, an interesting research field, while not equally straightforward.

10.4. Conclusions

This work is focused on using multitemporal SAR data for urban damage assessment after a disaster, and shows that a fast statistical analysis, performed at block level using ancillary data, may provide enough information to detect damage patterns. Additional research is required to characterize the damages in a more precise way, even if the methodology looks promising so far.

Future working lines, besides the fusion of amplitude and coherence-based damage evaluation, are aimed at validating the procedure using different data sets and to investigate the possibility to introduce different views in this scheme to reduce the time required for acquiring useful data.

Acknowledgments

The data sets used in this work were provided by MCEER. The authors are grateful to M. Sabbadini and M. Fornaroli for performing the experiments proposed in this paper.

References

1. Allenbach, B., R. Andreoli, S. Battiston, C. Bestault, S. Clandillon, K. Fellah, J.-B. Henry, C. Meyer, H. Scius, N. Tholey, H. Yesou, and P. de Fraiport, 2005, Rapid EO disaster mapping service: added value, feedback and perspectives after 4 years of Charter actions, Proc. of IGARSS05, Seoul, Korea.
2. Costamagna, E., P. Gamba, P. Lombardo, G. Chinino, 2000. Statistical analysis and neuro-fuzzy classification of polarimetric SAR images of

urban areas, Proc. of the ERS/ENVISAT Symposium, Gotheborg, Sweden, unformatted CD-ROM.

3. Gamba, P., F. DellAcqua, G. Trianni, 2006. Rapid damage detection in Bam area using multi-temporal SAR and exploiting ancillary data, IEEE Trans. Geoscience and Remote Sensing, in press.

4. Mansouri, B., Shinozuka, M., Huyck, C. and Houshmand, B. 2005. Earthquake-induced change detection in the 2003 Bam, Iran, earthquake by complex analysis using Envisat ASAR data, Earthquake Spectra, 21(81), pp. 8275-8284, 2005.

5. Matsuoka, M., and F. Yamazaki, 2005. Building damage mapping of the 2003 Bam, Iran, Earthquake using Envisat/ASAR intensity imagery, Earthquake Spectra, 21(81), 8285-8294.

6. Oliver, C., and S. Quegan, S. 1998. Understanding Synthetic Aperture Radar Images, Artech House, Boston.

7. SERTIT 2004. Available on-line at: http://unosat.web.cern.ch/unosat/freeproducts/.

8. Stramondo, S., M. Moro, C. Tolomei, F.R. Cinti and F. Doumaz, 2005. InSAR surface displacement field and fault modeling for the 2003 Bam earthquake (southeastern Iran), Journal of Geodynamics, 40(2-3), 347-353.

9. S. Stramondo A1, C. Bignami A2, M. Chini A3, N. Pierdicca A2, A. Tertulliani, 2006. Satellite radar and optical remote sensing for earthquake damage detection: results from different case studies. International Journal of Remote Sensing, Volume 27, Number 20 / 20 October 2006, pp. 4433-4447.

10. Yonezawa, C., and. S. Takeuchi, 2001. Decorrelation of SAR data by urban damages caused by the 1995 Hyogoken-nambu earthquake, Int. J. Remote Sens., 22(8), 1585-1600.

11. ZKI, Center for Satellite Based Crisis Information. Available online at http://www.zki.caf.dlr.de/.

Chapter 11

Intelligent Surveillance and Pose-invariant 2D Face Classification

Brian C. Lovell[1,2], Conrad Sanderson[1] and Ting Shan[1]

[1]*NICTA, 300 Adelaide St, Brisbane, QLD 4000, Australia and*
[2]*SAS, ITEE, University of Queensland, Brisbane, QLD 4072, Australia*

We describe recent advances in a project being undertaken to trial and develop advanced surveillance systems for public safety. One goal of the project is to trial commercial technologies in public spaces to evaluate their performance. Another is to develop and trial enhanced capabilities that will lead to more effective surveillance systems. A key technology being developed within the group is reliable face in the crowd identification from conventional CCTV cameras. While this is acknowledged to be a challenging problem, we have made considerable progress on several fundamental issues including recognition robust to large pose angles. We also describe a reconfigurable smart camera we are developing to handle the problem of obtaining high resolution face images while simultaneously surveilling large crowds in real-time.

Contents

11.1 Introduction 208
11.2 Methods Based on ASMs and AAMs 212
   11.2.1 Face modeling 212
   11.2.2 Pose estimation 213
   11.2.3 Frontal view synthesis 214
   11.2.4 Direct pose-robust features 215
   11.2.5 Remove pose effect using correlation model 216
   11.2.6 Face recognition using pose-independent features 217
11.3 Methods Based on Bag-of-Features Approach 217
   11.3.1 Feature extraction and illumination normalization 218
   11.3.2 Bag-of-features with direct likelihood evaluation 218
   11.3.3 Bag-of-features with histogram matching 218
11.4 Face Recognition Robust to Pose 219
11.5 NICTA Smart Camera 222
   11.5.1 Proposed smart camera architecture 222
   11.5.2 System design constraints 223
   11.5.3 Hardware specification of NICTA smart camera prototype 224

11.6 Conclusions 225
11.7 Future Work 226
References 227

11.1. Introduction

For isolated crimes such as assault and robbery, it is well-known that video surveillance is highly effective in helping to find and successfully prosecute the perpetrators. Moreover, electronic surveillance has been shown to act as a significant deterrent to crime. Cost is mitigated by recording most of the camera feeds without any human monitoring — if an event is reported to security, the relevant video is manually extracted and reviewed. In recent times the game has changed due to the human and political cost of successful terrorist attacks on soft targets such as mass transport systems. Traditional forensic analysis of recorded video after the event is simply not an adequate response from government and large business. This seachange in the security sector is due to the fact that in the case of suicide attacks there is simply no possibility of prosecution after the event, so simply recording surveillance video provides no terrorism deterrent. Video of successful attacks may indeed add impact to the political message of the perpetrators by highlighting the failure of Western governments to protect their populace. A pressing need is emerging to detect events and persons of interest using video surveillance before such harmful actions can occur. This means that cameras must be monitored at all times. Now the problem is how do we cost-effectively monitor thousands of surveillance cameras to detect the rare events of security interest in real-time.

The problem is that human monitoring of surveillance systems requires a large number of personnel, resulting in high ongoing costs and questionable reliability due to the attention span of humans decreasing rapidly when performing such tedious tasks. A solution may be found in advanced surveillance systems employing computer monitoring of all video feeds, delivering the alerts to human responders for triage. Indeed such systems may assist in maintaining the high level of vigilance required over many years to detect the rare events associated with terrorism — a well-designed computer system is never caught "off guard."

In 2006 NICTA was awarded a research grant to conduct long term trials of advanced ICCTV technologies in important and sensitive public spaces such as major ports and railway stations.[1] One such advanced technology is a system that projects all the CCTV video feeds on to a 3D model of the environment providing rapid situational assessment facilitating a rapid response to situations arising as shown in Figure 11.1. The trial will highlight operational and capability deficiencies in current ICCTV systems and will focus NICTA's research on capability gaps. The project is thus a unique collaboration of researchers, vendors, and user agencies aimed at delivering advances in computer vision and pattern recognition for human activity recognition.

One of the "test-beds" we are using for our advanced surveillance field trials is a railway station in Brisbane (Australia), which provides us with implementation and installation issues that can be expected to arise in similar mass-transport facilities. Capturing the camera feeds in a real-world situation can be problematic, as there must be no disruption in operational capability of existing security systems. The optimal approach would be to simply use IP camera feeds. However, in many existing surveillance systems the cameras are analog and often their streams are fed to relatively old analog or digital recording equipment. Limitations of such systems may include low resolution, recording only a few frames per second, non-uniform time delay between frames, and proprietary codecs. To avoid disruption

Figure 11.1.   Immersive 3-D Visual Presentation of Camera View and 3-D model of the railway platform.

while at the same time obtaining video streams which are more suitable for an intelligent surveillance system, it is useful to tap directly into the analog video feeds and process them via dedicated analog-to-digital video matrix switches.

Apart from the technical challenges, issues in many other domains may also arise. Privacy laws or policies at the national, state, municipal or organizational level may prevent surveillance footage being used for research even if the video is already being used for security monitoring — the primary purpose of the data collection is the main issue here. Moreover, without careful consultation and/or explanation, privacy groups as well as the general public can become uncomfortable with the needs of security research. Some people may simply wish not to be recorded as they have no desire in having photos or videos of themselves being viewable by other people. Plaques and warning signs indicating that surveillance recordings are being gathered for research purposes may allow people to consciously avoid monitored areas, possibly invalidating results.

A key technology being developed within our group for prevention of crime and terrorism is the reliable detection of "persons of interest" through face recognition. While automatic face recognition of cooperative subjects has achieved good results in controlled applications such as passport control, CCTV conditions are considerably more challenging. Examples of real life CCTV conditions captured at the railway station are shown in Figure 11.2.

Nuisance factors such as varying pose, illumination, and expression (PIE) can greatly affect recognition performance. According to Phillips *et al.* head pose is believed to be the hardest factor to model.[2] In mass transport systems, surveillance cameras are often mounted in the ceiling in places such as railway platforms and passenger trains. Since the subjects are generally not posing for the camera, it is rare to obtain a true frontal face image. As it is infeasible to consider remounting all the cameras (in our case more than 6000) to improve face recognition performance, any practical recognition system must have highly effective pose compensation.

A further complication is that in many practical situations there is generally only one frontal gallery image of each person of interest (*e.g.* a passport photograph or a mugshot). In addition to robustness and accuracy, scalability and fast performance are of prime importance for surveillance. A face recognition system should be able to handle large volumes of people (*e.g.* peak hour at a railway station), possibly processing hundreds of video streams. While it is possible to setup elaborate parallel computation machines, there are always cost considerations limiting the number of CPUs available for processing. In this context, a face recognition algorithm should be able to run in real-time or better, which necessarily limits complexity.

Previous approaches to addressing head pose variation include the synthesis of new images at previously unseen views,[3,4] direct synthesis of face model parameters[5] and local feature based representations.[6-8] We note that while true 3D based approaches in theory allow face matching at various poses, current 3D sensing hardware has too many limitations[9] including cost and range. Moreover unlike 2D recognition, 3D technology cannot be retrofitted to existing surveillance systems. Certainly 2D recognition presents much greater technical challenges due to difficulties presented by illumination and shadow effects as was famously noted by the great Leonardo da Vinci (1452-1519):

> After painting comes Sculpture, a very noble art, but one that does not in the execution require the same supreme ingenuity as the art of painting, since in two most important and difficult particulars, in foreshortening and in light and shade, for which the painter has to invent a process, sculpture is helped by nature.

The paper is structured as follows. In section 11.2 we overview the AAM-based face synthesis technique and present the modified form. Then in section 11.3 we overview the local feature approach. Section 11.4 evaluates the performance of several proposed pose robust face recognition techniques on the FERET and PIE databases. In section 11.5 we describe our NICTA smart camera for wide-area surveillance. Finally we draw our conclusions in section 11.6 and then describe future directions for the project in section 11.7.

Figure 11.2.   Examples of typical face pose under surveillance conditions.

11.2. Methods Based on ASMs and AAMs

In this section we describe face modelling based on deformable models popularised by Cootes et al., namely Active Shape Models (ASMs)[10] and Active Appearance Models (AAMs).[11] We first provide a brief description of the two models, followed by pose estimation via a correlation model and finally frontal view synthesis. We also show that the synthesis step can be omitted by directly removing the effect of the pose from the model of the face, resulting in (theoretically) pose independent features.

11.2.1. *Face modeling*

Let us describe a face by a set of N landmark points, where the location of each point is tuple (x, y). A face can hence be represented by a $2N$ dimensional vector:

$$\mathbf{f} = [\, x_1, x_2, \cdots, x_N,\ y_1, y_2, \cdots, y_N \,]^T. \tag{11.1}$$

In ASM, a face shape is represented by:

$$\mathbf{f} = \overline{\mathbf{f}} + \mathbf{P}_s \mathbf{b}_s \tag{11.2}$$

where $\overline{\mathbf{f}}$ is the mean face vector, $\mathbf{P}_s$ is a matrix containing the k eigenvectors with largest eigenvalues (of a training dataset), and $\mathbf{b}_s$ is a weight vector. In a similar manner, the texture variations can be represented by:

$$\mathbf{g} = \overline{\mathbf{g}} + \mathbf{P}_g \mathbf{b}_g \tag{11.3}$$

where $\overline{\mathbf{g}}$ is the mean appearance vector, $\mathbf{P}_g$ is a matrix describing the texture variations learned from training sets, and $\mathbf{b_g}$ is the texture weighting vector.

The shape and appearance parameters $\mathbf{b}_s$ and $\mathbf{b}_g$ can be used to describe the shape and appearance of any face. As there are correlations between the shape and appearance of the same person, let us first represent both aspects as:

$$\mathbf{b} = \begin{bmatrix} \mathbf{W}_s \mathbf{b}_s \\ \mathbf{b}_g \end{bmatrix} = \begin{bmatrix} \mathbf{W}_s \mathbf{P}_s^T (\mathbf{f} - \overline{\mathbf{f}}) \\ \mathbf{P}_g^T (\mathbf{g} - \overline{\mathbf{g}}) \end{bmatrix} \tag{11.4}$$

where $\mathbf{W}_s$ is a diagonal matrix which represents the change between shape and texture. Through Principal Component Analysis (PCA)[12] we can represent **b** as:

$$\mathbf{b} = \mathbf{P}_c \mathbf{c} \tag{11.5}$$

where $\mathbf{P}_c$ are eigenvectors, $\mathbf{c}$ is a vector of appearance parameters controlling both shape and texture of the model, and **b** can be shown to have zero mean. Shape **f** and texture **g** can then be represented by:

$$\mathbf{f} = \bar{\mathbf{f}} + \mathbf{Q}_s \mathbf{c} \tag{11.6}$$
$$\mathbf{g} = \bar{\mathbf{g}} + \mathbf{Q}_g \mathbf{c} \tag{11.7}$$

where

$$\mathbf{Q}_s = \mathbf{P}_s \mathbf{W}_s^{-1} \mathbf{P}_{cs} \tag{11.8}$$
$$\mathbf{Q}_g = \mathbf{P}_g \mathbf{P}_{cg} \tag{11.9}$$

In the above, $\mathbf{Q}_s$ and $\mathbf{Q}_g$ are matrices describing the shape and texture variations, while $\mathbf{P}_{cs}$ and $\mathbf{P}_{cg}$ are shape and texture components of $\mathbf{P}_c$ respectively, i.e.:

$$\mathbf{P}_c = \begin{bmatrix} \mathbf{P}_{cs} \\ \mathbf{P}_{cg} \end{bmatrix}. \tag{11.10}$$

The process of "interpretation" of faces hence entails finding a set of model parameters which code information about the shape, orientation, scale, position, and texture.

11.2.2. *Pose estimation*

Following,[13] let us assume that the model parameter **c** is approximately related to the viewing angle, θ, by a correlation model:

$$\mathbf{c} \approx \mathbf{c}_0 + \mathbf{c}_c \cos(\theta) + \mathbf{c}_s \sin(\theta) \tag{11.11}$$

where $\mathbf{c}_0$, $\mathbf{c}_c$ and $\mathbf{c}_s$ are vectors which are learned from the training data. (Here we consider only head turning. Head nodding can be dealt with in a similar way).

For each face from a training set Ω, indicated by superscript $[i]$ with associated pose $\theta^{[i]}$, we perform an AAM search to find the best fitting model parameters $\mathbf{c}^{[i]}$. The parameters $\mathbf{c}_0$, $\mathbf{c}_c$ and $\mathbf{c}_s$ can be learned via regression from $\left(\mathbf{c}^{[i]}\right)_{i \in 1,\cdots,|\Omega|}$ and $\left([1, \cos(\theta^{[i]}), \sin(\theta^{[i]})]\right)_{i \in 1,\cdots,|\Omega|}$, where $|\Omega|$ indicates the cardinality of Ω.

Given a new face image with parameters $\mathbf{c}^{[new]}$, we can estimate its orientation as follows. We first rearrange $\mathbf{c}^{[new]} = \mathbf{c}_0 + \mathbf{c}_c \cos(\theta^{[new]}) + \mathbf{c}_s \sin(\theta^{[new]})$ to:

$$\mathbf{c}^{[new]} - \mathbf{c}_0 = [\ \mathbf{c}_c\ \mathbf{c}_s\ ] \left[\ \cos(\theta^{[new]})\ \sin(\theta^{[new]})\ \right]^T. \qquad (11.12)$$

Let $\mathbf{R}_c^{-1}$ be the left pseudo-inverse of the matrix $[\ \mathbf{c}_c\ \mathbf{c}_s\ ]$. Eqn. (11.20) can then be rewritten as:

$$\mathbf{R}_c^{-1}\left(\mathbf{c}^{[new]} - \mathbf{c}_0\right) = \left[\ \cos(\theta^{[new]})\ \sin(\theta^{[new]})\ \right]^T. \qquad (11.13)$$

Let $[\ x_\alpha\ y_\alpha\ ] = \mathbf{R}_c^{-1}\left(\mathbf{c}^{[new]} - \mathbf{c}_0\right)$. Then the best estimate of the orientation is $\theta^{[new]} = \tan^{-1}(y_\alpha/x_\alpha)$. Note that the estimation of $\theta^{[new]}$ may not be accurate due to land mark annotation errors or regression learning errors.

11.2.3. *Frontal view synthesis*

After the estimation of $\theta^{[new]}$, we can use the model to synthesize frontal face views. Let $\mathbf{c}_{res}$ be the residual vector which is not explained by the correlation model:

$$\mathbf{c}_{res} = \mathbf{c}^{[new]} - \left(\mathbf{c}_0 + \mathbf{c}_c \cos(\theta^{[new]}) + \mathbf{c}_s \sin(\theta^{[new]})\right) \qquad (11.14)$$

To reconstruct at an alternate angle, $\theta^{[alt]}$, we can add the residual vector to the mean face for that angle:

$$\mathbf{c}^{[alt]} = \mathbf{c}_{res} + \left(\mathbf{c}_0 + \mathbf{c}_c \cos(\theta^{[alt]}) + \mathbf{c}_s \sin(\theta^{[alt]})\right). \qquad (11.15)$$

To synthesize the frontal view face, $\theta^{[alt]}$ is set to zero. Eqn. (11.15) hence simplifies to:

$$\mathbf{c}^{[alt]} = \mathbf{c}_{res} + \mathbf{c}_0 + \mathbf{c}_c. \qquad (11.16)$$

Based on Eqns. (11.6) and (11.7), the shape and texture for the frontal view can then be calculated by:

$$\mathbf{f}^{[alt]} = \overline{\mathbf{f}} + \mathbf{Q}_s \mathbf{c}^{[alt]} \qquad (11.17)$$

$$\mathbf{g}^{[alt]} = \overline{\mathbf{g}} + \mathbf{Q}_g \mathbf{c}^{[alt]}. \qquad (11.18)$$

Examples of synthesized faces are shown in Fig. 11.3. Each synthesized face can then be processed via the standard Principal Component Analysis (PCA) technique to produce features which are used for classification.[4]

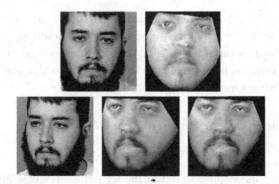

Figure 11.3. Top row: frontal view and its AAM-based synthesized representation. Bottom row: non-frontal view as well as its AAM-based synthesized representation at its original angle and $\theta^{[alt]} = 0$ (*i.e.* synthesized frontal view).

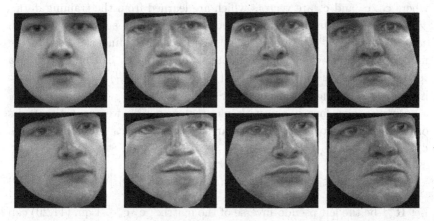

Figure 11.4. *Top row:* frontal mean-face and faces generated by adding person specific pose-independent features. *Bottom row:* mean-face at $+20^o$ and faces generated by adding person specific pose-independent features.

11.2.4. *Direct pose-robust features*

The bracketed term in Eqn. (11.14) can be interpreted as the mean face for angle $\theta^{[new]}$. The difference between $\mathbf{c}^{[new]}$ (which represents the given face at the estimated angle $\theta^{[new]}$) and the bracketed term can hence be interpreted as removing the effect of the angle, resulting in a (theoretically) pose independent representation. As such, $\mathbf{c}_{res}$ can be used directly for classification, providing considerable computational savings — the process of face synthesis and PCA feature extraction is omitted. Because of this, we're avoiding the introduction of imaging artefacts (due to synthesis) and information loss caused by PCA-based feature extraction. As such, the pose-robust features should represent the faces more accurately, leading to better discrimination performance. We shall refer to this approach as the *pose-robust features* method.

11.2.5. *Remove pose effect using correlation model*

11.2.5.1. *Correlation model and pose estimation*

Following,[13] let us assume that the model parameter $\mathbf{c}$ is approximately related to the viewing angle, θ, by a correlation model:

$$\mathbf{c} \approx \mathbf{c}_0 + \mathbf{c}_c \cos(\theta) + \mathbf{c}_s \sin(\theta) \tag{11.19}$$

where $\mathbf{c}_0$, $\mathbf{c}_c$ and $\mathbf{c}_s$ are vectors which are learned from the training data.

For each face from a training set Ω, indicated by superscript $[i]$ with associated pose $\theta^{[i]}$, we perform an AAM search to find the best fitting model parameters $\mathbf{c}^{[i]}$. The parameters $\mathbf{c}_0$, $\mathbf{c}_c$ and $\mathbf{c}_s$ can be learned via regression from $\left(\mathbf{c}^{[i]}\right)_{i \in 1, \cdots, |\Omega|}$ and $\left([1, \cos(\theta^{[i]}), \sin(\theta^{[i]})]\right)_{i \in 1, \cdots, |\Omega|}$, where $|\Omega|$ indicates the cardinality of Ω.

Given a new face image with parameters $\mathbf{c}^{[new]}$, we can estimate its orientation as follows. We first rearrange $\mathbf{c}^{[new]} = \mathbf{c}_0 + \mathbf{c}_c \cos(\theta^{[new]}) + \mathbf{c}_s \sin(\theta^{[new]})$ to:

$$\mathbf{c}^{[new]} - \mathbf{c}_0 = [\,\mathbf{c}_c\ \mathbf{c}_s\,] \left[\,\cos(\theta^{[new]})\ \sin(\theta^{[new]})\,\right]^T \tag{11.20}$$

Let $\mathbf{R}_c^{-1}$ be the left pseudo-inverse of the matrix $[\,\mathbf{c}_c\ \mathbf{c}_s\,]$. Eqn. (11.20) can then be rewritten as:

$$\mathbf{R}_c^{-1}\left(\mathbf{c}^{[new]} - \mathbf{c}_0\right) = \left[\,\cos(\theta^{[new]})\ \sin(\theta^{[new]})\,\right]^T \tag{11.21}$$

Let $[\,x_\alpha\ y_\alpha\,] = \mathbf{R}_c^{-1}\left(\mathbf{c}^{[new]} - \mathbf{c}_0\right)$, then the best estimate of the orientation is $\theta^{[new]} = \tan^{-1}\left(y_\alpha/x_\alpha\right)$.

11.2.5.2. *Removing pose effect in appearance*

After the estimation of $\theta^{[new]}$, we can use the correlation model to remove the effect of pose. Now

$$\mathbf{c}^{[new]} = \mathbf{c}_0 + \mathbf{c}_c \cos(\theta^{[new]}) + \mathbf{c}_s \sin(\theta^{[new]})$$

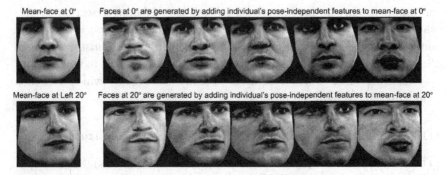

Figure 11.5. Faces generated by adding individual's pose-independent features to mean-face.

represents the standard parameter vector at pose θ, note that it's fixed at specific angle θ and changes when pose changes. Let $\mathbf{c}_{feature}$ be the feature vector which is generated by removing the pose effect from the correlation model: Note that the bracketed term in (11.14) can be interpreted as the mean face for angle $\theta^{[new]}$. Given any face image, we can use Active Appearance Models (AAMs) to estimate face model parameters $\mathbf{c}$ and use the correlation model as described above to remove pose effect. Each face image then can be characterized by $\mathbf{c}_{feature}$, which is pose-independent. Figure 11.5 shows different face images generated from mean face at certain angle by adding $\mathbf{c}_{feature}$. Note for recognition, there is no need to construct the face image itself.

11.2.6. *Face recognition using pose-independent features*

Both the gallery face images and the given unknown face image can be represented by parameter vector $\mathbf{c}_{feature}$. To recognize a given face image becomes a problem of measuring the similarity between the parameter vector of the given face image and the vectors of the gallery images stored in the database. We applied two well known pattern recognition techniques: Mahalanobis distance and cosine measure for classification.

11.3. Methods Based on Bag-of-Features Approach

In this section we describe two local feature based approaches, with both approaches sharing a block based feature extraction method summarised in section 11.3.1. Both methods use Gaussian Mixture Models (GMMs) to model distributions of features, but they differ in how the GMMs are applied. In the first approach (*direct bag-of-features*, section 11.3.2) the likelihood of a given face belonging to a specific person is calculated directly using that person's model. In the second approach (*histogram-based bag-of-features*, section 11.3.3), a generic model (not specific to any person), representing "face words", is used to build histograms which are then compared for recognition purposes.

11.3.1. *Feature extraction and illumination normalization*

The face is described as a set of feature vectors, $X = \{\mathbf{x}_1, \mathbf{x}_2, \cdots, \mathbf{x}_N\}$, which are obtained by dividing the face into small, uniformly sized, overlapping blocks and decomposing each block[a] via the 2D DCT.[16] Typically the first 15 to 21 DCT coefficients are retained (as they contain the vast majority of discriminatory information), except for the 0-th coefficient which is the most affected by illumination changes.[6]

11.3.2. *Bag-of-features with direct likelihood evaluation*

By assuming the vectors are independent and identically distributed (i.i.d.), the likelihood of X belonging to person i is found with:

$$P(X|\lambda^{[i]}) = \prod_{n=1}^{N} P(\mathbf{x}_n|\lambda^{[i]}) = \prod_{n=1}^{N} \sum_{g=1}^{G} w_g^{[i]} \mathcal{N}\left(\mathbf{x}_n|\mu_g^{[i]}, \Sigma_g^{[i]}\right) \qquad (11.22)$$

where
$\mathcal{N}(\mathbf{x}|\mu, \Sigma) = (2\pi)^{-\frac{d}{2}} |\Sigma|^{-\frac{1}{2}} \exp\left\{-\frac{1}{2}(\mathbf{x} - \mu)^T \Sigma^{-1} (\mathbf{x} - \mu)\right\}$ is a multi-variate Gaussian function,[12] while $\lambda^{[i]} = \{w_g^{[i]}, \mu_g^{[i]}, \Sigma_g^{[i]}\}_{g=1}^{G}$ is the set of parameters for person i. The convex combination of Gaussians, with mixing coefficients w_g, is typically referred to as a Gaussian Mixture Model (GMM). Its parameters are optimised via the Expectation Maximisation algorithm.[12]

11.3.3. *Bag-of-features with histogram matching*

The technique presented in this section is an adaption of the "visual words" method used in image categorisation.[17–19] First, a training set of faces is used to build a generic model (not specific to any person). This generic model represents a dictionary of "face words" — the mean of each Gaussian can be thought of as a particular "face word". Once a set of feature vectors

---

[a]While in this work we used the 2D DCT for describing each block (or patch), it is possible to use other descriptors, for example SIFT[14] or Gabor wavelets.[15]

for a given face is obtained, a probabilistic histogram of the occurrences of the "face words" is built:

$$\vec{h}_X = \frac{1}{N} \left[\sum_{i=1}^{N} \frac{w_1 p_1 (\vec{x}_i)}{\sum_{g=1}^{G} w_g p_g (\vec{x}_i)}, \sum_{i=1}^{N} \frac{w_2 p_2 (\vec{x}_i)}{\sum_{g=1}^{G} w_g p_g (\vec{x}_i)}, \cdots, \sum_{i=1}^{N} \frac{w_G p_G (\vec{x}_i)}{\sum_{g=1}^{G} w_g p_g (\vec{x}_i)} \right]$$

where w_g is the weight for Gaussian g and $p_g (x)$ is the probability of vector x according to Gaussian g.

Comparison of two faces is then accomplished by comparing their corresponding histograms. This can be done by the so-called χ^2 distance metric,[20] or the simpler approach of summation of absolute differences:[21]

$$d(h_A, h_B) = \sum_{g=1}^{G} \left| h_A^{[g]} - h_B^{[g]} \right| \tag{11.23}$$

where $h_A^{[g]}$ is the g-th element of h_A. As preliminary experiments suggested that there was little difference in performance between the two metrics, we've elected to use the latter one.

11.4. Face Recognition Robust to Pose

These pose robust face recognition algorithms were first proposed and compared in Sanderson, Shan, and Lovell (2007) .[22] The methods we compare are 1) baseline PCA or "eigenfaces" 2) Synthesis + PCA, where we synthesise frontal views from high pose angle views using deformable models popularised by Cootes *et al.* namely Active Shape Models (ASMs)[10] and Active Appearance Models (AAMs),[11] 3) Pose-robust features based on a modification of the previous method which avoids the synthesis step, 4) Direct bag of features based on GMMs, and 5) Histogram bag of features which is a faster and more scalable version of the previous method.

We are currently in the process of creating a suitable dataset for face classification in CCTV conditions. As such, in these experiments we instead used subsets of the PIE dataset[23] (using faces at -22.5°, 0° and $+22.5^\circ$) as well as the FERET dataset[24] (using faces at -25°, -15°, 0°, $+15^\circ$ and $+25^\circ$).

To train the AAM based approach, we first pooled face images from 40 FERET individuals at -15°, 0°, $+15^\circ$. Each face image was labelled with 58 points around the salient features (the eyes, mouth, nose, eyebrows and chin). The resulting model was used to automatically find the facial features (via an AAM search) for the remainder of the FERET subset. A new dataset was formed, consisting of 305 images from 61 persons with successful AAM search results. This dataset was used to train the correlation model and evaluate the performances of all presented algorithms. In a similar manner, a new dataset was formed from the PIE subset, consisting of images for 53 persons.

For the synthesis based approach, the last stage (PCA based feature extraction from synthesized images) produced 36 dimensional vectors. The PCA subsystem was trained as per.[4] The pose-robust features approach produced 43 dimensional vectors for each face. For both of the AAM-based techniques, Mahalanobis distance was used for classification.[12]

For the bag-of-features approaches, in a similar manner to,[5] we used face images with a size of 64×64 pixels, blocks with a size of 8×8 pixels and an overlap of 6 pixels. This resulted in 784 feature vectors per face. The number of retained DCT coefficients was set to 15 (resulting in 14 dimensional feature vectors, as the 0-th coefficient was discarded). The faces were normalised in size so that the distance between the eyes was 32 pixels and the eyes were in approximately the same positions in all images.

For the direct bag-of-features approach, the number of Gaussians per model was set to 32. Preliminary experiments indicated that accuracy for faces at around 25° peaked at 32 Gaussians, while using more than 32 Gaussians provided little gain in accuracy at the expense of longer processing times.

For the histogram-based bag-of-features method, the number of Gaussians for the generic model was set to 1024, following the same reasoning as above. The generic model (representing "face words") was trained on FERET "ba" data (frontal faces), excluding the 61 persons described earlier.

Tables 11.1 and 11.2 show the recognition rates on the FERET and PIE datasets, respectively. The AAM-derived pose-robust features approach obtains performance which is considerably better than the circuitous approach based on image synthesis. However, the two bag-of-features

Table 11.1.   Recognition performance on the FERET pose subset.

Method	Pose			
	−25°	**−15°**	**+15°**	**+25°**
PCA	23.0	54.0	49.0	36.0
Synthesis + PCA	50.0	71.0	67.4	42.0
pose-robust features	**85.6**	88.2	88.1	66.8
Direct bag-of-features	83.6	93.4	**100.0**	72.1
Histogram bag-of-features	83.6	**100.0**	96.7	**73.7**

Table 11.2.   Recognition performance on PIE.

Method	Pose	
	−22.5°	**+22.5°**
PCA	13.0	8.0
Synthesis + PCA	60.0	56.0
pose-robust features	83.3	80.6
Direct bag-of-features	**100.0**	90.6
Histogram bag-of-features	**100.0**	**100.0**

Table 11.3.   Average time taken for two stages of processing: (1) conversion of a probe face from image to format used for matching (one-off cost per probe face), (2) comparison of one probe face with one gallery face, after conversion.

Method	Approximate time taken (sec)	
	One-off cost per probe face	Comparison of one probe face with one gallery face
Synthesis + PCA	1.493	< 0.001
pose-robust features	0.978	< 0.001
Direct bag-of-features	0.006	0.006
Histogram bag-of-features	0.141	< 0.001

methods generally obtain better performance on both FERET and PIE, with the histogram-based approach obtaining the best overall performance. Averaging across the high pose angles ($\pm25°$ on FERET and $\pm22.5°$ on PIE), the histogram-based method achieves an average accuracy of 89%.

Table 11.3 shows the time taken to classify one probe face by the presented techniques (except for PCA). The experiments were performed on a Pentium-M machine running at 1.5 GHz. All methods were implemented in C++. The time taken is divided into two components: (1) one-off cost per probe face, and (2) comparison of one probe face with one gallery face.

The one-off cost is the time required to convert a given face into a format which will be used for matching. For the synthesis approach this involves an AAM search, image synthesis and PCA based feature extraction. For the pose-robust features method, in contrast, this effectively involves only an AAM search. For the bag-of-features approaches, the one-off cost is the 2D DCT feature extraction, with the histogram-based approach additionally requiring the generation of the "face words" histogram.

The second component, for the case of the direct bag-of-features method, involves calculating the likelihood using (11.22), while for the histogram-based approach this involves just the sum of absolute differences between two histograms (Eqn. (11.23)). For the two AAM-based methods, the second component is the time taken to evaluate the Mahalanobis distance.

As expected, the pose-robust features approach has a speed advantage over the synthesis based approach, being about 50% faster. However, both of the bag-of-features methods are many times faster, in terms of the first component — the histogram-based approach is about 7 times faster than the pose-robust features method. While the one-off cost for the direct bag-of-features approach is much lower than for the histogram-based method, the time required for the second component (comparison of faces after conversion) is considerably higher, and might be a limiting factor when dealing with a large set of gallery faces (i.e. a scalability issue).

When using a fast approximation of the exp() function, the time required by the histogram-based method (in the first component) is reduced by approximately 30% to 0.096, with no loss in recognition accuracy. This makes it over 10 times faster than the pose-robust features method and over 15 times faster than the synthesis based technique. In a similar vein, the time taken by the second component of the direct bag-of-features approach is also reduced by approximately 30%, with no loss in recognition accuracy.

11.5. NICTA Smart Camera

One of the challenges of face recognition in a surveillance environment is to obtain faces of sufficient resolution to allow accurate recognition. To facilitate this goal, we have been developing a smart camera which can surveil crowds while simultaneously extracting high resolution face images.[25,26]

11.5.1. *Proposed smart camera architecture*

Most existing smart camera designs use sensors ranging from 192x124 pixels to 640x480 pixels (VGA standard). In our design, we have decided to tailor the smart camera design to the task of face detection for crowd surveillance. Crowd surveillance usually surveils a wide area and often has multiple objects of interest in view. To classify these objects reliably we need high resolution images. However most of the scene is of little interest for automated analysis and can thus be acquired at much lower resolution. Our camera is designed to extract the objects of interest, in this case faces, at full sensor resolution while simultaneously obtaining a much lower resolution video of the entire scene. Figure 11.6 shows an example

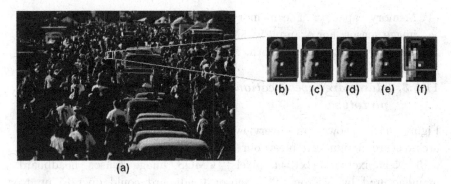

Figure 11.6.   Overall scene (a) ROI extracted from scene with resolution of 7Mp(b), 5Mp(c), 3Mp(d), 1Mp(e) and VGA(f).

of how obtaining such high resolution images affects the accuracy of face detection performance.

In the example, the region of interest (ROI) is extracted from an image of a crowd of people (a). The face (b) extracted from a 7 MP (MegaPixel) high resolution image is much more recognizable than (f) extracted from the lower resolution (VGA) image. The extracted faces were also tested for suitability for automatic detection using a Viola-Jones face detection module. The images (c), (d) and (e) taken with 5, 3, and 1MP sensors were suitable for face detection. However, face cannot be correctly detected in the VGA image (f) because the image does not have enough details for the face detection module to work correctly.

11.5.2. *System design constraints*

There are several constraints that we have taken into consideration in designing our smart camera the main ones being:

(1) Real-time constraint: Meeting real-time constraint is an important issue since our smart camera targeted application in the surveillance area with real-time response requirement.
(2) Hardware resources: In our smart camera design, we have chosen the Spartan FPGA-based series. A Spartan FPGA is a low cost version of the high performance Virtex family. Hence, the Spartan series has reduced hardware resources.
(3) Bandwidth constraint: Higher resolution image would require higher data transfer rate. In our current design, our smart camera has a limited communication bandwidth to a host PC of 800Mbps.

(4) Memory capacity: The memory storage is highly dependable on the image sensor. For example, a 5Mp image sensor has a total raw pixels value of 5Mp times Bit depth.

11.5.3. Hardware specification of NICTA smart camera prototype

Figure 11.7 shows an overview of our proposed smart camera architecture design. To meet our design requirement, we have chosen a 5 Megapixel (2592x1944 pixels) CMOS image sensor headboard manufactured by Micron. This sensor headboard could operate up to 14fps (frame-per-second) at full resolution. The main reasons to choose the CMOS image sensor are because unlike CCD image sensor, CMOS image sensor has parallel data access for faster data manipulation, low power consumption and the on-chip functionality. The main board of our smart camera has a Spartan-3 series FPGA chip (XS3C5000). For this project, Spartan FPGA is chosen as the processing target device primarily because of its low cost and low power consumption. The main board also has a DDR SDRAM slot. To ensure that our smart camera system could handle the high data rates (from the high resolution image sensor), we have installed a 1GB DDR SDRAM as the main frame buffer of the camera. As for the camera communication interface to the host PC, we have decided to use a FireWire 800 (1394b) communication protocol. A FireWire board that consists of Texas Instrument's 1394b Link Layer and Physical Layer controller chips and 3 FireWire 800 ports is used in our design. All three boards were interfaced together and powered using a custom-designed PCB board (interface board).

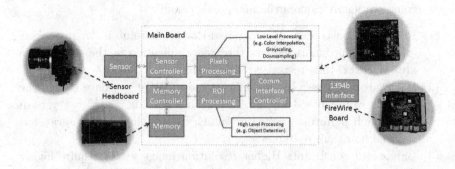

Figure 11.7.   Smart camera system architecture.

Figure 11.8 shows a picture of our smart camera prototype and Table 11.4 summarises the basic specification of our prototype.

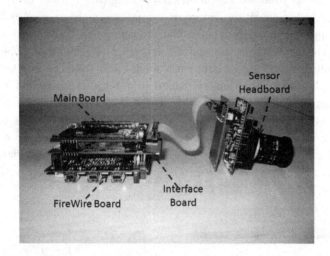

Figure 11.8.   NICTA smart camera prototype.

Table 11.4.   NICTA smart camera specification.

Parameter	Value)
Sensor Type	CMOS
Resolution	2592 x 1944
Processing Element	Spartan-3 FPGA
Comm. Interface	FireWire800
Physical Dimension	90 x 90 x 150 mm^3

11.6. Conclusions

In this paper we have described our advanced surveillance project and the need for computer based monitoring of CCTV video feeds. Next we described recent advances in robust face recognition primarily addressing the issue of pose compensation. We acknowledge that apart from pose variations, imperfect face localisation[27] is also an important issue in a real life surveillance system. Imperfect localisations result in translations as well as scale changes, which adversely affect recognition performance. Finally we described our reconfigurable smart camera project designed to deliver high quality face images from crowd scenes.

11.7. Future Work

In 2008 and beyond we are additionally targeting critical infrastructure protection in the maritime environment as illustrated in Figure 11.9. We will be applying intelligent surveillance techniques to address terrorism concerns through identity recognition as well as the day to day operational issues such as monitoring traffic on the land and ships in the 100km long shipping channel. Note that surveillance systems are installed primarily to address commercial concerns such as theft, property damage, and liability issues. They are typically not installed to address the very rare events associated with terrorism. So a system designed for enhanced counter-terrorism capabilities must also be operationally more efficient than a conventional surveillance system to justify the enormous cost of system upgrading.

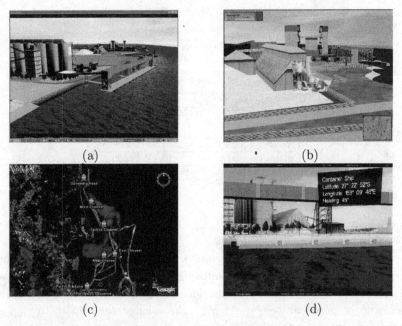

(a)

(b)

(c)

(d)

Figure 11.9. Images from port project: (a) Grain handling facilities (b) surveillance video of real fire projected on model of port (c) over 100 km of channel to protect (d) shipping labeled and positioned in the port model using AIS data feeds.

Ships currently use the Automatic Identification System (AIS) which provides a means for them to electronically exchange ship data including: identification, position, course, and speed, with other nearby ships and ports. The new project will require the integration of surveillance cameras with all other relevant information such as AIS data, harbour marine radar, weather stations, and possibly even CBR (Chemical, Biological, Radiation) wireless sensor networks. This will provide an integrated information system for the port which will lead to greater operational efficiency, less lost time, and faster recovery due to better management of incidents.

Acknowledgments

This project is supported by a grant from the Australian Government Department of the Prime Minister and Cabinet and by the Australian Research Council through the Research Network for Securing Australia. NICTA is funded by the Australian Government's *Backing Australia's Ability* initiative, in part through the Australian Research Council. The author thanks Abbas Bigdeli, Shaokang Chen, Amelia Azman, Yasir Mustafah, and Erik Berglund for their major contributions to this work.

References

1. A. Bigdeli, B. Lovell, and C. Sanderson. Vision processing in intelligent cctv for mass transport security. In *Proc. of SAFE 2007: Workshop on Signal Processing Applications for Public Security and Forensics*, (2007).
2. P. Phillips, P. Grother, R. Micheals, D. Blackburn, E. Tabassi, and M. Bone. Face recognition vendor test 2002. In *Proc. Analysis and Modeling of Faces and Gestures*, p. 44, (2003).
3. V. Blanz, P. Grother, P. Phillips, and T. Vetter. Face recognition based on frontal views generated from non-frontal images. In *Proc. IEEE Int. Conf. Computer Vision and Pattern Recognition*, vol. 2, pp. 454–461, (2005).
4. T. Shan, B. Lovell, and S. Chen. Face recognition robust to head pose from one sample image. In *Proc. 18th Int. Conf. Pattern Recognition (ICPR)*, vol. 1, pp. 515–518, (2006).
5. C. Sanderson, S. Bengio, and Y. Gao, On transforming statistical models for non-frontal face verification, *Pattern Recognition.* **39**(2), 288–302, (2006).
6. F. Cardinaux, C. Sanderson, and S. Bengio, User authentication via adapted statistical models of face images, *IEEE Trans. Signal Processing.* **54**(1), 361–373, (2006).
7. S. Lucey and T. Chen. Learning patch dependencies for improved pose mismatched face verification. In *IEEE Conf. Computer Vision and Pattern Recognition*, vol. 1, pp. 909–915, (2006).

8. L. Wiskott, J. Fellous, N. Kuiger, and C. V. Malsburg, Face recognition by elastic bunch graph matching, *IEEE Trans. Pattern Analysis and Machine Intelligence.* **19**(7), 775–779, (1997).

9. K. Bowyer, K. Chang, and P. Flynn., A survey of approaches and challenges in 3D and multi-modal 3D+2D face recognition., *Computer Vision and Image Understanding.* **101**(1), 1–15, (2006).

10. T. Cootes and C. Taylor. Active shape models - 'smart snakes'. In *Proc. British Machine Vision Conference*, pp. 267–275, (1992).

11. T. Cootes, G. Edwards, and C. Taylor, Active appearance models, *IEEE Trans. Pattern Analysis and Machine Intelligence.* **23**(6), 681–685, (2001).

12. R. Duda, P. Hart, and D. Stork, *Pattern Classification.* (Wiley, 2001), 2nd edition.

13. T. Cootes, K. Walker, and C. Taylor. View-based active appearance models. In *Proc. 4th IEEE International Conference on Automatic Face and Gesture Recognition*, pp. 227–232, (2000).

14. D. G. Lowe, Distinctive image features from scale-invariant keypoints, *International Journal of Computer Vision.* **60**(2), 91–110, (2004).

15. T. S. Lee, Image representation using 2D Gabor wavelets, *IEEE Trans. Pattern Analysis and Machine Intelligence.* **18**(10), 959–971, (1996).

16. R. Gonzales and R. Woods, *Digital Image Processing.* (Addison-Wesley, 1992).

17. G. Csurka, C. Dance, L. Fan, J. Willamowski, and C. Bray. Visual cetegorization with bags of keypoints. In *Workshop on Statistical Learning in Computer Vision (in conjunction with ECCV'04)*, (2004).

18. J. Sivic and A. Zisserman. Video google: A text retrieval approach to object matching in videos. In *Proc. 9th International Conference on Computer Vision (ICCV)*, vol. 2, pp. 1470–1477, (2003).

19. E. Nowak, F. Jurie, and B. Triggs. Sampling strategies for bag-of-features image classification. In *European Conference on Computer Vision (ECCV), Part IV, Lecture Notes in Computer Science (LNCS)*, vol. 3954, pp. 490–503, (2006).

20. C. Wallraven, B. Caputo, and A. Graf. Recognition with local features: the kernel recipe. In *Proc. 9th International Conference on Computer Vision (ICCV)*, vol. 1, pp. 257–264, (2003).

21. T. Kadir and M. Brady, Saliency, scale and image description, *International Journal of Computer Vision.* **45**(2), 83–105, (2001).

22. C. Sanderson, T. Shan, and B. Lovell. Towards pose-invariant 2d face classification for surveillance. In *Third IEEE International Workshop on Analysis and Modelling of Faces and Gestures at ICCV2007*, (2007).

23. T. Sim, S. Baker, and M. Bsat, The CMU pose, illumination, and expression database, *IEEE. Trans. Pattern Analysis and Machine Intelligence.* **25**(12), 1615–1618, (2003).

24. P. Phillips, H. Moon, S. Rizvi, and P. Rauss, The FERET evaluation methodology for face-recognition algorithms, *IEEE Trans. Pattern Analysis and Machine Intelligence.* **22**(10), 1090–1104, (2000).

25. A. Azman, Y. M. Mustafah, A. Bigdeli, and B. Lovell. Optimizing resources of an fpga-based smart camera architecture. In *Proc. of Digital Image Computing: Techniques and Applications*, pp. 600–606, (2007).

26. Y. M. Mustafah, T. Shan, A. W. Azman, A. Bigdeli, and B. Lovell. Real-time face detection and tracking for high resolution smart camera system. In *Proc. of Digital Image Computing: Techniques and Applications*, pp. 387–393, (2007).

27. Y. Rodriguez, F. Cardinaux, S. Bengio, and J. Mariethoz, Measuring the performance of face localization systems, *Image and Vision Computing*. **24**, 882–893, (2006).

Chapter 12

Simple Machine Learning Approaches to Safety-related Systems

Christian Moewes[*], Clemens Otte[†] and Rudolf Kruse[‡]

[*,‡]*Dpt. of Knowledge and Language Engineering, University of Magdeburg, Germany*
[†]*Siemens AG, Corporate Technology, Otto-Hahn-Ring 6, 81739 Munich, Germany*

The principles of machine learning become gradually more interesting to safety-related applications. This paper introduces a preprocessing method for such kind of applications. Here we concentrate on scenarios with highly unbalanced misclassification costs. Therefore we briefly introduce a variation of multiple-instance learning (MIL) and recall soft margin hyperplane classifiers. According to this classifier we present a training set selection method for multidimensional problems that combines the idea of support vector pruning with pattern weighting. The proposed method guarantees both high performance and interpretable decisions. The main advantage of our proposed filter method is the obtained training set that rather prefers quasilinear classifiers during model selection. We conclude with potential extensions for future research in this domain.

Contents

12.1 Introduction 232
    12.1.1 Multiple-instance problem 233
    12.1.2 Safety-related applications 233
    12.1.3 Outline of this chapter 235
12.2 Separating Hyperplanes 235
    12.2.1 Linear hyperplane classifiers 235
    12.2.2 Soft margin hyperplanes 237
    12.2.3 Support vector machines 238

[*]mailto:cmoewes@ovgu.de
[†]mailto:clemens.otte@siemens.com
[‡]mailto:kruse@iws.cs.uni-magdeburg.de

12.3 Creating Prerequisites for Simple Models 239
    12.3.1 Simplicity of support vector machines 240
    12.3.2 Support vector pruning 242
    12.3.3 Bag weighting 245
    12.3.4 Combination of both methods 246
12.4 Conclusions 246
References 247

12.1. Introduction

Safety-related systems can be found in manifold fields where a failure may lead to fatalities or severe injuries to human beings, loss or very bad damage of equipment, or environmental harm.[20] The usage of machine learning methods, e.g. for condition monitoring of plants, is not that straightforward compared to other applications where learning machines have been applied very successfully.

Main differences to other classification domains are highly unbalanced classification costs, the infrequency of positive events, e.g. trigger events or alarms. We try to compare this domain with an existing field of machine learning named multiple-instance (MI) learning of which problems partly resemble safety-related applications.

MI problems were first introduced to the machine learning community as supervised learning problems by Dietterich *et al.*[12] In contrast to single-instance supervised learning where one given example is represented by one feature vector (so-called instance), dealing with MI problems an example is a set of feature vectors. Therefore this setting of the learning problem is called *multiple-instance learning* problem. A set of multiple instances is called *bag*.

Concerning the circumstances of pattern recognition with two class labels $\{+1, -1\}$, a bag is positive if at least one of its instances is positive. It is negative if all of its instances are negative. This is called the *MI assumption* as it can be found in Xu.[25]

This assumption is too general for safety-related applications where the final model must be highly interpretable. Therefore we will tighten the MI assumptions in order to have a MIL framework for the present domain. Before we introduce our assumption and a possible approach to tackle safety-related problems, we will briefly recall the setting of MI problems and safety-related applications.

12.1.1. *Multiple-instance problem*

In multiple-instance problems, one single training example (a positive or negative bag) is constituted by many different feature vectors, so-called *instances*. At least one has to be responsible for the observed class of the given example if we follow the MI assumption. Thus the class label is attached to the bag instead of the instances themselves.

Let us denote positive bags as B_i^+ and the jth observation of this bag as $x_{ij}^+ \in \mathbb{R}^p$ where p is the dimensionality of input space. The bag B_i^+ consists of n_i^+ instances x_{ij}^+ for $j = 1, \ldots, n_i^+$. Consequently, the ith negative bag is denoted by B_i^-, its jth observation by x_{ij}^-. Likewise, n_i^- symbolizes the number of instances in this negative bag. We denote the number of positive and negative bags as l^+ and l^-. The overall number of instances is referred to $n = n^+ + n^- = \sum_{i=0}^{l^+} n_i^+ + \sum_{i=0}^{l^-} n_i^-$. Thus the sample of all instances in negative and positive bags is listed by $x_1, \ldots, x_n$.

Nowadays many learning problems have been treated as MI problems, e.g. drug activity prediction,[12,16] stock market prediction,[17] image retrieval,[26,27] natural scene classification,[17] text categorization,[2] and image categorization.[10] With the application to safety-related domains, another type of problem is identified as MI formulation under certain requirements.

Before we come up with a specialized MI assumption in the present domain, let us assume that there exists a certain class label for every instance. This is another main difference to the standard MI assumption where only single bags are labeled and instances are ambiguous. We can simplify the setting of MIL since we have this information in most safety-related systems.

12.1.2. *Safety-related applications*

Safety-related applications can be found in many real-world problems, e.g. condition monitoring of plants, automobiles, airplanes or trains. In our approach we focus on applications that can be considered as binary classification problems on multivariate time series. Every time series itself describes one certain event of multiple instances. Regarding the problem of MIL, we can thus state that every event (i.e. a time series) either belongs to the positive or negative class. One example may be the learning of the deployment decision for an airbag in the automobile industry where the positive class would consist of (crash) events requiring a deployment.

Due to the high imbalance of safety-related problems, no instance in time of a negative bag must be classified as positive. A false positive in such applications usually involves severe injuries or harm to humans or machines. On the other hand, all positive events or bags have to be correctly classified before a certain limiting time has passed. If a positive event is recognized early enough, then certain countermeasures can be performed to prevent or moderate heavy accidents. These requirements meet the MIL setting.

Since tests of such complex systems are very expensive and thus quite rare, there does not exist a vast of data (especially positive events). Hence a main disadvantage in those domains is the fact that formal proofs of the correctness of the learned classifier are not feasible.[20] Therefore the model has to be enriched by experts' knowledge in order to ensure security requirements, namely a high degree of interpretability. Furthermore, we can usually find unbalanced misclassification costs in safety-related domains such that constraints to handle them have to be added to the model as well.

Usually it is not trivial to find the best trade-off between accuracy and interpretability since their separate optimization normally excludes the other one. This challenge is called *bias-variance dilemma*.[14] In safety-related applications, the interpretability in terms of simple functional dependencies is very often the most important point.

Smooth functions with a good generalization performance have to be found to establish a physical interpretation of human experts. We will call these functions quasilinear as linearity is the simplest dependency between variables. The more complex a relation between input and output, the less accepted it will be. Hence we clearly prefer simpler models to more complex ones.

Moreover we assume that there exists a fairly simple classifier that distinguishes positive from negative bags in a quite accurate way. This comes from the fact that data generated by a safety-related system is drawn from an unknown but physical process that has to be understood. If the geometrical distances between positive and negative bags does not exceed a certain threshold for at least some instances, then we cannot expect our model to find a discriminant function that is easy to understand. This basically specializes the former MI assumption such that arbitrarily complicated classifiers are not preferred during model selection any longer.

A support vector machine (SVM) implicitly tries to find such a compromise between interpretability and accuracy. Taking advantages of the SVM's flexibility, one can incorporate knowledge to meet unbalanced misclassification costs as third objective as well. SV machines will be introduced as extension of separating hyperplane classifiers in the following section.

12.1.3. *Outline of this chapter*

The remainder of the chapter is organized as follows. Section 12.2 is dedicated to separating hyperplanes as special type of classifiers. Section 12.3 describes requirements for simple models regarding SV machines. After that, a combination of two methods named SV pruning and bag weighting is proposed in order to obtain a interpretable and accurate classifier. We conclude and discuss potential future work in Sec. 12.4.

12.2. Separating Hyperplanes

The present section is dedicated to techniques and procedures that are applied in the context of the presented studies. Section 12.2.1 defines an important type of learning machines, the linear separating hyperplane, that solve the problem of pattern recognition. In Sec. 12.2.2 a special class of this classifier, the soft margin hyperplane, that is more robust against outliers and noise is specified. This hyperplane classifier which must not classify every pattern correctly is very suitable for our unbalanced problem since it is sufficient to recognize one instance of a positive bags.

The concept of a support vector machine which is based on a separating hyperplane will be elaborated in Sec. 12.2.3. Every SVM enables the mapping of all patterns from the input space into a higher dimensional feature space where the optimal soft margin hyperplane is obtained by solving a convex optimization problem.

12.2.1. *Linear hyperplane classifiers*

Two finite subsets from the training data

$$(y_1, x_1), \ldots, (y_n, x_n), \qquad x \in \mathbb{R}^p, \quad y \in \{\pm 1\}, \qquad (12.1)$$

first subset X_1 for which $y = 1$ and second one X_2 for which $y = -1$, are called separable[23] by the hyperplane $\langle x, \phi \rangle = c$ if there exist both a unit vector ϕ and a constant c such that the inequalities

$$\langle x_k, \phi \rangle > c, \qquad \text{if } x_k \in X_1,$$
$$\langle x_m, \phi \rangle < c, \qquad \text{if } x_m \in X_2 \tag{12.2}$$

hold true where

$$\langle x, x' \rangle \equiv \sum_{d=1}^{p} (x)_d \cdot (x')_d. \tag{12.3}$$

is the scalar product of x and x' and $(x)_d \in \mathbb{R}$ the dth component of x. Since the number of possible hyperplanes is infinite and we are looking for the "best" one, the concept of the optimal hyperplane has to be introduced.[23]

Denote for any unit vector ϕ the values

$$c_1(\phi) = \min_{x_k \in X_1} \langle x_k, \phi \rangle,$$
$$c_2(\phi) = \max_{x_m \in X_2} \langle x_m, \phi \rangle.$$

Assume that the unit vector ϕ_0 maximizes the so-called margin

$$\rho(\phi) = \frac{c_1(\phi) - c_2(\phi)}{2}, \qquad \|\phi\| = 1 \tag{12.4}$$

when the inequalities (12.2) are fulfilled. Thus the vector ϕ_0 and the arithmetic mean of c_1 and c_2 ascertain the so-called *optimal hyperplane*.[15,24] It separates both classes of vectors x correctly and maximizes the margin (12.4). In addition, it can be shown very easily that the optimal hyperplane is unique.

So we are looking for a pair that consists of ψ_0 and a constant b_0 such that the inequalities

$$\langle x_k, \psi_0 \rangle + b_0 \geq +1 \qquad \text{if } y_k = +1,$$
$$\langle x_m, \psi_0 \rangle + b_0 \leq -1 \qquad \text{if } y_m = -1$$

do hold true and the vector ψ_0 must have the smallest vector norm

$$\|\psi_0\|^2 = \langle \psi_0, \psi_0 \rangle. \tag{12.5}$$

It can be shown[23] that the optimal hyperplane characterized by ψ_0 coincides with $\phi_0 = \psi_0 / \|\psi_0\|$. The margin between the optimal hyperplane and the separated training data equals $\rho(\phi_0) = 1/\|\psi_0\|$. Therefore we finally arrive at the following quadratic optimization problem: minimize the quadratic function (12.5) subject to the linear constraints

$$y_k(\langle x_k, \psi_0 \rangle + b_0) \geq 1, \qquad k = 1, \ldots, n. \tag{12.6}$$

Instead of solving this problem in the *primal space* of ϕ and b, one usually considers the *dual space* where the problem is more convenient to solve as Lagrangian

$$L(\psi, b, \alpha) = \frac{1}{2} \langle \psi, \psi \rangle - \sum_{k=1}^{n} \alpha_k \left(y_k(\langle x_k, \psi \rangle + b) - 1 \right),$$

whereas $\alpha = (\alpha_1, \ldots, \alpha_n)$ is the vector of Lagrange multipliers $\alpha_k \geq 0$. The Lagrangian L has to be maximized with respect to α and minimized with respect to ψ and b. Finally, we can reformulate the primal into the so-called dual optimization problem and get the dual

$$W(\alpha) = \sum_{k=1}^{n} \alpha_k - \frac{1}{2} \sum_{k=1}^{n} \sum_{m=1}^{n} y_k y_m \alpha_k \alpha_m \langle x_k, x_m \rangle. \tag{12.7}$$

subject to $a_k \geq 0$, $k = 1, \ldots, n$ and $\sum_{k=1}^{n} y_k \alpha_k = 0$. Denote the optimal solution with ψ_0, b_0 and α_k^0, respectively. Then we can expand the optimal hyperplane with the nonzero weights on support vectors by

$$\psi_0 = \sum_{k=1}^{n} y_k \alpha_k^0 x_k.$$

and the optimal hyperplane has the form

$$f(x, \alpha_0) = \sum_{k=1}^{n} y_k \alpha_k^0 \langle x_k, x \rangle + b_0.$$

12.2.2. *Soft margin hyperplanes*

Given a real-world data set, it might not be possible to find a separating hyperplane. Even if a solution can be found, it might not be the optimal one for these specific data. One single outlier that is labeled incorrectly can have heavy impacts on the hyperplane. Hence a much more tolerant concept is required to handle noisy data up to a certain fraction.

Cortes and Vapnik[11] developed a new type of hyperplane that allows certain samples to violate (12.6). A hyperplane $\langle \psi, x \rangle - b = 0$, $\|\psi\| = 1$ is called Δ-*margin separating hyperplane* if it classifies vectors x by

$$y = \begin{cases} +1 & \text{if } \langle \psi, x \rangle - b \geq \Delta \\ -1 & \text{if } \langle \psi, x \rangle - b \leq \Delta \end{cases}$$

The so-called *slack variables* $\xi_k \geq 0$ are introduced by

$$F(\xi) = \sum_{k=1}^{n} \xi_k \tag{12.8}$$

which is defined in order not to obtain a trivial solution where all slack variables reach huge values. Thus we have to minimize the functional $F(\xi)$ subject to $\langle \psi, \psi \rangle \geq \frac{1}{\Delta^2}$ and the constraints

$$y_k \left(\langle x_k, \psi \rangle - b \right) \geq 1 - \xi_k, \quad k = 1, \ldots, n.$$

Now we can make every ξ_k big enough to meet the constraint on (y_k, x_k). The generalized optimal hyperplane is determined by ψ that minimizes the functional

$$\Phi(\psi, \xi) = \frac{1}{2} \langle \psi, \psi \rangle + C \left(\sum_{k=1}^{n} \xi_k \right) \tag{12.9}$$

subject to (12.8) where C is a parameter that regularizes the strength of the slack variables. By applying the same techniques as above, this leads to the regularizing term (12.7) with respect to

$$\sum_{k=1}^{n} y_k \alpha_k = 0, \qquad 0 \leq \alpha_k \leq C, \qquad k = 1, \ldots, n.$$

12.2.3. *Support vector machines*

The idea of a support vector machine (SVM)[11,23] is based on the principle of structural risk minimization (SRM). Basically, a support vector machine tries to learn a linear decision rule (12.2). Finding the hyperplane that maximizes the margin (12.4), however, an SVM chooses the function out of a set of functions for which the smallest error probability is guaranteed.

Mapping the input vectors x into a higher-dimensional *feature space* $\mathcal{H}$, a nonlinear decision rule can be learned.[4] Then the optimal separating hyperplane is found in the new space. The feature space, however, does not need to be considered explicitly. Moreover, only the inner products between the support vectors x_k of which $\alpha_k \neq 0$ and the input vectors have to be calculated in order to learn nonlinear decision rules. The inner product is carried out by a kernel $K(x, x_k)$ which is a symmetric function that satisfies Mercer's condition.[18]

This leads to the decision function in the input space

$$f(x, \alpha) = \text{sgn} \left(\sum_{k=1, \alpha_k^0 \neq 0}^{n} y_k \alpha_k^0 K(x, x_k) + b \right)$$

which can be obtained by constructing a linear separating hyperplane of which inner product is substituted by the kernel function $K(x, x_k)$ into (12.7), respectively. Different support vector machines can be defined by different kernel functions. Aside the so-called linear kernel (12.3), the following three kernels were successfully used in many real-world applications:

(1) kernels that return polynomials of degree d:

$$K(x, x') = (\langle x, x' \rangle + 1)^d.$$

(2) kernels generating radial basis functions:

$$K(x, x') = K(\|x - x'\|),$$

for example

$$K(\|x - x'\|) = \exp\left(-\gamma \|x - x'\|^2\right). \tag{12.10}$$

(3) kernels that generate two-layer neural networks:

$$K(x, x') = S(v \langle x, x' \rangle + c)$$

where $S(\cdot)$ is an sigmoid function, e.g. $\tanh(\cdot)$ or $\frac{1}{1+\exp(\cdot)}$.

12.3. Creating Prerequisites for Simple Models

In this section we elucidate a robust method to select a training set which will prefer a simple classifier in the model selection step. The training set selection is based on a combination of two methods.[19] Concerning safety-related systems, requirements for a classifier that has to solve a real-world problem in the present domain are very restrictive. Two important requirements are underlined in the next paragraphs.

At any point of time, *the model in a safety-related system shall be transparent.* This fact enables a very high degree of interpretability, especially when false positive/negative decisions have to be analyzed. The correctness of every decision can then be approved by human experts.

For instance, a fuzzy-rule based decision can be expressed by natural language easily. Its sequence of commands for the decision-making can simply be understood by humans. On the contrary, black box classifier like artificial neural networks do not offer many insights into neither the learning process nor the decision. Unfortunately the acceptance of an SVM is similar to an ANN due to their missing transparency. The vast number of support vectors and the similarity measure of the used kernel function in a high-dimensional space is not traceable for human beings. This might explain why the usage of the SV method is unpopular for safety-related systems.

The second requirement can be formulated as follows. *The model shall be rather simple than complex.* Complex models might suffer from overfitting[3] which is fatal for unseen bags that are not located around the given data for training and testing. Tests of safety-related systems are usually normed and take place in standardized environments. It is understood that not all different conditions of complex systems can be performed since their procedure is very often expensive. Complex models that separately cover nearly all positive and negative bags might cause non-interpretable decisions in an unknown situation. As a consequence, simple and flexible models do not suffer from this kind of overfitting.

12.3.1. *Simplicity of support vector machines*

With respect to the SVM principle as introduced in Sec. 12.2.3, simplicity of an SV machine can be expressed by the capacity of the function chosen by the principle of SRM. This principle of minimizing the expected risk controls the capacity such that the chosen hyperplane will guarantee the lowest error on unseen patterns. Thus it heavily influences the complexity of the SVM.

Problems that are hard to classify will lead to a rather high fraction of support vectors with big weights α_k close to the constant $C > 0$. The sum of all positive (or negative) weights α_k and the number of support vectors are reasonable measures for simplicity of an SVM. The more complex the discriminant function has to be, the more support vectors are needed.

The classification problem we deal with does not demand to correctly classify all positive instances. A positive bag will be correctly discriminated by only one of its instances (or two instances to have more confidence). On the contrary, all instances of negative bags have to be correctly recognized.

Thence a pruning of positive examples that are hard to classify before the actual training might be a striking idea to simplify the decision function. The actual discrimination function will be then selected by any suitable binary classifier, e.g. an SVM. An approach to prune the "worst" positive examples is introduced in Sec. 12.3.2.

Another measure of simplicity is motivated as follows. A priori, the user has to define an appropriate kernel function for the given learning problem.

The linear kernel (12.3) will force the SVM to find a linear separating hyperplane in the input space. Hence the decision boundary will be linear and easy to interpret. Other, more complex kernels (cf. Sec. 12.2.3) enable the SV machine to choose more sophisticated decision boundaries in order to solve the problem linear in a very high-dimensional feature space.

So the following question arises: How can we determine the "linearity" of nonlinear kernels e.g., Gaussian kernels (12.10)? Schölkopf and Smola[22] argue that the linearity of this kernel type depends on γ. For small values of γ, the resulting feature space corresponds geometrically to the input space. The SV method then determines a nearly linear discriminant function. On the other hand, a large γ causes narrow kernels that lead to complex nonlinear functions in the input space.

The simplicity of an SV machine might be necessary in order to accept and approve such a model. By decreasing the number of possible functions that an SVM can choose, the potential solution becomes probably simpler. The overall risk, however, will increase in general. As a consequence, the actual pattern recognition problem that one deals with may not be solved properly enough anymore.

A priori, there does not exist any information for the SVM if a bag is hard or even not to classify. An approach to that problem is the following idea. The user defines certain weights for those bags B_i which impose classification problems. The weights will determine the importance of the weighted bags and influence the decision-making of the SVM. With the objective of minimizing both the capacity of the chosen function and the expected risk, there has to be a trade-off between *the global simplicity and the local complexity* of the decision function. Such a concept is explained thoroughly in Sec. 12.3.3.

The following ideas establish an approach to both simplicity of the model and local complexity, respectively. First of all, a promising concept for linearizing a subsequent hyperplane classifier by pruning of positive support vectors is presented in Sec. 12.3.2. This pruning method named *support vector pruning* is based on a sequence of linear SV machines such that the remainder of positive patterns is easier to separate linearly from the negative patterns.

The pruning guarantees less complex discriminant functions, however, the separating hyperplane might not generalize well on some unseen bags. Thus the hyperplane shall locally become more complex in order to ensure a higher accuracy. An approach towards local complexity is proposed in Sec. 12.3.3 as trade-off to the SV pruning method.

12.3.2. *Support vector pruning*

As we already sketched in Sec. 12.1.2, a learning machine that shall discriminate events of security-related systems has to be interpretable in order to be approved due to security standards. Usually easier machines are favored instead of those that are hard to understand. The SVM principle might be theoretically very well motivated, however, the feature space where the decision is carried out is never expressed explicitly. If we construct a feature space that is geometrically similar to the input space without using the linear kernel (12.3), then it will be possible to interpret and understand the resulting machine to a higher degree.

The idea is to favor linear classifiers by pruning a certain amount of instances that are very hard to classify linearly. Since we deal with MI problems in security-related domains, a pruning of negative instances is strictly forbidden. On the other hand, we only need one positive instance in order to correctly classify the complete corresponding bag. Therefore pruning is only feasible for positive bags.

The pruning shall remove candidates for critical positive instances from the dataset. It shall not remove complete positive bags since all bags have to be considered for the discrimination. After that, a nonlinear classifier, e.g. a Gaussian SVM should come up with an easier decision boundary than without applying SV pruning. The margin should become wider since a better linear separation of positive and negative samples can be achieved for unseen patterns.

The pruning process is motivated by the fact that a linear discriminant function of positive and negative instances is geometrically the easiest one. Furthermore, misclassified points, no matter if positive or negative patterns, will automatically become support vectors of the linear machine. The farthest positive support vectors on the negative side of the hyperplane are the ones that will have a big influence on the model selection step since it is very probable that they will become support vectors again even with a more sophisticated kernel.

This kind of support vectors are the reason for two major influences that may occur after training set selection during the actual training process. First of all, there might be an undesired shift of the hyperplane. Second, it is possible to obtain so-called *island solutions* by applying a nonlinear kernel. The farthest positive support vectors "pull" and shift the decision boundary locally by their weights such that undesired complex structures of the hyperplane can occur. On the other hand, their distance to the next negative support vector might be big compared to the distances among the negative support vectors. Their weights may radiate very much so that islands of positive areas next to their positions can occur. Since such a complex decision boundary would form positive islands surrounded by negative areas, we refer to such a discriminant function as island solution. An island solution is very hard to interpret and justify since there does not exist one unique linear functional dependency between the chosen input variables.

It is natural to remove those positive patterns that might cause conflicts. It shall be guaranteed, however, that every positive bag is represented by at least m positive patterns in the final training set. This is an important prerequisite for the subsequent SVM training since a minimal number of training instances for every bag ensures the generalization performance.

The pruning can be briefly explained by the following 4 procedures:

(1) Train a linear SV machine with all positive and negative patterns.
(2) Identify misclassified positive support vectors.
(3) Create a training set without these positive samples.
(4) Start training again and repeat this process until a stable model is obtained.

The third procedure has to assure that none of the bags is totally pruned. This is done by pruning every bag separately. Concerning one positive bag, only the farthest wrong positive support vectors are pruned such that the number of remaining positive instances is at least m. After all positive bags have been pruned for the first time, a new linear classifier is trained. The procedure begins again until the number of pruned support vectors equals zero.

Figure 12.1 shows an artificial two-dimensional application of SV pruning. The training of the linear SV machines has been performed with $C = 10$ in order to allow instances to be on the wrong side. Minimal $m = 10$ instances of every bag had to remain after pruning to ensure a certain generalization performance of the subsequent classifier. The first pruning step is shown on the left side where nearly 400 instances of some positive bags are pruned.

The second step on the right side of Fig. 12.1 shows the remaining instances after SV pruning has been applied once. Many positive (white) instances have been removed compared to the left side. The decision

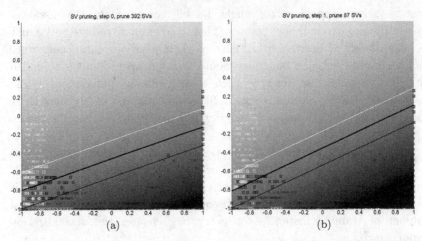

Figure 12.1.   First two steps of SV pruning on an artificial two-dimensional MI problem. Positive (negative) instances are shown as white (black) crosses. The thick black line represents the decision boundary whereas the thinner white (black) line symbolizes the margin of 1. Positive (negative) SVs are distinguished by white (black) squares around the corresponding instances. The gray-shaded colors clarify the distance to the hyperplane. (a) Initial step found 392 positive instances that will be pruned. (b) Second step with pruned dataset determined 87 further positive instances which will be removed.

boundary of the new SVM does not produce so many classification errors than the one of the SVM on the left side. In the present step, 87 instances would have been pruned. A new linear SVM would have been trained until there is not any instance that can be pruned.

For this given problem, there does not exist any perfect linear separation. This is due to the fact that at least one positive bag (lower left corner in the plots) is completely located in the negative classification area. Hence such bags cannot be pruned by SV pruning. They rather represent conflicts that have to be analyzed by human experts. Only then an interpretable and understandable model can be obtained.

Note that this iterative procedure of SV pruning is somehow related to boosting[13] where a weak classifier, e.g. a linear SVM is used to find hard to classify instances. Applying boosting, their weights are then increased. Using SV pruning, we drastically set these weights to zero by removing them from the training set. Boosting is not applied since it would complicate and not simplify the classifier. Nevertheless, Andrews and Hofmann[1] employed boosting successfully to general MI problems that must not be that restrictive as problems originating from safety-related systems.

12.3.3. *Bag weighting*

The simplicity of both the SV machine and its discriminant function is very nice to have. On the contrary, the model shall also deploy all positive bags and prevent deployment of all negative bags. As a consequence, a trade-off between simplicity and complexity has to be found. Whereas the last section already presented an approach to global simplicity, this section will introduce a slight modification of the standard C-SV machine which enables us to locally enrich the discriminant function.

Customer requirements of the safety-related system like "Ensure high accuracy for all positive (or negative) bags!" may exist since some bags may be more important to classify than others. These demands can be modeled by assigning weights to prioritized bags. The higher the weight of a bag, the more its misclassification has to be prevented by all means. If such knowledge is available, it can be incorporated into our learning machine.

It is important to note that standard implementations of the SVM principle do not offer the weighting of single patterns or multi instances, e.g. bags[a]. Usually one can only set different class weights which is only partly appropriate in the case of MI problems.

To have an understanding of what is changed compared to the standard SVM, we have to recall the problem of minimizing the functional (12.9) subject to (12.8). In general, the global parameter C expresses the costs for a misclassification for every pattern. It is set to one by default. As a consequence, a priori all patterns are treated the same without any information of priority. By minimizing

$$\Phi(\psi, \xi) = \frac{1}{2} \langle \psi, \psi \rangle + C \left(\sum_{k=1}^{n} C_k \xi_k \right)$$

subject to (12.8), we can define weights C_k for the training instances x_k, $1 \leq k \leq n$. In addition, it is straightforward to assign weights C_i to complete bags where $i = 1, \ldots, l$ and the number of bags $l = l^+ + l^-$. Thus incorporating available bag weights as experts' knowledge into the learning machine, the user can have an influence on the learning step[a].

In combination with the pruning method that was introduced in the last section, the assignment of priorities by weighting of single training bags can be a powerful tool to ensure both an interpretable model and the fulfillment

---

[a]Using a distinct implementation of SV machines, e.g. the package LIBSVM,[5] there exists already a tool based on LIBSVM that enables to apply a different weight to every training instance.[6]

of customer requirements, e.g. high accuracy. It might be a good procedure to first apply the pruning methods and then have a look which bags have been misclassified. Then SV pruning can be coupled to the assignment of weights in order to solve the conflicts that arose before.

12.3.4. *Combination of both methods*

Combining the methods of SV pruning and bag weighting is straightforward. Since the training set (12.1) which is returned after pruning strongly favors quasilinear classifiers (see Sec. 12.3.1 for linearity of SV machines), the introduction of weights for some bags shall complicate the discriminant function in order to solve remaining unrecognized bags.

Remember that SV pruning only prunes positive bags and thus gives strong preference to negative bags. The subsequent weighting of (usually positive) bags that have not been correctly classified after pruning shall overcome the bias-variance trade-off. It compromises between global simplicity of a linear classifier and local complexity which is necessary to solve our special MI problem.

The search for appropriate bag weights C_i is another challenging task which is not discussed in this paper. However, note that big weights may force the SVM to finally correctly discriminant every bag which did not work even after SV pruning and bag weighting with small $C_i \approx 1$. Smaller values may not make any change big enough to solve conflicting bags. A positive bag that is located in an area of only negative instances cannot be classified. Then such a conflict can be found easily and must be analyzed by experts. This is necessary since we deal with problems in safety-related domains where every classification decision has to be justifiable.

12.4. Conclusions

In this paper we presented a hybrid approach for preprocessing MI problems in safety-related domains. Whereas classifiers for standard MI datasets aim to be as accurate as possible, we focused on problems where the interpretability is essential, too. Therefore we introduced SV pruning to favor quasilinear classifiers. Bag weighting has been suggested to enable both the input of expert's knowledge and the trade-off between model simplicity and accuracy. The presented idea has been successfully applied to the off-line analysis of a safety-related system in automobile industry.[19]

Using SV machines to prune instances of the given bags, there are many possible extensions and improvements one can think of. Especially the generation of fuzzy rules based on SV learning should be considered since this type of decision-making has been successfully implemented in safety-related applications, e.g. in the automobile industry.[20] Some approaches recently came up to construct fuzzy graphs from support vectors.

Chen and Wang[9] initially came up with this idea by introducing one fuzzy rule for every support vector. Although the number of rules did not depend on the dimensionality of the problem any more, their approach leaded to many fuzzy rules which does not help to understand the model. [21] then improved the original idea in order to massively reduce the number of fuzzy rules. Chaves *et al.*[7] proposed a similar approach to extract fuzzy rules from support vector machines where the rule's antecedents are associated with fuzzy sets. Two years later they extended their method to multi-class problems.[8]

Preprocessing the bags by methods like SV pruning and bag weighting can be the basis for the following approach. Incorporating the learning problem of fuzzy rules directly into the SVM may be the key to this problem. Therefore one would have to either define a special kernel that already includes knowledge about the setting or formulate a differentiated optimization problem with sophisticated constraints. Both ways might result in understandable fuzzy rules that still guarantee a high accuracy on unseen data. The principle of SV machines would allow the experts to comprise their knowledge to the learning step. The whole concept might establish a powerful framework to tackle classification problems in safety-related domains.

Acknowledgment

We would like to thank Prof. Dr. Eyke Hüllermeier for valuable discussions about relationships between our approach and multiple-instance learning.

References

1. Andrews, S. and Hofmann, T. (2003). Multiple-instance learning via disjunctive programming boosting, in S. Thrun, L. K. Saul and B. Schölkopf (eds.), *NIPS* (MIT Press), ISBN 0-262-20152-6.

2. Andrews, S., Tsochantaridis, I. and Hofmann, T. (2002). Support vector machines for multiple-instance learning, in S. Becker, S. Thrun and K. Obermayer (eds.), *NIPS* (MIT Press), ISBN 0-262-02550-7, pp. 561–568.
3. Bartlett, P. L. (1996). For valid generalization the size of the weights is more important than the size of the network, in M. Mozer, M. I. Jordan and T. Petsche (eds.), *NIPS* (MIT Press), pp. 134–140.
4. Boser, B. E., Guyon, I. and Vapnik, V. (1992). A training algorithm for optimal margin classifiers, in *COLT*, pp. 144–152.
5. Chang, C.-C. and Lin, C.-J. (2001). *LIBSVM: a library for support vector machines*, Software available at http://www.csie.ntu.edu.tw/~cjlin/libsvm.
6. Chang, M.-W. and Lin, H.-T. (2005). *Weighted Training Instances for LIBSVM*, Software available at http://www.csie.ntu.edu.tw/~cjlin/libsvmtools/libsvm-weight-2.81.zip.
7. Chaves, A., Vellasco, M. B. R. and Tanscheit, R. (2005). Fuzzy rule extraction from support vector machines, in N. Nedjah, L. de Macedo Mourelle, A. Abraham and M. Köppen (eds.), *HIS* (IEEE Computer Society), ISBN 0-7695-2457-5, pp. 335–340.
8. Chaves, A., Vellasco, M. B. R. and Tanscheit, R. (2007). Fuzzy rules extraction from support vector machines for multi-class classification, in P. Melin, O. Castillo, E. G. Ramirez, J. Kacprzyk and W. Pedrycz (eds.), *ASC*, *Advances in Soft Computing*, Vol. 41 (Springer-Verlag, Berlin/Heidelberg, Germany), ISBN 978-3-540-72431-5, pp. 99–108.
9. Chen, Y. and Wang, J. Z. (2003). Support vector learning for fuzzy rule-based classification systems, *IEEE-FS* **11**, 6, pp. 716–728.
10. Chen, Y. and Wang, J. Z. (2004). Image categorization by learning and reasoning with regions, *Journal of Machine Learning Research* **5**, pp. 913–939.
11. Cortes, C. and Vapnik, V. (1995). Support-vector networks, *Machine Learning* **20**, 3, pp. 273–297.
12. Dietterich, T. G., Lathrop, R. H. and Lozano-Pérez, T. (1997). Solving the multiple instance problem with axis-parallel rectangles, *Artif. Intell.* **89**, 1-2, pp. 31–71.
13. Freund, Y. and Schapire, R. E. (1996). Experiments with a new boosting algorithm, in *ICML*, pp. 148–156.
14. Geman, S., Bienenstock, E. and Doursat, R. (1992). Neural networks and the bias/variance dilemma, *Neural Computation* **4**, 1, pp. 1–58.
15. Guyon, I., Boser, B. E. and Vapnik, V. (1992). Automatic capacity tuning of very large vc-dimension classifiers, in S. J. Hanson, J. D. Cowan and C. L. Giles (eds.), *NIPS* (Morgan Kaufmann), ISBN 1-55860-274-7, pp. 147–155.
16. Maron, O. and Lozano-Pérez, T. (1997). A framework for multiple-instance learning, in M. I. Jordan, M. J. Kearns and S. A. Solla (eds.), *NIPS* (The MIT Press), ISBN 0-262-10076-2.
17. Maron, O. and Ratan, A. L. (1998). Multiple-instance learning for natural scene classification, in J. W. Shavlik (ed.), *ICML* (Morgan Kaufmann), ISBN 1-55860-556-8, pp. 341–349.

18. Mercer, J. (1909). Functions of positive and negative type and their connection with the theory of integral equations, *Philos. Trans. Roy. Soc. London* **A 209**, pp. 415–446.
19. Moewes, C. (2007). *Application of Support Vector Machines to Discriminate Vehicle Crash Events*, Diploma thesis, Faculty of Computer Science, University of Magdeburg.
20. Otte, C., Nusser, S. and Hauptmann, W. (2006). Machine learning methods for safety-related domains: Status and perspectives, in *Proceedings of FSCS* (Magdeburg, Germany), pp. 139–148.
21. Papadimitriou, S. and Terzidis, C. (2005). Efficient and interpretable fuzzy classifiers from data with support vector learning, *Intell. Data Anal.* **9**, 6, pp. 527–550.
22. Schölkopf, B. and Smola, A. J. (2002). *Learning with Kernels* (MIT Press, Cambridge, MA).
23. Vapnik, V. (1998). *Statistical Learning Theory* (Wiley, New York).
24. Vapnik, V. and Chervonenkis, A. (1974). *Theory of Pattern Recognition [in Russian]* (Nauka, Moscow), (German Translation: W. Wapnik & A. Tscherwonenkis, *Theorie der Zeichenerkennung*, Akademie–Verlag, Berlin, 1979).
25. Xu, X. (2003). *Statistical Learning in Multiple Instance Problems*, Master's thesis, Department of Computer Science, University of Waikato.
26. Yang, C. and Lozano-Pérez, T. (2000). Image database retrieval with multiple-instance learning techniques, in *ICDE*, pp. 233–243.
27. Zhang, Q., Goldman, S. A., Yu, W. and Fritts, J. E. (2002). Content-based image retrieval using multiple-instance learning, in C. Sammut and A. G. Hoffmann (eds.), *ICML* (Morgan Kaufmann), ISBN 1-55860-873-7, pp. 682–689.

Chapter 13

Nonuniform Multi Level Crossings for Signal Reconstruction

Nagesh Poojary[1], Hemantha Kumar[2] and Ashok Rao[3]

[1] *Computing Department, Middle East College of Information Technology,*
Knowledge Oasis Muscat, P.B. No. 79, Al Rusayl,
Sultanate of Oman
E-mail: nagesh.bk@gmail.com

[2] *Dept. of Studies in Computer Science,*
University of Mysore, Mysore-570 006, India

[3] *Dept. of Electronics and Communication, CIT,*
Gubbi-Tumkur-572216, Karnataka, India

Level crossing based sampling might be used as an alternative to Nyquist theory based sampling of a signal. Level crossing based approach takes advantage of statistical properties of the signal, providing cues to efficient nonuniform sampling. This paper presents new threshold level allocation schemes for level crossing based nonuniform sampling. Intuitively, it is more reasonable if the information rich regions of the signal are sampled finer and those with sparse information are sampled coarser. To achieve this objective, we proposed non-linear quantization functions which dynamically assign the number of quantization levels depending on the importance of the given amplitude range. Various aspects of proposed techniques are discussed and experimentally validated. Its efficacy is investigated by comparison with Nyquist based sampling.

Contents

13.1 Introduction 252
13.2 Level Crossing Based Irregular Sampling Model 254
13.3 Weight Functions for Irregular Sampling 254
    13.3.1 Linear function 256
    13.3.2 Logarithmic function 256
    13.3.3 Incomplete beta function 256
    13.3.4 Level estimation 258

13.4 Experimental Evaluation 259
13.5 Conclusion 266
References 266

13.1. Introduction

In recent years, there has been considerable interest in level crossing algorithms for sampling continuous time signals. Driven by a growing demand for intelligent and high speed analog-to-digital converter (ADC) with low-power processor, increasing efforts have been made to improve level crossing based sampling techniques. An asynchronous level crossing sampling scheme records a new sample whenever the source signal crosses a threshold level. Consequently, more samples are recorded during fast changing intervals and fewer samples are recorded during relatively quiescent intervals. As a result, the signal is sampled nonuniformly. If the quiescent intervals are long and the number of these long intervals is large, then the average number of samples recorded would be relatively low. However, the recorded samples contain sufficient information that enables a fairly accurate reconstruction of the source signal. The recorded samples can be represented with very high accuracy; essentially because highly accurate clocks are much easier to build than circuits that quantize amplitudes very accurately. Also, asynchronous level crossing sampling is attractive because it can be implemented with a single-comparator circuit.[8]

Several case studies in ADC's show that level crossing based on asynchronous sampling technique can be more effective than synchronous ADCs. The 1-bit ADC (bipolar) is optimized improving the dynamic range such that quantization error effectively decreases.[9,20] The level crossing sampling scheme has been demonstrated for speech applications using CMOS technology and a voltage mode approach for the analog parts of the converter. Electrical simulations prove that the Figure of Merit of asynchronous level crossing converters increased compared to uniform sampling ADCs.[4,11] Level crossing sampling scheme have also been suggested in literature for non-bandlimited signals,[5] random processes,[10] band limited gaussian random processes,[6] reconstruction from nonuniform sampling[8,21] and for monitoring and control systems.[12–16] The level crossing sampling strategy is also known as an event-based sampling,[17,18] Lebesgue sampling,[19] send-on-delta concept[14] or deadband concept.[16]

In general, conventional uniform sampling is with uniform time-step and variable amplitude. There is a trade-off between the requirements of bandwidth and the dynamic range to obtain a certain resolution. Sampling at the Nyquist rate requires smallest bandwidth but large number of quantization levels to achieve high resolution. Increasing the bandwidth decreases the need for large number of quantization levels, thus reducing the quantization error power and increasing the number of samples. At the extreme, the signal can be sampled capturing its characteristics using level crossing concept. Several signals have interesting statistical properties, but uniform sampling does not take advantage of them. Signals such as electro cardiograms, speech signals, temperature sensors, pressure sensors, seismic signals are almost always constant and may vary significantly during brief moments. In level crossing, the characteristics of the waveform play a vital role in approximation of the input signal. It has been proved in[1,4] that level crossing sampling approach can lead to reduction in number of samples. The other advantage of level crossing sampling is that sampling frequency and quantization levels are decided by the signal itself. However, the methods developed for various cases use either constant threshold step size quantization levels (linear levels) or manually determined levels. The problem of primary interest is to determine statistical information on automatic distribution of quantization levels based on the characteristics of the input signal. Linear threshold level allocation scheme is simple but not efficient in terms of data bit usage for the following reason. The linear threshold allocation will result in a higher SNR at the region of higher amplitude than the region of lower amplitude. This increased SNR at the higher signal amplitude does not increase the perceived audio quality because humans are most sensitive to lower amplitude components.[23] To overcome these problems, we propose a non-linear quantization approach based on logarithmic and Incomplete Beta Function (IBF) which dynamically assign the number of quantization levels exploiting this auditory motivation.

The paper is organized as follows. In section §13.2 level crossing based sampling approach with the proposed nonuniform threshold allocation scheme is described. The incorporation of linear, logarithmic and IBF functions to formulate a rule for allocation of nonuniform threshold levels in multi level crossing is discussed in Section §13.3. In section §13.4 experimental setup for testing the proposed approach and results are discussed. Also, the performance and analysis of the proposed method is discussed. Section §13.5 is devoted to conclusions as well as indicate directions for future lines of work.

13.2. Level Crossing Based Irregular Sampling Model

Level Crossing Analysis represents an approach to interpretation and characterization of time signals by relating frequency and amplitude information. Measurement of level crossing of a signal is defined as the crossings of a threshold level l by consecutive samples.

Definition 13.1. Let $w(x)$ be a deterministic weight function and $p(x)$ be the probability density function of a source signal. The level sampler $L_{f(.)}$ density distribution with a deterministic level allocation weight function $f(.)$ is a mapping

$$L_{f(.)} \colon R \longrightarrow f(p(x), w(x), Z) : L_{f(.)} = (p(x) \otimes w(x)) \times N$$

where N is the total number of nonuniform levels. R and Z denotes the set of real and integer numbers respectively. The $\otimes$ symbol represents convolution.

Since the quantization levels are irregularly spaced across the amplitude range of the signal, it increases the efficiency of bit usage. The spacing of the levels is decided by the importance of the amplitude segments which is discussed in section III. A sample is recorded when the input signal crosses one of the nonuniformly spaced levels. The precession of time of the recorded sample is decided by the local timer τ.

Definition 13.2. Let $L_{f(.)} = \{l_1, l_2, \dots l_N\}$ be the set of nonuniformly spaced levels and $2^b = N$ quantization levels with b bit resolution. The level crossing of the threshold level l_i by a signal $s(t)$ with period T is given by

$$L_{f(.)}(I_{ni}) = l_i \quad iff \quad \left(s\left(\frac{i-1}{N}T\right) - l_i\right) \times \left(s\left(\frac{i}{N}T\right) - l_i\right) < 0 \quad (13.1)$$

where n sub intervals are defined by $I_{ni} = \left(\frac{i-1}{N}T, \frac{i}{N}T\right)$, $i = 1, 2, \dots n$

The level crossing problem is depicted in Figure 13.1 where the samples are recorded whenever the input signal crosses the threshold levels. If a sample is recorded and transmitted every time a level crossing occurs, the encoding procedure is called asynchronous delta modulation.[2]

13.3. Weight Functions for Irregular Sampling

Determining the positions of threshold levels on an amplitude scale is very important as it has a huge impact on the performance of coding.

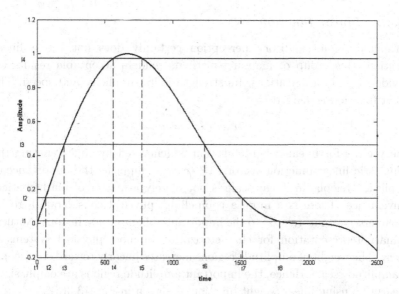

Figure 13.1. Level Crossing sampling. $t_1, t_2, t_3, t_4, t_5, t_6, t_7, t_8$ denotes the recorded samples due to levels l_1, l_2, l_3, l_4 which are nonuniformly spaced.

Unfortunately there is no theory available to determine the locations of threshold levels which exploit the statistics of a random variable under a particular distribution. Furthermore, the uniform threshold levels are not the efficient coding of the levels because they do not take advantage of the statistical properties of the signal. The basic idea behind the weight functions is to emphasize the amplitude regions where (speech) signal is dominant, and to attenuate the amplitude regions which are less important considering auditory properties. As a result, signals with lesser activity in higher amplitude regions compared to the lower amplitude regions, will have less number of levels at higher amplitude region. Hence, basic methodology in level crossing based irregular sampling is to choose a weight function which encourages the important amplitude regions. The present study discusses distribution of nonuniform threshold levels based on the three weight functions namely linear, logarithmic and Incomplete Beta Functions (IBF). IBF probability distribution function (PDF) can attain variety of shapes; this allows the user to select the distribution which exploits the auditory properties. This viewpoint suggests family of distributions for weight functions. Hence, we have proposed two more weight functions namely linear and logarithmic, to study and analyze the characteristics of proposed approach.

13.3.1. *Linear function*

Although human auditory perception certainly does not use a linear function, this group of mapping methods renders acceptable results for a wide range of applications. Its strength is its simplicity and speed. The linear function is defined by

$$linear\,(n) = n$$

The vectors for linear weight function is generated by concatenating the symmetric linear function vectors. However, computing the importance of amplitude regions in linear scale is not merely a matter of mathematical convenience. There is a more a compelling, physical consideration to be taken into account, related to the importance of amplitude regions. Natural primary representation for characterization of most physical systems is linear. The weight of amplitude regions increases linearly towards the center of amplitude scale. Hence, the important amplitude regions are emphasized linearly by using linear weight function as shown in Fig. 13.3(a).

13.3.2. *Logarithmic function*

A logarithm of a number x in base b is a number n such that $x = b^n$, where the value b must be neither 0 nor a root of 1. It is usually written as

$$log_b\,(x) = n.$$

When x and b are further restricted to positive real numbers, the logarithm is a unique real number. Our sense of hearing perceives equal ratios of frequencies as equal differences in pitch. Representation of importance of amplitude on a logarithmic scale can be helpful when the importance of regions varies monotonically. Logarithmic rule assigns less number of levels to the corner amplitude regions and more levels are assigned logarithmically in important amplitude regions. The center amplitude regions (near zero amplitude regions) are considered to be important amplitude regions. This issue, however is not whether to accept or reject logarithmic rule but to appreciate where it fits in, and where it does not.

13.3.3. *Incomplete beta function*

The Beta function is a continuous distribution defined over a range of real values. Additionally, both of its end points are fixed at exact locations and it belongs to the flexible family of distributions. The lack of data to decide the exact positions of levels for a given signal creates problems concerning the quality of level sampled data. In such cases, an expert will have to assume the level positions on amplitude scale. For this reason, the flexible incomplete beta distribution, capable of attaining a variety of shapes could be used in level crossing applications. Because of its extreme flexibility, the distribution appears ideally suited for the computation of number of levels for a specific amplitude region of a speech signal. A generalization of the incomplete beta function is defined by[7]

$$B\left(z, \alpha, \beta\right) \equiv \int_0^z u^{\alpha-1} \left(1 - u^{\beta-1}\right) du \qquad (13.2)$$

$$= z^\alpha \left[\frac{1}{\alpha} + \frac{1-\beta}{\alpha+1} z + \right.$$

$$\left. \cdots + \frac{(1-\beta)\cdots(n-b)}{n!(\alpha+n)} z^n + \cdots\right] \qquad (13.3)$$

The Incomplete beta function $I\left(z, \alpha, \beta\right)$ is defined by

$$I\left(z, \alpha, \beta\right) \equiv \frac{B\left(z, \alpha, \beta\right)}{B\left(\alpha, \beta\right)} \qquad (13.4)$$

$$\equiv \frac{1}{B\left(\alpha, \beta\right)} \int_0^z u^{\alpha-1} \left(1 - u^{\beta-1}\right) du \qquad (13.5)$$

Eq. 13.5 has the limiting values $I_0\left(\alpha, \beta\right) = 0$ and $I_0\left(\alpha, \beta\right) = 1$. The shape of the incomplete beta function obtained from equation 13.5 depends on the choice of its two parameters α and β. The parameters are any real number greater than zero; depending on their values, the incomplete beta function generated will have the inverted U, the triangle or the general bell shape of the unimodal function as shown in Figure 13.2. Estimating these parameters is a challenge since these parameters control the number of levels for a given amplitude range of a speech signal along with the signal probability density function. The lower amplitude regions are important than the extreme corner amplitude regions in speech signal since humans are more sensitive to the lower amplitude regions. With the knowledge of this auditory information, one can obtain the approximation for the perceptually motivated IBF weight function. We have empirically chosen the values of $\alpha = 0.2$ and $\beta = 0.2$. When $\alpha = 0.2$ and $\beta = 0.2$ the near zero amplitude regions are more highlighted compared to the corner amplitude regions. However, the selection was made under worst case assumption to provide some general criterion to obtain best PDF out of family of PDF

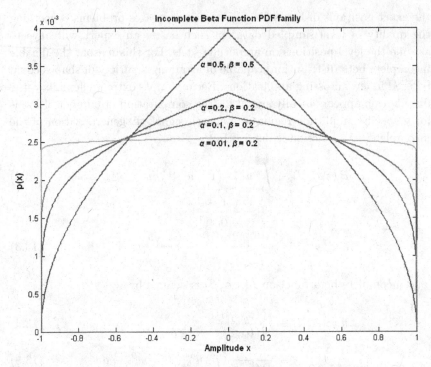

Figure 13.2.   IBF distribution for various α, β. The IBF distribution is characterized by the parameters α, β values.

curves. Keeping the auditory motivation information, we use the IBF for estimating levels.

13.3.4. *Level estimation*

In a deterministic environment, the accuracy of the signal reconstruction depends on several parameters such as positioning of the levels, total number of levels, statistical properties of the signal etc. If weight functions are directly applied for level estimation, amplitude activity information of a given signal will not be used, which results in biased level estimation. Hence, level distribution PDF is convolved with signal PDF to correct for the biased distribution of levels. This ensures that level distribution is unbiased. Specifically, for a given signal we analyze its structural behavior by estimating its PDF. The signal histogram is approximated to obtain the signal PDF $p(x)$.

Now, consider a signal with amplitude PDF $p(x)$ and weight function $w(x)$. Let N be the total number of levels. The locations of N levels are estimated by the distribution

$$L_{f(.)}(x) = p(x) \otimes w(x) \qquad (13.6)$$

$L_{f(.)}(x)$ gives the probability distribution of levels and guides the distribution of N levels over the amplitude range. As expected, the spacing of N levels are not uniform and they are nonuniformly spaced over the amplitude range. Each level can be represented with $log_2(N)$ bits. Since the levels are nonuniformly spaced depending on the importance of the amplitude segment, we efficiently utilize the quantization levels by ignoring the amplitude regions with less activity. Hence only amplitude regions with higher activity and important lower amplitude regions will be allocated more number of levels using the weight function $w(x)$ and signal amplitude PDF $p(x)$. The histogram of sample speech signal is shown in Fig. 13.3(a), along with plot of PDF of linear weight function(Fig. 13.3(b)), PDF of logarithmic weight function(Fig. 13.3(c)) and IBF weight function for $\alpha = 0.2, \beta = 0.2$ (Fig. 13.3(d)). The steps employed for the proposed approach are summarized as follows.

(1) Input signal s[n] is normalized to lie within [-1, 1] and made zero mean.
(2) Find the signal histogram. Approximate the signal histogram to find the PDF of the speech signal.
(3) For each weight function and for varying number of bins(used to compute the weight function)

    (a) Find the distribution of quantization levels
    (b) Find the level crossings of the input signal. Store the level crossed sample value and its position.

13.4. Experimental Evaluation

In this section, the performance of the proposed approach is evaluated for speech signals. We have run simulations for the level crossing based sampling of speech signals from TIMIT database.[22] The TIMIT speech signals are sampled at 16 KHz sampling rate and each sample size is 16 bit. Speech signals are chosen from TEST/DR1 folder which contains seven male and four female adult speakers thereby yielding a total of 100 signals. The PDF of the speech signal is estimated by computing the amplitude histogram of the signal with 100 bins. The total number of quantization

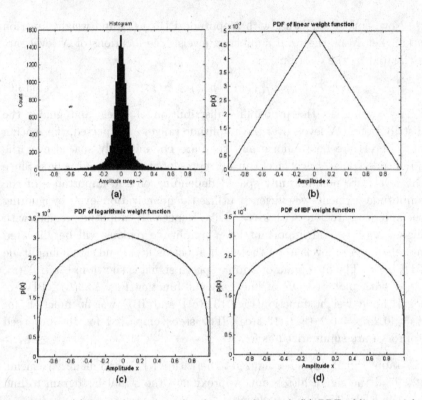

Figure 13.3. (a) Signal histogram of a clean speech signal. (b) PDF of linear weight function (c) PDF of logarithmic weight function (d) PDF of Incomplete Beta Function for values $\alpha = 0.2 \beta = 0.2$.

levels required to sample the given signal are set to 16, 32, 64 and 128. The accuracy of distribution of the levels computed from equation 6 also depends on the number of bins used to compute convoluted PDF of the signal with weight function. The levels are estimated for 20, 40, 60, 80, 100 bins for comparison and analysis. We evaluated the system with proposed linear, logarithmic and IBF weight functions. The performance of the proposed method is evaluated computing SNR and compression ratio. The performance measure SNR can be interpreted as

$$SNR = 10 log_{10} \left(\frac{\frac{1}{N} \sum_{i=1}^{N} s\,(i)^2}{\frac{1}{N} \sum_{i=1}^{N} s\,(i)^2 - s'\,(i)^2} \right)$$

where $s\,(i)$ represents the original speech signal and $s'\,(i)$ denotes the reconstructed signal. Computation of SNR can be interpreted as the speed-up factor by which level crossing sampler achieves the same precision as the uniform sampling method. The ability to recover the uniform samples from its data representation of unequal sample values is also important. In our study, we applied direct interpolation scheme, polynomial curve fitting to approximate original signal from level crossed signal. Compression ratio is used to quantify the reduction in data-representation size produced by the proposed method and is defined as the ratio between the uncompressed size (original signal size) and the compressed size (level crossed sample size).

$$compressionratio = \frac{number\ of\ samples\ in\ original\,signal}{number\ of\ samples\ used\ in\ reconstruction\ of\ signal}$$

The simulation results are approximated analytically using quadratic polynomial. By comparing IBF, logarithmic and linear rule results, we analyze the performances. We investigated relationship between SNR and the histogram bins used to compute the signal amplitude histogram. The simulation results are depicted in Fig. 13.4(a), Fig. 13.5(a) and

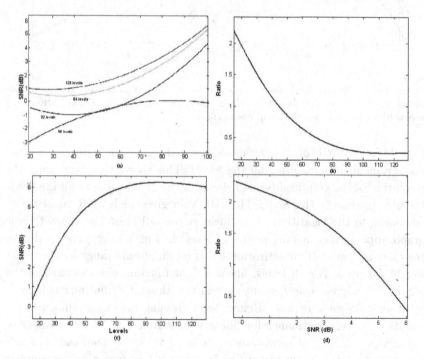

Figure 13.4. Performance of linear weight function (a) Histogram bin versus SNR. (b) Quantization level versus Compression ratio. (c) Quantization level versus SNR. (d) SNR versus Compression ratio.

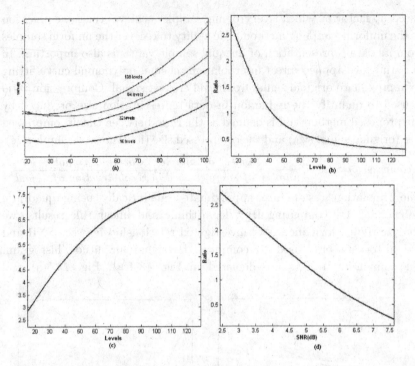

Figure 13.5.   Experimental results for logarithmic weight function (a) Histogram bin versus SNR. (b) Quantization level versus Compression ratio. (c) Quantization level versus SNR. (d) SNR versus Compression ratio.

Fig. 13.6(a). SNR of the resampled signal generally improves as the histogram bins increase for all the levels. This shows that increasing the resolution of the amplitude scale helps in accurate distribution of the levels thereby increasing the SNR. The IBF rule gives high SNR consistently compared to the logarithmic and linear rule at all bins. The characteristic graph appears non monotonic for 16 levels in Fig. 13.4(a). This is due to the distribution of 16 quantization levels on amplitude range by the linear weight function. For 16 levels, linear weight function clusters most of the quantization levels near 0 amplitude region without distributing much levels to other amplitude regions. Hence, level crossing based sampling process results in poor performance for linear weight function. As the number of histogram bins and quantization levels increase, more quantization levels are spread across amplitude range. Hence, SNR increases as the number of histogram bins and quantization levels increases. The performance of logarithmic rule (Fig. 13.5(a)) is slightly less than that of IBF rule

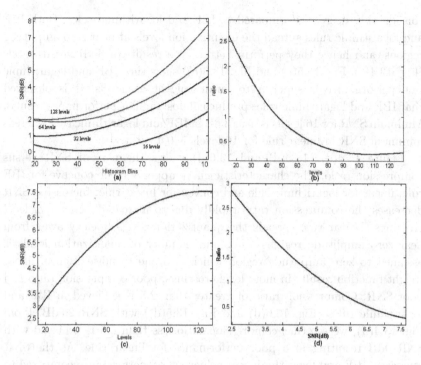

Figure 13.6.   Performance of IBF weight function (a) Histogram bin versus SNR. (b) Quantization level versus Compression ratio. (c) Quantization level versus SNR. (d) SNR versus Compression ratio.

(Fig. 13.6(a)) for all the levels. The best performance is observed for IBF rule with 128 levels. In case of linear rule, 1 dB drop in SNR is observed compared to IBF for 128 levels. Similarly, higher SNR is achieved for IBF and logarithmic rule compared to linear rule at all levels (Fig. 13.4(a), Fig. 13.5(a) and Fig. 13.6(a)). This proves that increasing the quantization levels increases the SNR.

However, increasing the quantization levels considerably decreases the compression ratio. The comparison of compression ratio at various levels for the three rules is shown in Fig. 13.4(b), Fig. 13.5(b) and Fig. 13.6(b). We observe that logarithmic rule slightly outperforms IBF rule. The logarithmic rule gives higher SNR for lesser levels and the ratio decreases as the levels are increased. Linear rule results in low compression ratio for all levels. For higher levels all the rules give similar results. Since, the linear rule forces quantization levels to cluster near zero amplitude segments, which are more prone to noise in speech signals, the compression ratio considerably decreases compared to IBF and logarithmic rules. Both IBF and logarithmic rules spread the quantization levels at near zero amplitude regions, and hence they perform better. The results of SNR versus levels (Fig. 13.4(c), Fig. 13.5(c) and Fig. 13.6(c)) show that IBF and logarithmic rule performance is superior to linear rule at all levels. It is observed that IBF and logarithmic rules produce almost similar performance results. Minimum SNR for 16 levels is near 3 dB in IBF and logarithmic rule whereas minimum SNR in linear rule for 16 levels is 0.4 dB.

Figure 13.4(d), 13.5(d) and 13.6(d) shows the plot of SNR versus compression ratio. The characteristic curve appears to be concave for IBF rule, linear for logarithmic rule and convex for linear rule. Increasing SNR decreases the compression ratio rapidly due to increased number of level crossings. Linear rule spreads the quantization levels linearly away from near zero amplitude regions. Maximum number of quantization levels is assigned to zero amplitude region which is prone to noise. Hence, linear weight function results in more level crossings, poor compression ratio and poor SNR. Compression ratio of greater than 2.5 is achieved in IBF and logarithmic rules (Fig. 13.6(d) and Fig. 13.5(d)) with SNR 2.5dB. From Fig. 13.4(d), we see that compression ratio less than 2.5 is achieved with SNR 0dB resulting in a poor performance for linear rule. As the SNR increases, IBF and logarithmic rule achieve good performance compared to linear rule due to the spread of quantization levels. Furthermore for higher SNR values the compression ratio drops drastically for IBF and logarithmic rule, whereas the drop in compression ratio for increasing SNR is much slower due to the distribution of levels by the linear rule. The IBF and logarithmic rules consistently outperformed linear rule for all SNR values as shown in Fig. 13.4(d), Fig. 13.5(d) and Fig. 13.6(d). Performance of IBF and logarithmic rules are considerably better than linear rule, with higher SNR for higher compression ratio, which is nonetheless better performance. Comparison of IBF, logarithmic and linear rule shows that, the IBF rule and logarithmic outperforms linear rule. Also, performances of IBF slightly outperforms logarithmic rule in compression ratio and SNR. Fig. 13.7 compares the plot of input signal(speech signal from TIMIT database) with reconstructed signal.

The behavioral patterns of IBF, logarithmic and linear rule appear to be similar except in SNR versus ratio analysis. IBF rule is based on the auditory properties of the humans. IBF rule distributes more levels in the critical amplitude regions. Similar to IBF, logarithmic rule also considers that near zero amplitude regions are important than the corner amplitude

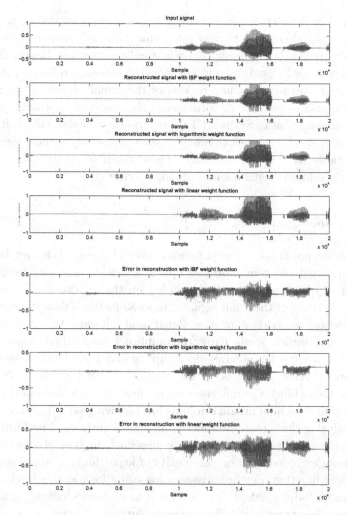

Figure 13.7. Comparison of input signal and reconstructed signal with linear, logarithmic and IBF weight functions. In this example, thirty two quantization levels are distributed using deterministic weight functions. The reconstructed signals from logarithmic and IBF functions appear to be approximately similar compared to the linear weight function. Linear weight function assigns more levels near corner amplitudes (-1,+1) compared to logarithmic and IBF weight functions. Hence the plot of linear rule has more samples near the corner amplitude regions than IBF and logarithmic weight function. However, humans are not very much sensitive to the corner amplitude regions. Therefore, reconstruction by logarithmic and IBF are better than linear weight function. Furthermore, the error graphs of signal reconstructions show that the error is less in logarithmic and IBF weight functions compared to linear weight function.

regions. The priority of the amplitude regions varies logarithmically from corner amplitude regions to near zero value amplitude regions. Linear rule considers that each amplitude region is equally important. Hence, the SNR of the resampled signal remains consistently superior to linear rule. Lack of levels at critical amplitude regions of the signal decreases the SNR of the resampled signal. The performance of the proposed approaches is fairly consistent with that of Sayiner.[3] This experimental analysis illustrates that signal with special statistical behavior such as speech, medical signals are not suitable for uniform sampling. These types of signals can be more efficiently sampled using a level crossing scheme.

13.5. Conclusion

This paper presents a new threshold level allocation schemes for level crossing based on nonuniform sampling which dynamically assigns the number of quantization levels depending on the importance of the given amplitude range of the input signal. Proposed methods take the advantage of statistical properties of the signal and allocate the nonuniformly spaced quantization levels across the amplitude range. The proposed level allocation scheme for nonuniform sampling based on level crossing may motivate directed attempts to augment traditional methods that will improve their ability. Overall, these results motivate continued work on level crossing based on nonuniform sampling for improving sampling performance and analyzing the signals. Simplicity but significantly good performance of logarithmic weight function is what is observed. In general logarithmic is best because implementation complexity of logarithmic is much lesser than IBF wight function. Further investigation could look at this level crossing problem for 2-dimensional signals. This is much more challenging and also not a simple extension of 1-dimensional solution.

References

1. Mitchell, R. J. and Gonzalez, R. C. (1978) "Multilevel crossing rates for automated signal classification", *Proc. of ICASSP 78* **3**, 218.
2. Inose, H., Aoki, T., Vitjko, Wantanable, K. (1966) "Asynchronous delta modulation systems", *Electron. Commun.*, 34.
3. Sayiner, N., Sorensen, H. V. and Viswanathan, T. R. (1996) "A level crossing sampling scheme for A/D conversion", *IEEE Transactions on Circuits and Systems.* **II 43**, 335.

4. Allier, E., Sicard, G., Fesquet, L. and Renaudin, M. (2005) "Asynchronous level crossing analog to digital converters", *Measurement Journal*. **37**, 296.

5. Guan, K., Andrew, C. S. (2006) "A Level Crossing Sampling Scheme for Non-Bandlimited Signals", *Proc. of ICASSP*. **3**, 381.

6. Marek Miskowicz (2006) "Efficiency of Level-Crossing Sampling for Bandlimited Gaussian Random Processes", *Proc. of IEEE International Workshop on Factory Communication Systems*, 137.

7. William, H. P., Saul A. T., William, T.V and Brian, P. F. (2002) "Numerical Recipes in C++", *Cambridge university press*. **II**.

8. Lim, M., Saloma, C. (1998) "Direct signal recovery from threshold crossings", *Phys. Rev***E-58**, 6759.

9. Tapang, G., Saloma, C. (2002) "Dynamic range enhancement of an optimized 1-bit AD converter", *IEEE Trans. Circuits Syst II***49**, 42.

10. Blake, I. F and Lindsey, W. C. (1973) "Level-crossing problems for random processes", *IEEE Transactions on Information Theory***3**, 295.

11. Akopyan, F., Manohar R. and Apsel, A. B. (2006) "A level-crossing flash asynchronous analog-to-digital converter", *Proc. of IEEE International Symposium on Asynchronous Circuits and Systems*, 12.

12. LonMark Interoperability Association (2002) "Layer 7 LonMark Interoperability Guidelines", **Ver 3.2**.

13. Guptha, S. C. (1963) "Increasing the sampling efficiency for a control system", *IEEE Transactions on Automatic Control***8(3)**, 263.

14. Miskowicz, M. (2006) "Send-on-delta concept: an event-based data reporting strategy", *Sensors, Special Issue: Wireless Sensor Networks and Platforms***6(1)**, 49.

15. Astrom, K. J. and Bernhardsson,B . (1999) "Comparison of periodic and event based sampling for first-order stochastic systems", *Proc. of IFAC World Congress*, 301.

16. Otanez, P., Moyne,J. and Tilbury, D. (2002) "Using deadbands to reduce communication in networked control systems", *Proc. of American Control Conference*, 3015.

17. Miskowicz, M. (2006) "Asymptotic Effectiveness of the Event-Based Sampling according to the Integral Criterion", *Sensors, Special Issue: Wireless Sensor Networks and Platforms*,**6(1)**, 49.

18. Bernhardsson, B., Trngren, M. and Sanfridson, M. (2006) "Event triggered sampling", *Research problem formulations in the DICOSMOS project 1998*.

19. Astrom, K. J. and Bernhardsso, B. (2002) "Comparison of Riemann and Lebesgue Sampling for First Order Stochastic Systems", *Proc. of the 41st IEEE Conference on Decision and Control*,**2**, 2011.

20. Daria, V. and Saloma, C. (2000) "High-Accuracy Fourier Transform Interferometry, Without Oversampling, with a 1-Bit Analog-to-Digital Converter", *Appl. Opt.*,**39**, 108.

21. Nazario, M. A. and Saloma, C. (1998) "Signal Recovery in Sinusoid-Crossing Sampling by use of the Minimum-Negativity Constraint", *Appl. Opt.*,**37**, 2953.

22. Garofolo, J. S. and Lamel, L. F. (1993) "DARPA TIMIT Acoustic-phonetic Continuous Speech Corpus", *U.S.Department of Commerce.*

23. G. Lu (1996) "Communication and Computing for Distributed Multimedia Systems", *Artech House, ISBN: 0-89006-884-4.*

Chapter 14

Adaptive Web Services Brokering

Kalyan Moy Gupta[1] and David W. Aha[2]

[1] *Knexus Research Corp.; Springfield, VA 22153; USA*
[2] *Navy Center for Applied Research in Artificial Intelligence;*
Naval Research Laboratory (Code 5514); Washington, DC 20375; USA
kalyan.gupta@knexusresearch.com, david.aha@nrl.navy.mil

Web services provide a means to architect and operate large-scale distributed information systems. However, syntactic and semantic differences among Web services complicate their interoperability and service composition. Brokers can facilitate their interoperability by providing discovery and mediation services, yet existing approaches are impractical for dynamic applications. We address this limitation by formulating three discovery tasks as supervised learning tasks. In particular, we apply textual case-based and decision tree induction approaches to these tasks and investigate the use of multiple representations. We evaluate their performance in a broker that discovers and mediates requests and responses for meteorological and oceanographic data. Our evaluations show that, for our evaluation tasks, classifiers learned by either approach can effectively perform service discovery in a broker.

Contents

14.1 Introduction 270
14.2 Web Services Brokering Overview 271
14.3 A Meteorological and Oceanographic Application 272
14.4 Integrated Web Services Broker 273
    14.4.1 User interface 275
    14.4.2 Service discovery and mediation engine 275
    14.4.3 Service discovery engine 275
    14.4.4 Knowledge base 279
14.5 Evaluations 279
    14.5.1 Web service classification evaluation 280
    14.5.2 Web service method classification evaluation 282
    14.5.3 Web service data category classification evaluation 283

14.5.4 Discussion 285
14.6 Conclusion 286
References 287

14.1. Introduction

System architects are abandoning traditional monolithic information systems architectures in favor of distributed architectures that enable component reuse, improve scalability, and reduce the total cost of ownership (i.e., cradle to grave costs for a system). Web services provide a standard for developing and deploying distributed information processing components that are accessible over the Web, and more generally over a network. For example, if a known Web service provides information about worldwide airports (Airport, 2007), then an airline reservation system can use it rather than require the development of a similar system. However, the set of available and relevant Web services changes rapidly, discovering them is a challenging task, and communicating and exchanging information across them can be problematic due to their syntactic and semantic differences.

A *broker* is an intermediary software agent that resolves syntactic and semantic differences and facilitates the communication between Web services. Brokers perform several functions. For example, they can help two parties communicate when they do not share a common language, or provide a trusted intermediary such as an escrow service for e-commerce transactions (Paolucci *et al.*, 2004). Brokering information between Web services involves two primary tasks: (1) *Discovery* - the identification of services that can provide relevant information, and (2) *Mediation* - the translation of requests and responses, which requires addressing their syntactic and semantic differences. Most brokers perform manually assisted discovery and use hand-crafted rules for mediation (e.g., Malley *et al.*, 2005), while some other brokers prescribe that Web services should include additional domain information represented with Web ontology languages such as OWL-S (Paolucci *et al.*, 2004; Howard & Kerschberg, 2004). However, mandating such ontological annotations in distributed and unknown organizational settings could be impractical.

We instead investigate a fully automated methodology for Web services discovery and mediation that does not make these demands.,Instead, we formulate the discovery task as a sequence of supervised learning tasks, and implement this methodology in the *Integrated Web Services Broker* (IWSB). To our knowledge, this is the first application of supervised learning methods for these tasks (Ladner *et al.*, 2006). Consequently, the choice of suitable methods for them is unclear. For the design and development of IWSB, we consider two promising methods: (1) textual case-based reasoning (TCBR) (Weber *et al.*, 2005) and (2) top-down induction of decision trees (TDIDT) (Quinlan, 1986). We include the XML Web service descriptions in the representations of the Web services. This semi-structured textual content makes the tasks amenable to suitable TCBR methods (e.g., Gupta *et al.*, 2006). Some of the IWSB learning tasks can be performed using alternative representations. Consequently, we investigate the effect of alternative representations on classification accuracy. We evaluate selected supervised learners that employ these methods in an application involving meteorological and oceanographic (MetOc) data. We found that they perform comparably on all the tasks.

We discuss Web services and brokering in Section 14.2, and describe the MetOc application in Section 14.3. In Section 14.4, we introduce the IWSB, including the specific supervised learning methods we use for Web services discovery, focusing on the TCBR methods. We evaluate them in Section 5. Section 6 concludes with a discussion and directions for future research.

14.2. Web Services Brokering Overview

A Web service supports interoperable machine-to-machine interaction over a network, especially over the Web (W3C, 2007). Usually, Web services use SOAP-formatted XML and interfaces described using WSDL (Web Service Description Language) XML schemas (or *WSDLs*), which provide a standard method for describing services operating on the Web. For example, a Web service might provide a list and the associated details of airports for a country, which can be accessed by an airline reservation application.

Service providers advertise the availability of their Web services by publishing them in a Web service registry such as UDDI (Universal Description Discovery and Integration). Users must first discover it by searching publicly available registries. Once located, they can issue information requests that conform to the exact syntax and vocabulary specified in its WSDL. In practice, locating and using relevant Web services is problematic due to differences in vocabulary and semantics. For example, the exact syntax of querying for airports in the USA from a service that provides such information (e.g., (Airport, 2007)) depends on which of several syntactic and semantic equivalents is used (e.g., *USA*, *U.S.A.*, *United States*, and *United States of America*).

Brokering can automatically discover and mediate information requests and responses across Web services (Sample *et al.*, 2006). As explained in Section 1, brokering information between Web services involves discovery and mediation tasks. In this paper, we focus on automating the discovery task, which involves identifying application-relevant Web services. For example, a financial application may wish to utilize Web services that publish mortgage rates from different regions across the world. Various WSDL registries can be searched to identify relevant services. However, formulating suitable search queries can be problematic. This may involve creating a broad query using a preliminary domain vocabulary (e.g., to identify mortgage-related Web services, query terms such as *mortgage* and *rates* could be used). Unfortunately, general queries typically return many irrelevant services, and these must be filtered. Additional discovery tasks could include identifying relevant components in a Web service and other application-specific characteristics that must be considered. In Section 14.4, we describe these tasks for a MetOc application, which we summarize in Section 14.3.

14.3. A Meteorological and Oceanographic Application

Accurate and timely MetOc information is critical for many military operations. For example, the wind speed and its direction for a particular location at sea is a critical input for landing aircrafts on carriers. To facilitate the acquisition of MetOc information from a variety of DoD MetOc sources, the US Department of Defense (DoD), as part of Net Centric Enterprise Services (NCES), is developing a Web service standard called the *Joint MetOc Broker Language* (JMBL). This standard has been mandated for adoption by the DoD MetOc community. The Navy MetOc information providers (e.g., the Naval Oceanographic Office, the Fleet Numerical Meteorology and Oceanography Center) are chartered to make data available via Web services through a MetOc Web portal (Malley *et al.*, 2005). In the envisioned application, a client is expected to discover MetOc Web services via the core enterprise discovery service and then use the core mediation service to translate requests to and responses from these services.

Although the planned NCES standard will be a substantial improvement over the current practice of independent and heterogeneous MetOc information providers, it will have several shortcomings that are typical of distributed applications which lack an automated brokering capability. For example, the core enterprise discovery service will constrain service discovery to only DoD Web services via a strict taxonomy, which will prevent access to non-DOD Web services. Also, the mediation service will be limited to only those Web services whose schemata have been manually mapped. Finally, as JMBL standards change, mappings and change services will need to be updated, which will increases the effort of maintaining these mappings.

The methods for automated discovery and mediation that we present in this paper can ameliorate these limitations. For example, IWSB, our integrated broker, enables discovery of non-DoD MetOc information services thereby substantially increasing the scope of information sources that can be accessed; we have already identified over a dozen non-DoD MetOc Web services that can be accessed using IWSB. In addition, IWSB does not require any manual mapping of Web service schemas. Instead, it can automatically translate requests and responses by using a service index that is automatically created during the discovery process. This fully automated approach, which includes three machine learning components, eliminates all manual mapping and maintenance effort. Thus, it relieves DoD MetOc information providers from having to constantly upgrade their implementations to conform to the latest JMBL specification. We next describe the IWSB.

14.4. Integrated Web Services Broker

IWSB's functional architecture (Figure 14.1) includes three components:

(1) Two *user interface* components, namely the Service Discovery Console, which allows users to initiate and administer a service discovery process, and the Web Service Client, which allows end users to submit information requests to the mediation component and view the responses.

(2) A *Service Discovery and Mediation Engine* (SDME), which discovers and mediates Web services using classifiers derived using supervised machine learning methods. In this paper, we detail how TCBR methods can be used to induce these classifiers, and also include TDIDT methods in our analysis.

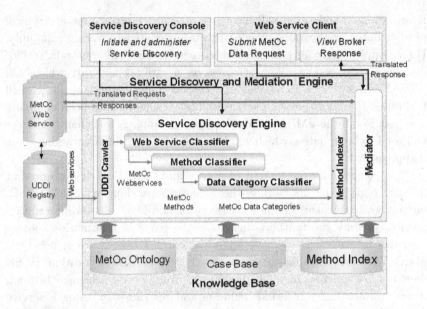

Figure 14.1.   The Integrated Web Services Broker's functional architecture.

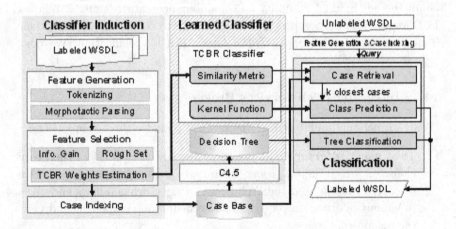

Figure 14.2.   IWSB's architecture for learning and applying classifiers.

(3) A *knowledge base* that includes three information sources used by SDME.

We next describe each of these components.

14.4.1. *User interface*

The IWSB has the following two user interface components:

(1) *Service Discovery Console*: This allows a systems administrator to initiate and manage a web services discovery process, which is the focus of this paper.
(2) *Web Service Client*: This component provides forms to users for submitting information requests and viewing responses. For example, using a form in a Web browser, a user may request *wave height* in a particular *area of interest* and receive a suitable response. The user can then, for example, use this information to help guide a search and rescue mission.

14.4.2. *Service discovery and mediation engine*

The SDME includes two main sub-components:

(1) *Service Discovery Engine*: This discovers Web services of interest, identifies the relevant methods that they can invoke, and identifies specific categories of responses these methods can provide. We investigate both case-based and TDIDT methods for inducing its classifiers.
(2) *Mediator*: This component receives information requests from users, translates them, and forwards them to appropriate Web services. Also, after it receives the Web service's responses, the Mediator translates and forwards them to the user. We detail these two sub-components below.

14.4.3. *Service discovery engine*

This includes the UDDI Crawler, a set of three classifiers, and the Method Indexer, all of which we describe below. ***

UDDI Crawler. This component uses the conceptual vocabulary of the MetOc domain (e.g., *weather, ocean, temperature, wave height*) from the MetOc Ontology described below to formulate queries for searching WSDL schemas. It submits the queries to known UDDI directories such as xMethods[a] and WSIndex[b]. The relevant WSDLs are then downloaded for further processing by the classifiers.

---

[a][http://www.xmethods.net] ****
[b][http://www.wsindex.org]

Classifiers. Web service discovery requires performing three classification tasks, which requires the following three classifiers:

(1) *Web Service Classifier*: This identifies Web service categories. That is, it identifies whether a WSDL downloaded by the UDDI Crawler can provide MetOc information. Thus, it performs a binary classification task.

(2) *Method Classifier*: Each MetOc-relevant WSDL schema includes multiple methods for submitting requests and receiving responses, only a subset of which return MetOc-related information. Therefore, this binary classifier evaluates whether a method in WSDL classified as MetOc-relevant returns MetOc-related information.

(3) *Data Category Classifier*: This is a multi-label classifier. In the MetOc domain, each Web service method can supply one or more categories of data. Some example labels of these categories are *Observation*, *Gridded Forecast*, and *Imagery*. Thus, this classifier identifies the categories of these methods.

Figure 14.2 displays IWSB's process for learning and applying classifiers, which use a bag-of-words representation for Web services and their methods. We refer to these representations as *cases*, although other terms (e.g., instances, objects) are synonymous. We also think of these as being stored in a *case base*. Given this terminology, the TCBR and TDIDT learning processes both require three data preparation tasks:

(1) *Feature Generation*: Depending on the classification task, the inputs may vary. For example, the inputs for the Web Service Classifier are labeled WSDLs. We disregard any XML tag structure and treat all input as free text. The input files are tokenized, which decomposes compound terms written in "camel script" into their constituent words. For example, *waveHeight* is decomposed into *wave* and *height*. IWSB then morphotactically parses these atomic terms into their canonical baseforms. For example, it reduces the terms *production* or *producer* to their baseform *produce*. This operation is performed by RuMoP, a rule-based morphotactic parser that outperforms a traditional parser such as PC-KIMMO (Gupta & Aha, 2004). These baseforms are then used as features in a bag-of-words case representation.

(2) *Feature selection*: WSDLs and their methods contain thousands of tokens that can be used as features. However, a large number of features in a textual case base can reduce classification accuracy. Hence,

in IWSB, the classifier induction process includes a feature selection step. Broadly speaking, two types of feature selection approaches exist: *filters*, which use a surrogate metric to assess feature quality, and *wrappers*, which select features by directly testing their ability to improve performance (e.g., here, to increase accuracy) (Kohavi & John, 1997). These represent a tradeoff; wrappers often attain higher accuracies, but typically have higher computational complexity, which can preclude their use on high-dimensional textual classification tasks. Thus, we will apply two filter approaches: information gain (IG) (Yang & Pederson, 1997) and a rough set method (Gupta *et al.*, 2006).

(3) *Case indexing*: For each case base, IWSB assigns indices to the cases (i.e., WSDLs for the first classification task, or WSDL methods for the latter two tasks) using only the selected features.

As mentioned above, we evaluate two methods for learning classifiers. The first is a TCBR method while the other is a standard TDIDT method (i.e., C4.5 (Quinlan, 1993)). Both yield a classifier that partitions the case space by defining class prediction boundaries. The TCBR method does this implicitly through the use of a similarity function, while the TDIDT method does this explicitly by inducing a decision tree that recursively partitions the case space. We provide more detail on each of these in turn.

TCBR is a subfield of CBR that focuses on retrieving and reusing cases whose content is predominantly text (Weber *et al.*, 2005). Common applications of TCBR include email categorization, news categorization, and spam filtering (e.g., Wiratunga *et al.*, 2004; Gupta *et al.*, 2006). Classifiers derived using TCBR methods have outperformed those induced using logistic regression, Nave Bayes, TDIDT, and support vector machines methods on text classification tasks such as topic assignment to newswire text and keyword assignment to medical abstracts (Sebastiani, 2002).

To learn the classifiers, our TCBR method applies two functions (see Figure 14.2):

(1) *Similarity metric*: This uses a contrast function specified using the selected features. That is, we define the similarity between a *query* (i.e., an unlabelled case) and a stored case as the ratio of the weighted combination of feature similarities across both cases and the summed weights of features that belong to the set, which is the union of features in the two cases (Montazemi & Gupta, 1997). More formally, for a query q and a case c, each described by a set of F features, then

$$sim(q, c) = \sum_{f \in F} w_f * sim_f(q_f, c_f) / \sum_{f \in F} w_f \qquad (14.1)$$

where simf(qf, cf) is the identity function. We use IG to assign weights to features. The selected features and their respective weights are used in IWSB's metric for computing the similarity of two cases.

(2) *Kernel function*: Given a query q (e.g., a WSDL schema), our TCBR method generates its features, assigns them as q's indices, and sets their values. It then retrieves q's k most similar cases; each contributes its similarity as the vote for its label. For example, if k=5 and three of the k-nearest neighbors have the class label *MetOc* with similarities 0.5, 0.25 and 0.1, the overall voted score for that label is 0.85 (0.5 + 0.25 + 0.1). The label with the highest vote is chosen as the predicted class

C4.5 (Quinlan, 1993) is a popular TDIDT algorithm that has performed well on a large number of classification tasks and is frequently included in benchmark performance comparisons. For this application, it selects the binary feature (each of which indicates the presence or absence of a term for describing a Web service or method) that maximizes information gain, uses it to split the data into two subsets, and acts recursively on these subsets. We used its default parameter values to set the stopping criterion and control post-pruning.

Method Indexer. The learned classifiers identify the available WSDL methods capable of providing MetOc data and the particular type(s) of data they return. The Method Indexer takes this as input and further analyzes their return parameters by looking up the parameter terms with the MetOc ontology for associated concepts (see Section 4.3). The methods, their parameters (i.e., retrieved meteorological concepts), and associated request formats are stored in an index for use by the Mediator. See Ladner et al. (2006) for additional details on the Method Indexer.

14.4.3.1. *Mediator*

Upon receiving a request for information (e.g., salinity at a certain ocean depth in a region of interest) from a Web service client, the Mediator looks up the method's index using the requested parameter as the key to identify the Web services and their particular methods capable of responding to the request. The parameters from the request are extracted and used to complete request schemas appropriately structured for each of the candidate methods, which are submitted to their respective Web services. The Web services send their responses to these customized requests using their respective response schemas. Upon receiving these disparately structured responses from the candidate Web services, the Mediator extracts the response values, completes a return schema that a specific client can interpret, and forwards it back to the user. See Ladner et al. (2006) for additional details on the Mediator.

14.4.4. *Knowledge base*

The IWSB Knowledge Base includes three components:

(1) *MetOc Ontology*: This includes the conceptual vocabulary of the MetOc domain. It includes standard taxonomic (is-a-type) and meronymic (is-a-part-of) relations among relevant concepts such as *salinity, depth,* and *location.* The concepts are represented using a Generative Sublanguage Ontology (Gupta & Aha, 2003). This ontology is used for reducing vocabulary, syntactic, and semantic differences. For example, the terms *Sal* and *Salinity* may be specified as synonyms. This ontology is also used by the Mediator for request and response translation.

(2) *Case Bases*: These are the case bases for the three classifiers, respectively. For the Web service classification task, WSDLs were used whose class labels were *MetOc* and *Not-MetOc.* For the method classification task, we used method names and their parameter descriptions. Finally, for the data category classification task, the case base was a subset of cases used for training the Method Classifier (i.e., only those methods that are classified as *MetOc*).

(3) *Method Index*: This contains the outputs of the discovery process that can be used to translate requests and responses. It indexes candidate Web service methods by their ability to serve requests containing specific concepts.

14.5. Evaluations

We performed three evaluations, one for each of the three classification tasks, for the MetOc Web services brokering application. Our objectives were the following:

(1) Assess the suitability of inducing and using classifiers for the MetOc classification tasks.

(2) Compare the performance of classifiers induced by TCBR methods versus a TDIDT method, namely C4.5 (Quinlan, 1993).

(3) Investigate the impact of contextual information on classification accuracy, where applicable.

14.5.1. *Web service classification evaluation*

Our objective in this first study was to establish a baseline performance for the Web Service Classifier, investigate the effectiveness for our textual case-based method for this application, and compare its utility with C4.5 (Quinlan, 1993).

Hypothesis. Our TCBR method will attain higher accuracies than C4.5 on the WWW service classification task. We posit this hypothesis because prior research indicates that classifiers induced by case-based approaches routinely outperform those induced by decision tree approaches and other competing machine learning algorithms on textual data (Sebastiani, 2002).

Data. We crawled and searched publicly available UDDI directories such as xMethods and WSIndex and collected 63 WSDLs (see Table 14.1). These Web services were examined by subject matter experts and labeled as *MetOc* or *Non-MetOc*. For example, the 25 MetOc WSDLs that we located are from both DoD (e.g., JMBL version 2.13) and non-DoD providers (e.g., AirportWeather). The 38 non-MetOc WSDLs we located includes, among others, one that monitors and reports earthquakes and another that provides address verification services.

Table 14.1.   Web service classification data.

Number of cases	63
Terms per case	158 (Avg.), 52 (Min), 1134 (Max)
Number of class labels	2
Class probabilities	MetOc (39.68%) Non-MetOc (60.32%)

Classifiers.   We used a suite of text classification tools within a software environment we developed called the *Classification Workbench* (CLAW). We tested the following configurations and components to evaluate our approach:

(1) *TCBR-D*: A textual case-based reasoner with a default (D) configuration for the Web Service classification task. This configuration

uses IG feature selection and weighting. We found that the optimal number of features for the Web service classification task was 850, a subset of over 1700 possible features used to describe the 63 WSDLs.

(2) *C4.5*: This is a popular supervised learning algorithm for inducing decision trees (Quinlan, 1993).

(3) *TCBR-RS*: This configuration uses a rough set feature selection method instead of IG. It utilizes Johnson's Reduct Heuristic (Gupta *et al.*, 2006).

All TCBR methods used the similarity voting kernel function and set $k = 5$.

Method. Due to the relatively small size of this case base, we used the leave-one-out cross-validation (LOOCV) evaluation methodology. This involved, for each case, removing it from the case base to serve as a test case and evaluating it against a case base containing the remaining cases. We report the average results over 63 runs and analyze performance using the one-tailed paired-t statistic.

Measures. We measured classification accuracy, which is the proportion of test cases correctly classified. To account for the varying probability of class labels in a data set, we also report *label-wise precision* (LWP) and *label-wise recall* (LWR). LWP is the proportion of correctly classified instances among the classifications that pertain to a particular label. LWR is the ratio of all instances belonging to a label that were correctly classified.

Results. Table 14.2 shows that TCBR-D attains the same classification accuracy as C4.5 on this task (92.06%). Therefore, we reject our hypothesis that TCBR-D outperforms C4.5.

Table 14.2.   Web service average classification accuracy results (in %).

Measures	Classifiers			
	TCBR-D	**C4.5**	**TCBR-RS**	**TCBR-A***
Accuracy	92.06	92.06	65.07	33.33
LWP (MetOc)	95.45	95.45	84.21	84.00
LWR (MetOc)	84.00	84.00	64.00	84.00
LWP (Non-MetOc)	90.24	90.24	75.75	0.00
LWR (Non-MetOc)	97.36	97.36	65.79	0.00
* TCBR adjusted to use the same number of features as TCBR-RS (i.e., 8 features)				

The TCBR-RS configuration allowed us to assess the utility of a rough set feature selection method for this classification task. TCBR-RS's accuracy was significantly lower than TCBR's (65.07% vs. 92.06%,

$p<0.001$), which uses IG for feature selection. We hypothesize that this occurred because the case base is small. As a result, the rough set method selected only eight features. Our rough set feature selection algorithm can select a maximum number of features equal to the size of the training case base. Typically, the number of selected features (i.e., the reduct) is much smaller. In comparison, TCBR's best performance using IG was achieved using 850 features. For a fair comparison, we constrained IG feature selection in TCBR to use only its eight highest-rated features (see TCBR-A in Table 14.2). The results show that TCBR-RS attains higher average accuracy than TCBR-A (65.07% vs. 33.33%), which indicates that, when so constrained, the rough set method selects more informative features than IG. This is consistent with our previously reported findings (Gupta et al., 2006). Nonetheless, we concluded that IG feature selection and weighting is more suitable than rough set feature selection for the Web service classification task.

14.5.2. *Web service method classification evaluation*

For this task, our goal was to assess the impact of alternative case representations on classification accuracy and to establish a baseline performance for the Method Classifier. Additionally, we compared the performance of TCBR with C4.5.

Hypotheses. (1) Adding contextual information (see details below) to the case representation will significantly increase classification accuracy and (2) our TCBR method will attain higher accuracies than C4.5.

Data. From the 25 known MetOc WSDLs, we extracted 74 methods (see Table 14.3). This included method names and, optionally, the type parameters (i.e., context) associated with them. Our subject matter experts labeled each method as *MetOc* or *Non-MetOc*.

Table 14.3.   Method classification data.

Number of cases	74
Terms per case	3.8 (Names Only), 49.6 (With context)
Number of class labels	2
Class probabilities	MetOc (86.48%), Non-MetOc (13.52%)

Classifiers. We tested the following configurations for the Method Classifier:

(1) *TCBR-N*: A TCBR method in which only the Web service method names (N) are used in the case representation. Due to the small number of tokens in the names (see Table 14.3), we did not perform any feature selection. We used IG to learn feature weights.

(2) *TCBR-NC*: A TCBR method that, in addition to the method names (N), uses type information as context (C). No feature selection was performed. Features were weighted using information gain.

(3) *C4.5-N*: In this case, C4.5 is given only the terms in method names.

(4) *C4.5-NC*: In this case, C4.5 is also given the contextual information.

All versions of TCBR use the similarity voting kernel function with $k = 3$.

Method. We used LOOCV.

Measures. We used classification accuracy, LWP, and LWR to measure performance.

Results. Introducing context in the representation by including parameter information produces mixed results on classification accuracy (see Table 14.4). For example, TCBR-NC performs marginally better than TCBR-N (93.24% vs. 91.89%; p=0.16). For C4.5, the result is reversed. That is, C4.5-NC marginally underperforms C4.5-N (90.54% vs. 91.89%). Therefore, we reject Hypothesis #1 that including context in the representation improves classification.

Overall, TCBR-NC is the most accurate classifier (93.24%). This data set has a skewed class distribution, with *MetOc* being the majority class at 87.67%. All the learned classifiers attained higher average classification accuracies than the nave method that always predicts the majority class label.

Table 14.4.   Method classification results.

Measures	Classifiers			
	TCBR-N	**TCBR-NC**	**C4.5-N**	**C4.5-NC**
Accuracy	91.89	93.24	91.89	90.54
LWP(MetOc)	93.94	92.75	93.94	93.46
LWR(MetOc)	96.87	100.00	96.87	96.87
LWP(Non-MetOc)	80.0	100.00	80.00	71.42
LWR(Non-MetOc)	60.00	50.00	60.00	50.00

14.5.3.   *Web service data category classification evaluation*

Our goal in this final study was to establish a base line performance for the Data Category Classifier and to investigate the performance of alternative representations.

Hypothesis. The addition of contextual information to the case representation will significantly increase TCBR's classification accuracy.

Data. Only 65 of the 74 WSDL methods in our original data set were MetOc-related. From these, six of the JMBL methods were removed as special cases and 59 cases were retained for category classification (See Table 14.5).

Table 14.5. Data category classification data.

Number of cases	59
Terms per case	3.8 (Names Only), 41 (With context)
No. of class labels	2
Class probabilities	AN-Message (89.84%) Observation (10.16%)

Classifiers. We tested the following four classifiers: (1) TCBR-N, a TCBR method that uses a case representation based only on method names, and (2) TCBR-NC, a TCBR method that uses method names (N) and context (C) (i.e., object type schema) for case representation, (3) C4.5-N, which uses only the method names, and (4) C4.5-NC, which uses both method names and signatures.

Method. We used LOOCV.

Measures. We used classification accuracy, LWP, and LWR as our measures.

Results. Introducing the contextual information in the case representation marginally reduces classification accuracy for TCBR (93.22% [TCBR-N] vs. 91.52% [TCBR-NC]), but it is not statistically significant. For C4.5, context does not have any impact on its classification performance (see Table 14.6) (94.91% [TCBR-N] vs. 94.91% [TCBR-NC]). Therefore, we reject our hypothesis. C4.5-N marginally outperforms TCBR, although the difference is statistically insignificant ($p > 0.34$).

Table 14.6. Data category classification results.

Measures	Classifiers			
	TCBR-N	**TCBR-NC**	**DTC-N**	**DTC-NC**
Accuracy	93.22	91.52	94.91	94.91
LWP(Observation)	75.00	60.00	71.42	71.42
LWR(Observation)	50.00	50.00	83.33	83.33
LWP(AN-Message)	94.54	94.44	96.29	96.29
LWR(AN-Message)	98.11	96.22	98.11	98.11

This dataset has a highly skewed class distribution; the majority class is (89.84%). Both the TCBR and C4.5 variants outperform the nave classification strategy of always predicting the majority class as the label for a query.

14.5.4. *Discussion*

Applying classifiers learned via a TCBR method and C4.5 for the three IWSB discovery tasks shows that they perform acceptably. For example, in the Web service classification task, *MetOc* is the category of interest and its precision is 95.45% (See Table 14.2). This exceeded the expectation of our MetOc application experts. Moreover, in practice, we expect Web service classification errors to be substantially reduced or completely eliminated during the subsequent method classification, data category classification, and indexing tasks. The recall performance for the *MetOc* label is 84%. This implies that the classifier fails to identify approximately 1 in 6 *MetOc* WSDLs. This performance needs to be improved and we will investigate appropriate methods in our future research. There was no significant difference in performance between the classifiers learned by our TCBR method and C4.5 on most tasks. Hence either supervised learning method could be used in IWSB.

The latter two classification tasks involve skewed class distributions. For example, in the method classification task, the probability of the majority class *MetOc*, which is IWSB's category of interest, was 87.67%. In this task, TCBR-NC attained perfect accuracy on MetOc (see Table 14.4). Like the Web service classification task, we expect its imperfect precision (92.75%) to be improved or completely corrected by IWSB's downstream processes. Finally, in the method classification and data category classification tasks, injecting the selected type of contextual information into the case representation did not increase classification accuracy.

The class distribution in the data category classification task was even further skewed than for the method classification task. However, all the categories in this task are of interest to IWSB. Although TCBR's average accuracy was higher than the percentage of cases in the majority class, its accuracy for minority class instances suffered. We will investigate suitable methods for further increasing its accuracy in our future research.

Our algorithm is similar to previous TCBR classification methods (e.g., Wiratunga *et al.*, 2004; Delaney *et al.*, 2005; Gupta *et al.*, 2006).

For example, we used a bag-of-words case representation, information gain feature selection, and a weighted similarity-voting kernel function. However, our investigation also has a few novel contributions. This is the first application of classifiers to Web service discovery for a brokering application. It is also a first application of a TCBR method in which the raw data is XML content instead of free form text. In this context, we explored the impact of considering contextual information from the XML tags for some of the classification tasks.

14.6. Conclusion

Brokering requests and responses across Web services is challenging due to their syntactic and semantic differences. Unlike existing hand-crafted and/or purely ontology-based approaches, we investigated a completely automated approach to Web services brokering. We developed IWSB, an integrated Web service brokering architecture that formulates service discovery as a sequence of three classification tasks. Based on the textual nature of the input used in the application (i.e., WSDLs represented by XML tags), we applied a textual case-based reasoning (TCBR) algorithm and an algorithm for top-down induction of decision trees to three classification tasks. We investigated the effectiveness of various TCBR design choices such as the use of context in case representation and alternative feature selection approaches (information gain vs. rough sets). We found that the TCBR and TDIDT methods perform comparably for these tasks, and their performance was acceptable to subject matter experts.

We identified several issues for future research. We will investigate methods for improving the recall of selected class labels without compromising their precision. Additionally, we will investigate methods for increasing classification performance when the class distributions are highly skewed. With these goals in mind, we will also evaluate the utility of classifier ensembles for these tasks.

Acknowledgment

This research was supported by the Naval Research Laboratory.

References

1. Airport (2007). Airport locator Web service, Retrieved from http://www. Webservicex.net/airport.asmx?wsdl on 6 February 2007.
2. Delaney, S.J., Cunningham P. & Coyle, L. (2005). An assessment of case-based reasoning for spam filtering. *Artificial Intelligence Review,* **24**(3-4), 359-378.
3. Gupta K.M., Aha D.W., & Moore P.G. (2006). Rough set feature selection algorithms for textual case-based classification. *Proceedings of the Eighth European Conference on Case-Based Reasoning* (pp. 166-181). Ölündeniz, Turkey: Springer.
4. Gupta, K.M, & Aha, D.W (2003). Nominal concept representation in sublanguage ontologies. *Proceedings of the Second International Workshop on Generative Approaches to the Lexicon,* (pp. 53-62) Geneva, Switzerland: School of Interpretation and Translation, University of Geneva.
5. Gupta, K.M., & Aha, D.W. (2004). RuMoP: A rule-based morphotactic parser. *Proceedings of the International Conference on Natural Language Processing* (pp. 280-284). Hyderabad, India: Allied Publishers.
6. Howard, R., & Kerschberg, L. (2004). A knowledge–based framework for dynamic semantic Web services brokering and management. *Proceedings of the Fifteenth International Workshop on Database and Expert Systems Applications.* Zaragoza, Spain: IEEE Computer Society.
7. Kohavi, R., & John, G.E. (1997). Wrappers for feature subset selection. *Artificial Intelligence,* **97**(1-2), 273-324.
8. Ladner, R., Warner, E., Petry, F., Gupta, K.M., Moore, P, Aha, D.W., & Shaw, K. (2006). Case-based classification alternatives to ontologies for automated Web service discovery and integration. *Proceedings of the Defense and Security Symposium* (volume 6201) (pp. 17.1-17.8). Bellingham, WA: SPIE.
9. Malley, D., Bennett, T., Kerr, B., & Estrada, M. (2005). A NAVOCEANO and FNMOC initiative to implement network-centric MetOc support to the U.S. Military. *Proceedings of the Oceans Systems Conference* (pp. 2463-2467). Washington, DC: MTS/IEEE.
10. Montazemi, A.R. & Gupta, K.M. (1997). Empirical evaluation of retrieval in case-based reasoning systems using modified cosine matching function. *IEEE Transactions on Systems, Man, and Cybernetics,* **27**(5), 601-612.
11. Paolucci, M., Soudry J., Srinivasan, N., & Sycara, K. (2004). A broker for OWL-S Web services. In T. Payne (Ed.) *Semantic Web Services: Papers from the AAAI Spring Symposium* (Technical Report SS-04-06). Menlo Park, CA: AAAI Press.
12. Quinlan, J.R. (1986). Induction of decision trees. *Machine Learning,* **1**, 81-106.
13. Quinlan, J.R. (1993). *C4.5: Programs for machine learning.* San Mateo, CA: Morgan Kaufmann.

14. Sample, J.T., Ladner, R., Ioup, E., Petry, F., Warner, E., Shaw, K., McCreedy, & F.P. Shulman, L. (2006). Enhancing the US Navy's GIDB portal with Web services. *Internet Computing*, **10**(5), 53-60.

15. Sebastiani, F. (2002). Machine learning in automatic text categorization. *Computing Surveys* **30**(1), 1-47.

16. W3C (2007). World Wide Web Consortium. [http://www.w3.org]

17. Weber, R.O., Ashley, K.D., & Brninghaus, S. (2005). Textual case-based reasoning. *Knowledge Engineering Review*, **20**(3), 255-260.

18. Wiratunga, N., Koychev, I., & Massie, S. (2004). Feature selection and generalization for retrieval of textual cases. *Proceedings of the Seventh European Conference on Case-Based Reasoning* (pp. 806-820). Madrid, Spain: Springer.

19. Yang, Y., & Pederson, J. (1997). A comparative study of feature selection in text categorization. *Proceedings of the Fourteenth International Conference on Machine Learning* (pp. 412-420). Nashville, TN: Morgan Kaufmann.

Chapter 15

Granular Support Vector Machine Based Method for Prediction of Solubility of Proteins on Over Expression in Escherichia Coli and Breast Cancer Classification

Pankaj Kumar[2], B. D. Kulkarni[1,*] and V. K. Jayaraman[3,†]

[1] Chemical Engineering Division, National Chemical Laboratory,
Pune-411008, India
[2] Department of Chemical Engineering, Indian Institute of Technology,
Kharagpur-721302, India
[3] Scientific and Engineering Computing Group,
Center for Development of Advanced Computing,
Pune University Campus, Pune-411021, India

We employed a granular support vector Machines (GSVM) for prediction of soluble proteins on over expression in Escherichia coli and to classify the Wisconsine breast cancer diagnosis data set (WBCD) into two classes. Granular computing splits the feature space into a set of subspaces (or information granules) such as classes, subsets, clusters and intervals.[1] By the principle of divide and conquer it decomposes a bigger complex problem into smaller and computationally simpler problems. Each of the granules is then solved independently and all the results are aggregated to form the final solution. For the purpose of granulation association rules were employed. The results indicate that a difficult imbalanced classification problem can be successfully solved by employing GSVM.

Contents

15.1 Introduction 290
15.2 System and Methods 291
   15.2.1 Granular computing 291
   15.2.2 Association rules 292
   15.2.3 Support vector machines 293
   15.2.4 Granular Support Vector Machine (GSVM) 296
15.3 Modeling Method 297

*Corresponding author: bd.kulkarni@ncl.res.in
†Corresponding author: jayaramanv@cdac.in

     15.3.1 Association rules formation as granulation methodology 297

     15.3.2 GSVM modeling 298

15.4 Experimental Evaluation 299

     15.4.1 Case study 1: Protein solubility classification 299

     15.4.2 Case study 2: Wisconsin breast cancer dataset 301

15.5 Conclusions 303

References 303

15.1. Introduction

The enteric bacterium Escherichia coli is the most commonly used organism for the production of recombinant proteins. E.coli has been preferred over other expression hosts because it is well characterized, is easy to handle and manipulate genetically, and has a relatively high growth and production rate.[2] However only some proteins are soluble upon overexpression in E.coli and others are generally expressed as insoluble aggregate folding intermediates known as inclusion bodies.[2] It has been observed that primary sequence of the protein is the most important determinant of the solubility status of the overexpressed protein.[3] Protein sequences are difficult to understand and model because of their random length; furthermore solubility of protein on overexpression in E coli is manifestation of the net effect of several sequence dependent and sequence independent factors.[4] Wilkinson and Harrison[5] observed that inclusion body formation is correlated, in descending order, to charge average, turn forming residue fraction, cysteine fraction, proline fraction, hydrophobicity and molecular weight. But later it was found by Ref. 6 that only the first two features are critical in distinguishing soluble and insoluble proteins. This problem was further investigated by several authors.[7-9]

Aliphatic index, the frequency of occurrence of Asn, Thr and Tyr and the dipeptide and tripeptide-composition were found to be the most informative features by Ref. 4. Recently, Ref. 3 employed Support Vector Machines(SVM) to predict solubility on overexpression. As the data was unbalanced they had employed the weighted version of the SVM which yielded an accuracy of 74.5% with a specificity of 81% and sensitivity of 57%. The algorithm could satisfactorily predict the change in solubility for most of the point mutations reported in literature. Due to the immense importance of this classification problem, it would be highly desirable to increase the prediction accuracy and the sensitivity. In the present work a granular computing based machine learning approach has been employed with a view to improve the prediction performance. Granular

computing, unlike traditional, computing, is knowledge oriented. It reduces
the complexity of a problem by splitting it into smaller, simpler problems.
In this work association rules have been used to make granules while
SVM is employed as a classifying method. Our result shows superiority
of the proposed method over building a single contiguous hyperplane
to classify the data using SVM. As a second case study we analyzed
Wisconsine Breast cancer classification problem to test the robustness of our
methodology. Breast cancer is the most common form of cancer in women. It
can be diagnosed as an abnormality in memogram or a lump on the breast.
Studies in this field attributes genetic and hormonal factor to be the cause of
breast cancer. Surgery, mastectomy, radiation therapy, hormonal therapy,
chemotherapy are some of the common treatment method available. In
this paper we presents a method to diagnose cancer The model is able to
discriminate between malign and benign tumor based on features computed
from a digitized image of a fine needle aspirate (FNA) of a breast mass with
substantially high accuracy.

15.2. System and Methods

In this section a brief introduction of the principle of granular computing
and support vector machine is presented. Subsequently the methodology
employed in building Granular Support vector machines (GSVM) is
explained. GSVM combines statistical machine learning algorithm with
knowledge-based classification to build a robust model.

15.2.1. *Granular computing*

Granular computing('GrC') was first introduced by Ref. 1 in 1997. Since
then it has been successfully employed in various fields like diakoptics,
divide and conquer structured programming, interval computing, cluster
analysis, fuzzy and rough set theories, neutrosophic computing, quotient
space theory, belief functions, machine learning, databases, and many
others.[1,10,11]

Granular computing splits the feature space into a set of subspaces (or
information granules) such as classes, subsets, clusters and intervals.[1] By
the principle of divide and conquer it decomposes a bigger complex problem
into smaller and computationally simpler problems. Each of the granules
is then solved independently and all the results are aggregated to form the
final solution. Proper granulation is capable of removing some redundant

and irrelevant information and at the same time facilitates getting rid of overfitting problem.[12] Thus granulation helps in building a computationally more efficient model for a complex problem.

In granular computing information granules are first constructed and computations are subsequently carried out with the granules.[11] In the literature several methods have been used for granulation like clustering,[13] fuzzy sets,[14] decision tree and association rules. In this work association rules[12] have been used for the purpose of granulation.

15.2.2. *Association rules*

Association rules tend to capture the underlying hidden patterns in datasets.[15] It provides information in the form of $IF - THEN$ statements. In the most general form an association rule has the form IF C_1 $THEN$ C_2 where C_1 and C_2 are conjunctions of condition and each condition is of form either $A_i = V_i$ or $A_i \in (L_i, U_i)$. For e.g.; IF frequency of occurrence of Cysteine (Cys) lies between 0.024 and 0.3279 $THEN$ that protein belongs to class -1(inclusion bodies) The antecedent part ('IF part') can have one or more than one condition joined by an operator 'and'. It must, however, be beneficial to form association rules with short IF-parts to avoid overfitting, yielding better generalization. To estimate the quality of a rule formed the confidence and support parameters are used:

(1) *Confidence:* Confidence is defined as the fraction of instances that are correctly classified by the rule among the instances for which it makes any prediction. Thus if the confidence of a rule is one, we can say that all the data in the training sample that satisfies the rule are correctly classified. Mathematically confidence for an association rule can be represented as,

$$con = \frac{count\_then}{count\_if} \qquad (15.1)$$

Where, $count_{then}$, the number of sample that satisfies the 'THEN' part of the rule, and $count_{if}$, is the number of samples that satisfy only the 'IF' part of association rule.

(2) *Support:* Support is defined as the ratio of the training data that are correctly classified by the rule to the size of training data with same class label as then part. Hence a support indicates the fraction of data in a class correctly classified by the rule:

$$\text{sup} = \frac{count\_then}{size(class_{then})} \qquad (15.2)$$

Where, $size(class_{then})$ is the size of training data with same class label as rule consequent.

While making a rule a threshold for support and confidence is used to prune out all the rules that will have support and confidence below the user defined threshold.[16] This is done so as to obtain a set of association rules that will enable efficient and reliable classification of unseen test instances. If the threshold confidence of the rule is kept high then less number of association rules will be mined but their prediction accuracy will be quite high. Similarly if support is kept very high generalization will be more but number of rules obtained will be very few while if support is too low then rule obtained will tend to overfit the training sample.

15.2.3. *Support vector machines*

SVM are a machine learning algorithm introduced by Vapnik.[17] It classifies a nonlinearly separable problem by building a linear separating hyperplane in a high dimensional feature space. The general hyperplane equation is of the form $w^T . x + b = 0$, where w is the weight vector, b is the bias and (.) denotes the dot product. Here w and b are selected so as to maximize the margin,$(1/\|w\|)$ between the hyperplane and the closest data points belonging to the different classes. The computational intractability problem introduced due to the high dimensionality is over come by defining an appropriate Kernel function.

Given a training dataset of the form (x_i, y_i), $i = 1, 2, \dots N$ where $x_i \in \Re^m$ and $y_i \in \{-1, 1\}$, the final SVM classifier function can be given as:

$$f(x) = \sum_{i=1}^{m} y_i \alpha_i K(x_i, x) + b \qquad (15.3)$$

Here, x_i represent the ith vector of input pattern and y_i is the target output corresponding to the ith vector and K is the kernel matrix and $m(\leq N)$ is the number of input pattern having non zero Langrangian multipliers (α_i); these are also called support vectors. The Langrangian multiplier is found by solving the following dual form of quadratic programming problem,

$$w(\alpha) = \sum_{i=1}^{N} \alpha_i - \frac{1}{2} \sum_{i,j=1}^{N} \alpha_i \alpha_j y_i y_j K(x_i, x_j) \qquad (15.4)$$

Subject to the constraints,

$$0 \le \alpha_i \le C, i = 1, 2, \dots N \qquad (15.5)$$

$$\sum_{i=1}^{N} \alpha_i y_i = 0 \qquad (15.6)$$

Where, C is the regularization parameter known as cost function that determines the tradeoff between the model complexity and the misclassification. So our task of binary classification reduces to the above maximization problem i.e. Eq. (15.4) - Eq. (15.6). It can be seen from Eq. (15.4) that the Lagrangian dual is cast entirely in terms of the training data. Also, we notice that the data points appear only inside the dot product.

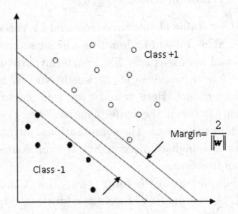

Figure 15.1.   Maximum margin-minimum norm classifier.

Solution of Eq. (15.4) - Eq. (15.6) determines the optimal separating hyperplane. The points for which Lagrange multipliers α_i, are non-zero and which lie on the margin of the separation, are termed as Support Vectors. For the linearly separable data, all the support vectors will lie on the margin of separation and the number of support vectors will be very small, the optimal hyperplane can be determined by a small subset of the training set. The hyperplane can be found out just by using these support vectors. Thus, a support vector machine summarizes information-content of a data-set using support vectors.

The above formulation of the SVM optimization problem is called the hard margin formulation since no training errors are allowed. If the separating hyper plane is allowed to pass through origin by selecting a fixed value $b = 0$, then in that case the SVM formulation is called the hard margin SVM without threshold. In that case, the optimization problem remains the same except that the constraint $\sum_{i=1}^{n} \alpha_i y_i = 0$ disappears.

For imbalanced classification problem SVM uses different error cost for the positive C^+ and negative C^- classes. Here the langrangian equation is modified to

$$L_p = \frac{\|w\|^2}{2} + C^+ \sum_{i|y_i=+!}^{n_+} \xi_i + C^- \sum_{j|y_j=-!}^{n_-} \xi_j - \sum_{i=1}^{n} \alpha_i \left[y_i \left(w.x_i + b \right) - 1 + \xi_i \right] - \sum_{i=1}^{n} r_i . \xi_i$$

(15.7)

Subject to the constraint,

$$0 \leq \alpha_i \leq C^+ \, if \, y_i = +1, \, and \, 0 \leq \alpha_i \leq C^- \, if \, y_i = -1 \qquad (15.8)$$

After the optimal value of α_i is found the decision function is based on the sign of $f(x)$ as given by Eq. (15.3). Different types of kernel function[18] are used for transformation of input space to a higher dimension feature space. Most commonly used kernel function are shown in Table 15.1.

Table 15.1. Different types of kernel functions.

S.No.	Name of the kernel	Expression
1	Polynomial	$K\left(\mathbf{x}_i, \mathbf{x}_j\right) = \left(\left(\mathbf{x}_i \bullet \mathbf{x}_j\right) + 1\right)^p \quad p = 1, 2, \ldots$
2	Gaussian Radial Basis Function	$K\left(\mathbf{x}_i, \mathbf{x}_j\right) = \exp\left(\frac{\|\mathbf{x}_i - \mathbf{x}_j\|^2}{-2\sigma^2}\right)$
3	Exponential Radial Basis Function	$K\left(\mathbf{x}_i, \mathbf{x}_j\right) = \exp\left(\frac{\|\mathbf{x}_i - \mathbf{x}_j\|}{-2\sigma^2}\right)$
4	Multi-layer Perceptron	$K\left(\mathbf{x}_i, \mathbf{x}_j\right) = \tanh\left(b\left(\mathbf{x}_i \bullet \mathbf{x}_j\right) - c\right)$
5	Fourier Series	$K\left(\mathbf{x}_i, \mathbf{x}_j\right) = \frac{\sin\left(N + \frac{1}{2}\right)\left(\mathbf{x}_i - \mathbf{x}_j\right)}{\sin\left(\frac{1}{2}\left(\mathbf{x}_i - \mathbf{x}_j\right)\right)}$ $N = $ dimension of the space
6	Tensor Product Splines	$K\left(\mathbf{x}_i, \mathbf{x}_i\right) = \prod_{m=1}^{n} K_m\left(\mathbf{x}_{im}, \mathbf{x}_{jm}\right)$

In the present work RBF kernel was found to provide the best possible results.

15.2.4. *Granular Support Vector Machine (GSVM)*

For many complex problems it can never be guaranteed that a contiguous hyperplane as discussed above will be able to classify the data correctly. Better classification performance can be achieved by judicious granulation of the feature space. For example, consider the traditional XOR problem; as such without any transformation it is non-linearly separable but if we divide the whole feature into two equal halves then each half becomes linearly separable.

Even in the case where a single linear hyperplane is available the use of granulation will help in maximizing the margin between the hyperplane and the closest data points belonging to the different classes. Furthermore for the case of imbalanced data where the number of instances in one class is far more than the number of instances in other, the separating hyperplane tends to shifts towards the minority class so SVM misclassifies most of the instances into the majority class, thus giving higher accuracy for the majority class but poor predictivity for minority class. In such cases granulation may become an effective means to handle data imbalance. In GSVM the whole feature space is first divided into granules, viz., pure (where almost all the instances belong to one class) and mixed granules (where instances from both classes are present). After separating out pure granules instances present in the mixed granule may become more balanced and hence the probability of prediction accuracy of SVM can be expected to be higher.

Feature Selection It is of immense importance to perform feature selection to find an informative subset before performing an analysis on any real world data. This is particularly true for multivariate dataset containing large number of features. Feature selection not only improves prediction accuracy but also eliminates cost of computation of unnecessary features making it computationally efficient. In this work Ant colony optimization(ACO) based feature selection was employed.

ACO was first proposed by Ref. 19 as a multiagent approach for difficult combinatorial optimization problems such as traveling salesman problemand the quadratic assignment problem. This method is based on the observation that ants in real world are able to find an optimal path from their nest to food source without making use of any apparent visual clue. Ants secretes an odorous chemical called pheromone in their path. Each ant follows a path rich in pheromone, depositing further pheromone along that path. As the pheromones also decay or evaporate with time, thus the less preferred path will gradually loose its pheromone trail and eventually all ants end up with an optimal path.

In the employed methodology, two phase feature selection method was used. Different hybrid model of ACO has been tried in literature.[20] In our approach we first ranked all the features using WEKA infogain attribute selector. This ranking forms the basis for assigning weights to each feature. Then ACO was employed to obtain an optimal path. The steps required can be summarized as, First a random intial population is generated. All the features were initialized with equal pheromone value. Then the fitness of each ant is evaluated using SVM. Based on fitness, Pheromone values are updated by increasing the pheromones of path with maximum fitness by an amount propotional to its fitness value while reducing the pheromones for other by an appropriate decay ratio. Then a roulette wheel based selection is employed to generate the new generation. The above steps are repeated until an optimal path is obtained.

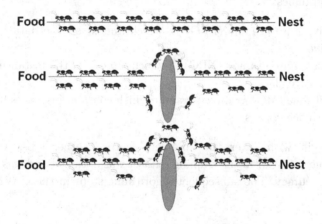

Figure 15.2.   Ant colony optimization.

15.3. Modeling Method

15.3.1. *Association rules formation as granulation methodology*

In this work we employed the association rules methodology of Ref. 12 for the purpose of granulation. As explained in Sec. 15.2.2 association rules with optimal support and confidence were mined. Among all the association rules formed with different attributes the one with highest confidence was added to the set called *selected_rule_set*. After a rule was chosen, all instances classified by the rule were removed and the rule formation process was repeated until no further rule with support and confidence greater than the predetermined threshold is formed or all the instances has already been classified. Care was taken to apply them in the order in which they are discovered. Table 15.1 shows the *selected_rule_set* for dataset with all 446 features.

15.3.2. *GSVM modeling*

After all the association rules were obtained GSVM model was built by iteratively combining the association rules from *selected_rule_set* to find the optimal granules which were both pure and significant. Thus using association rules the complete feature space can be divided into three different granules:[12]

(1) Positive pure granule (PPG) in which almost all the data belong to positive class
(2) Negative pure granule (NPG) in which almost all the instances belong to negative class
(3) Mixed zone (MG) or mixed granule which contains instances belonging to both the classes

To begin with, over the complete feature space, cross validation performance of SVM in the training dataset was obtained and was taken as baseline accuracy. The subsequent algorithmic steps in the GSVM model are:

(1) A rule from *selected_rule_set* was taken
(2) All the instances that satisfy the antecedent (IF part) part of rule was removed as pure granules and was assigned the class label as predicted by consequent part of rule.
(3) The remaining instances that do not satisfy the rule, form the mixed granule. SVM model was built with the instances in the mixed granule by tuning the algorithm parameters to obtain the best accuracy.
(4) If the considered rule was added to set called *final_rule_set* if it was found to improve the classification performance. The improved accuracy was now considered to be the new baseline accuracy.

(5) Otherwise the next rule in the list from *selected_rule_set* was taken and Steps 3 to 5 were repeated.

(6) The above steps were continued until the entire set of rules in the list had been processed.

Table 15.2 shows the *final_rule_set* for the dataset comprising of all 446 features. When unseen test instances are to be classified, they are first checked by the formed association rules in *final_rule_set*. All the instances that satisfy the antecedent of rule are assigned the class predicted by the rule and the class label for the remaining instances (not predicted by rule) were predicted by the SVM model built on mixed granule.

15.4. Experimental Evaluation

15.4.1. *Case study 1: Protein solubility classification*

The Dataset of Idicula-Thomas et al[3] were employed for the GSVM experiments. This dataset consist of 192 protein sequences, 62 of which are soluble on overexpression in and the remaining 130 sequences form inclusion body. The 446 features extracted by them include i) six physiochemical properties(Attribute nos. 1-6), viz., aliphatic index, instability index of the entire protein, instability index of the N-terminus and net charge. ii) twenty single aminoacid residues(Attribute nos. 7-26) arranged in alphabetical order (A,C,D) followed by 20 reduced alphabets(attribur nos. 27-46). The reduced alphabets employed includes 7 reduced class of conformational similarity,8 reduced class of BLOSUM50 substitution matrix and 5 reduced class of hydrophobicity.[3] Finally the features in the list includes 400 attributes (attribute nos. 47-446) comprising of the dipeptide compositions.

Model Building The instances(each comprising of 446 features)were randomly divided into training and test sets keeping the inclusion body forming and the soluble proteins approximately in ratio of 2:1. The training dataset comprised 128 sequences, 87 inclusion body-forming and 41 soluble proteins. The test dataset comprised 64 sequences, 43 inclusion body forming and 21 soluble proteins.[3]

The modeling process was initiated by first forming association rules with the instances in the training dataset. As explained in Sec. 15.3.1, only single feature association rules with substantial support and confidence were mined to form *selected_rule_set*. Table 15.2 shows the mined set of association rules in the form: $IF X_0 \leq attribute_i \leq X_1 THEN class = y$.

GSVM model was built employing these rules for pure zones and SVM classification for the mixed zone. However before applying SVM, as a preprocessing step all the features were scaled by making their mean zero and standard deviation one. SVM experiments done in this work were performed using an implementation of LIBSVM.[21] As our data was imbalanced weighted SVM was used. The SVM parameters C, γ and weights were tuned by grid search. Table 15.2 shows the final set of rule selected by GSVM algorithm to make a model. Out of the 4 rules shown in Table 15.2 only the rules shown in Table 15.3 were found to increase the cross-validation performance over training data, so only those two rules were selected.

Table 15.2.   Mined association rule on original unscaled training data.

S.No.	X_0	X_1	Attribute Number	Confidence	Support	Class
1	0.0051	0.0242	443	1	0.1954	-1
2	0.0059	Inf	435	1	0.1609	-1
3	0.0078	0.0127	296	1	0.1609	-1
4	0.0084	0.0141	330	0.9231	0.2927	1

Table 15.3.   Set of rules selected by GSVM algorithm.

S.No.	X_0	X_1	Attribute Number	Confidence	Support	Class
1	0.0078	0.0127	296	1	0.1609	-1
2	0.0084	0.0141	330	0.9231	0.2927	1

The algorithm performance was subsequently tested on unseen test dataset using the same test measure as used by Ref. 3. 50 random splits of the dataset were taken (with the same ratio of nearly 1:2 between the two classes of proteins), and their average performance was measured. Table 15.4 shows the comparison of results obtained by using GSVM and SVM (as reported by Ref. 3. These results shows that the GSVM is capable of capturing inherent data distribution more accurately as compared to a single SVM build over complete feature space.

Table 15.4.   Set of rules selected by GSVM algorithm.

Number of features	Algorithm	ROC	Accuracy (%)	Specificity (%)	Sensitivity (%)
446	SVM	0.5316	72	76	55
446	GSVM	0.7227	75.41	81.40	63.14
27	GSVM	0.7635	79.22	84.70	68

As the number of proteins forming inclusion bodies is far more than number of soluble proteins(nearly 2 times,) our dataset is imbalanced. So accuracy alone does not give the correct measure of performance. For an imbalanced data, receiver operation characteristic (ROC) curve is generally used as test measure. Our result shows a marked increase in the value of ROC from 0.5316 using SVM over complete feature to 0.72227 using GSVM for the "best classifier" reported by Ref. 3 using 446 features. The value of sensitivity and specificity has also gone up which has increased the overall accuracy to 75.41%. The increased ROC shows that our model is not biased towards majority class and is capable of predicting the minority class (soluble proteins) as well with equally good accuracy.

We also tried feature selection in the mixed granule with the original 446 features to find the most informative subset. After feature selection only 27 features were found critical for predicting the solubility. The selected features were aliphatic index, frequency of occurrence of residues Cysteine (Cys), Glutanic acid (Glu), Asparagine (Asn) and Tyrosine (Tyr). Among the reduced alphabets, only the reduced class [CMQLEKRA] was selected from the seven reduced classes of conformational similarity. Similarly from the five reduced classes of hydrophobicity originally reported, only [CFILMVW] and [NQSTY] were selected. And from the eight reduced classes of BLOSUM50 substitution matrix the only reduced class selected was [CILMV]. The 18 dipeptide whose composition were found to significant. These include [VC], [AE], [VE], [WF], [YF], [AG], [FG], [WG], [HH], [MI], [HK], [KN], [KP], [ER], [YS], [RV], [KY], and [TY].

A new GSVM model was built with these most informative features. In this case we didn't get any positive rule, which satisfied our minimum support and confidence threshold condition (kept as 0.18 and 0.85 respectively for positive rule while for negative rule the values are 0.15 and 0.95 respectively). After applying GSVM all 3 rules were selected in the final model. So our final model with 27 selected features comprised of association rules shown in Table 15.5 and SVM parameters $C = 32, \gamma = 0.0039$ and $w = 1.3$. Our result (Table 15.4) shows that performance was further improved by feature selection.

15.4.2. *Case study 2: Wisconsin breast cancer dataset*

As a second example of the application of GSVM, the methodology was employed to classify the Wisconsine breast cancer diagnosis data set obtained from UCI database. The dataset consists of 569 instances distributed in two classes, malignant and benign with class distribution of 212 and 357 respectively. Each sequence is comprised of 30 real valued input features. The features describe characteristic of cell mass nuclei present in the image of a fine needle aspirate (FNA) of a breast mass. The detailed description on how these features are computed can be found in Ref. 22.

Table 15.5.   Mined association rule on original unscaled training data after feature selection.

S.No.	X_0	X_1	Attribute Number	Confidence	Support	Class
.1	0.0059	Inf	26	1	0.1954	-1
2	0.0240	0.3279	2	1	0.1609	-1
3	0.0027	0.3279	12	1	0.1954	-1

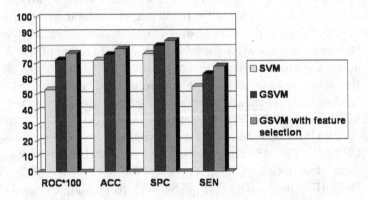

Figure 15.3.   Test results for protein solubility prediction.

The methodology employed was similar to that explained in above problem. The complete dataset was normalized before forming association rules. The model was validated by training it on 80% of dataset and then testing it on remaining 20% (42 from malignant and 72 benign). The results are reported on 50 such random. Our final model consist of the rule set shown in Table 15.6 and SVM parameters $C = 8$ and $\gamma = 0.0078$. The average training ROC and accuracy was found to be 0.9838 and 98.34% respectively. The test results are shown in Table 15.7.

Table 15.6.   Selected rule set.

S.No.	X_0	X_1	Attribute Number	Confidence	Support	Class
1	-1.2213	-0.6556	24	1	0.3754	-1
2	-1.2607	-0.6663	8	0.9885	0.2409	-1

Table 15.7.   Classification results on test dataset averaged over 50 random splits.

Number of features	Algorithm	ROC	Accuracy (%)	Specificity (%)	Sensitivity (%)
30	GSVM	0.9729	97.29	97.48	97.10

From the above result, we can observe that both specificity and sensitivity are very high, giving another proof that our model is not biased toward majority class. We also tried feature selection with the given dataset. From the attribute ranking using WEKA info-gain attribute selector, it was found that out of 30 only 3 features had zero info-gain value. With 22 features the training accuracy rose to 98.66%, however in that case no rule got selected implying that splitting of feature space into separate granules was not required.

15.5. Conclusions

In this work Granular Support Vector Machines(GSVM) was successfully employed for classification of soluble and insoluble proteins and Wisconsine Breast cancer dataset. GSVM systematically combines statistical learning theory with granular computing to build a hybrid system exhibiting superior performance with the inherently unbalanced data set. By splitting the feature space into granules it reduces the complexity of problem thereby improving the classification efficiency. The significant increase in ROC values as compared to that obtained using SVM alone bears testimony to the excellent generalization capability of the hybrid model.

Acknowledgment

Dr. V.K. Jayaraman gratefully acknowledges Department of Biotechnology, New Delhi, India for financial support.

References

1. Lin, T.Y. (1997) Granular computing, Announcement of the BISC Special Interest Group on Granular Computing
2. Baneyx, F. (1999.) Recombinant protein expression in Escherichia coli. Curr. Opin. Biotechnol. 10: 411-421.
3. Idicula-Thomas S, Kulkarni A.J., Kulkarni B.D., Jayaraman V.K., and Balaji P.V .(2006) A support vector machine-based method for predicting

the propensity of a protein to be soluble or to form inclusion body on overexpression in Escherichia coli. Bioinformatics 22: 278-284.

4. Idicula-Thomas,S. and Balaji,P.V. (2005) Understanding the relationship between the primary structure of proteins and its propensity to be soluble on overexpression in Escherichia coli. Protein Sci., 14, 582-592.

5. Wilkinson, D.L. and Harrison, R.G. (1991). Predicting the solubility of recombinant proteins in Escherichia coli. Biotechnology 9: 443-448.

6. Davis, G.D.,Elisee, C Newham, D.M. and Harrison,R.G.(1999). New Fusion Protein Systems Designed to Give Soluble Expression in Escherichia coli.Biotechnol Bioeng 65, 382-388

7. Bertone,P. et al. (2001) SPINE: an integrated tracking database and data mining approach for identifying feasible targets in high-throughput structural proteomics.Nucleic Acids Res., 29, 2884-2898.

8. Goh,C.S. et al. (2004) Mining the structural genomics pipeline: identification of protein properties that affect high-throughput experimental analysis. J. Mol. Biol., 336,115-130.

9. Luan,C.H. et al. (2004) High-throughput expression of C. elegans proteins. Genome Res., 14, 2102-2110.

10. Hirota, K. and Pedrycz,W.(1999) Fuzzy computing for data mining, Proceedings of the IEEE, 87, 1575-1600

11. Yao, Y.Y.,(2000) Granular computing: basic issues and possible solutions, Proceedings of the 5th Joint Conference on Information Sciences, Volume I, Atlantic City, New Jersey, USA, P.P. Wang (Ed.), Association for Intelligent Machinery, pp. 186-189.

12. Tang Yuchun, Jin Bo and Zhang Y-Q (2005) Granular support vector machines with association rules mining for protein homology prediction, Artificial Intelligence in Medicine, Volume 35, Issues 1-2, Computational Intelligence Techniques in Bioinformatics, Pages 121-134

13. Zhong W, He Jieyue, Harrison R, Phang C. Tai and Pan Yi,(2006) Clustering support vector machines for protein local structure prediction, Expert Systems with Applications, In Press, Corrected Proof,

14. Zadeh L.A. (1997) Toward a theory of fuzzy information granulation and its centrality in human reasoning and fuzzy logic. Fuzzy Sets and Systems, 90(2):111–127

15. Agrawal et al. Mining association rules between sets of items in large databases. In Proceedings of the ACM SIGMOD Conference on Management of Data, pages 207-216, Washington, D. C., May 1993.

16. Agrawal R and Srikant Ramakrishnan. (1994) Fast algorithms for mining association rules. In Proc. 20th Int. Conf. Very Large Data Bases, VLDB, pages 487– 499. Morgan Kaufmann, 12–15

17. Vapnik, V. (1995) The Nature of Statistical Learning Theory. Springer, New York.

18. Burges CJC. A tutorial on support vector machines for pattern recognition. Data Mining Knowledge Disc 1998; 2(2):121-67.

19. Dorigo M, Gambardella LM. Ant colonies for the traveling salesman problem. BioSystems 1997;43:73-81.

20. Diwakar Patil, Rahul Raj, Prashant Shingade, V.K.Jayaraman and B.D Kulkarni, Feature Selection and Classification employing hybrid ACO-Random Forest methodology, Combinatorial Chemistry and High Throughput Screening (In Press)
21. Chih-Chung Chang and Chih-Jen Lin (2001). LIBSVM: a library for support vector machines, http://www.csie.ntu.edu.tw/ cjlin/libsvm
22. W.H. Wolberg, W.N. Street, and O.L. Mangasarian, Machine learning techniques to diagnose breast cancer from fine-needle aspirates. Cancer Letters 77 (1994) 163-171